A Candle Within Her Soul
Mary Elizabeth Mahnkey and Her Ozarks
(1877-1948)

What Others Say About this Book . . .

"An engaging portrait of a remarkable woman and an authentic view of the time and place in which she lived."

Robert K. Gilmore, Author
Ozark Baptizings, Hangings, and Other Diversions,
Consulting Editor of *OzarksWatch*

"I'm so pleased this long-awaited book is now in print. The story of Mary Elizabeth Mahnkey is one to be told and Ellen Gray Massey is just the person to tell it."

Barbara Wehrman, Publisher
Ozarks Mountaineer

"A rare echo of rural America. Ellen Massey's commitment to reminding us of our heritage and culture, and her skills as a researcher, writer, and teacher make her the perfect chronicler for Mahnkey's remarkable story. I am delighted to recommend this book to you."

John E. Moore, Jr., President
Drury College, Springfield, Missouri

"She was not widely traveled nor formally educated nor exposed to the myriad stimuli of modern urbanity, yet by the innate insight that was uniquely hers, the breadth of her observations from an isolated rural environment as expressed in her life and writings encompasses a universe of human experience with which we all can identify and find hope and instruction.

"Yet there is much high drama in her story: floods, fires, tornados, familiar spirits, fortune-telling gypsies, covered-wagons, birth and death, murder, kidnapping, marauding Indians, raiding vigilantes, rattle snakes, mad dogs, bitter winters, summer droughts, politics, bankruptcies, the Great Depression, grief, ecstasy, recognition, ridicule, romance, and boy-meets-girl—all within the confines of marriage in a time when women were often prisoners of that institution.

"At a time when life was hard beyond our modern mind's ability to imagine, Mary Elizabeth Mahnkey was a light and an inspiration to those whom she touched from her obscure corner of the Ozarks. Through the marvelous window of this book she is yet a light and inspiration to us today wherever we are. We thank you, Ellen, for this work of love and pray that these enlightening pages will keep Mary Elizabeth's warm candle of wisdom and wit brightly lit for the ages."

Dr. David Stewart, Author/Editor
The Earthquake America Forgot and other books.
Gutenberg-Richter Publications

A Candle Within Her Soul

Mary Elizabeth Mahnkey and Her Ozarks
(1877-1948)

by

Ellen Gray Massey

Bittersweet, Inc.

Publisher of Ozark Magazines & Books

Lebanon, Missouri

1996

A Candle in Her Soul by Ellen Gray Massey
Cover Photograph by Townsend Godsey
(Used with permission of Townsend Godsey)

ISBN 0-934426-71-6   LCCN 96-78751

Available from:

BITTERSWEET, INC.
126 Maple Drive
Lebanon, MO 65536

PRICE $14.95
(subject to change)

Manufactured in the
United States of America by

Stewart Printing & Publishing Co.
Route 1, Box 646
Marble Hill, Missouri 63764
(800) 758-8629

Library of Congress Cataloging-in-Publication Data

Massey, Ellen Gray
    Candle within her soul : Mary Elizabeth Mahnkey and
her Ozarks, 1877-1948 / by Ellen Gray Massey.
    p. cm.
    Includes bibliographical references and index.
    Preassigned LCCN: 96-78751
    ISBN: 0-934426-71-6
    1. Women journalists—United States—Biography.
2. Ozark Mountains Region—social life, customs, folklore.
I. Title.
PN487.M4755M37 1996
070'.92—dc20

For Doug, Pat, Mary Jo, and Winnie Bee

CONTENTS

Contents

Contents

PHOTOS, ILLUSTRATIONS, AND MAPS

ACKNOWLEDGEMENTS

I would like to thank the following for their help
in preparing this book:

Pete and Clarabelle Box

Robert L. Church

Dr. Graham Clark

Maude Freeland

Frieda Freeland Ingenthron

Alva and Lois Kenner

Mary Jo Mahnkey Kirkey

Lorene Mahnken

Douglas Mahnkey

Patrick Mahnkey

Audra Orr Marchbank

David G. Massey

Gordon McCann

Cecil McClary

May and Leonard McFarland

Charles and Ella Moore

Ira Rittenhouse

Phyllis Rossiter

John Strahan, Jr.

Susan and Mark Theriac

Carolyn Gray Thornton

Lucile Morris Upton

Kathleen Van Buskirk

Winnie Bee Jones Wolf

FOREWORD

Life's fabric has worn thin;
   'tis darned and patched
   and tied;
It has been turned so many times
To show the brighter side.
       Mary Elizabeth Mahnkey (ca 1930)

This is the story of a native Ozark woman's role in the Ozark scene and of events during her lifetime. It is the world that Mary Elizabeth Mahnkey recorded in prose and poetry while it was happening and in retrospect.

To appreciate Mary Elizabeth and what she accomplished, we must understand her place and time. Otherwise we might overlook her simple metaphors of nature and women's work, such as mending clothes in the poem above to express fundamental values of the human condition.

The area where she lived is still there—the rugged and forested hills of the Ozark Plateau in southern Missouri and northern Arkansas, an area of karst topography, characterized by a thin, below average soil, many springs, caves, and clear-running streams hemmed in by limestone bluffs. However, the negative reputation of its residents has changed with the growing popularity of the region and better understanding of its people. In her time, north Missouri and the rest of the country belittled and stereotyped the men and women who lived in this isolated land area as ignorant, lazy hillbillies. In reality they worked every daylight hour using mostly hand labor to support their families on small, self-sufficient farms. They depended on themselves, sometimes trading work with neighbors in the close-knit, conservative, and religious communities.

Mary Elizabeth's story includes Indians, vigilante terrorism, gypsies, near-fatal accidents, tornadoes, tragedies, endless moving, love, and merriment. As a farm girl of the latter part of the nineteenth century and a woman in the first half of the twentieth, she lived the life of a typical Ozark woman, experiencing the joys and hardships of post-pioneer living in the hills.

Thus her life story lets the modern reader experience what it was like to be a daughter, wife, mother, and grandmother of that time and place where women were second-class citizens.

But Mary Elizabeth Mahnkey was not a typical woman in many ways. She could not slide anonymously into a woman's accepted role—lifelong service to her man and children, denying her own desires and abilities. Though fulfilling that role to her family's and society's satisfaction, she inwardly rebelled at the restrictions. Continually developing her verbal and observational talents, she retained some independence by writing. She wrote in an area where most women received little education and were discouraged from any literary pursuits. When the world ridiculed Ozark people and their heritage, Mary Elizabeth recognized their value. She wrote about her life and about her neighbors. She chronicled more than seventy years of Ozark living from the post-Civil War period to the late nineteen forties when the twentieth century discovered the Ozarks.

In her daily journals and in her published writings, she captured the pain of life's problems as well as the wonder and excitement of its beauty, weaving all into the life fabric of those who knew her or read her "pieces." For fifty-seven years Mary Elizabeth's weekly column appeared in her home newspapers in Taney County, Missouri, and for eighteen years her monthly column was published in the dailies of Springfield, Missouri.

In addition to these published writings, she left dozens of

journals which reveal the pain, frustration, and unhappiness she experienced in her struggles to fit into her woman's role.

In spite of the problems, she always found beauty in commonplace things—both a literal and a spiritual beauty which pervades her prose and poetry. Sharing this beauty through her writing was almost a mission, as she explained in a letter in 1936. "Sometimes I feel a vague hurt, almost physical pain, that people fail to realize the real beauty in these little simple things."

This simplicity appealed to her readers during her life. It still does to those who know about her work. Over several years I have given more than 200 talks about the Ozarks to groups all over Missouri using some of her poems and anecdotes to illustrate my points. Without exception these modern audiences, young or old, in rural or urban areas, in the Ozarks or in north Missouri, have responded emotionally to her lyric images. Her simply expressed insight still speaks to us today. But if we look only at its literal meaning or become snagged on her use of out-of-date references—such as recycling a garment by turning the faded cloth to show its brighter side—we can easily overlook the depth of her poetry and classify it as "old-fashioned and not very good," as one recent critic said. Perhaps her very simplicity is why academic critics, then and now, have largely ignored her work.

By choice Mary Elizabeth remained in the Ozarks, although she had several opportunities to move away; when she did leave briefly, the beauty, peace, and the comfort of the hills reclaimed her. The character of the Ozark people sustained her. All these gave her strength. In this unlikely setting—rural, backward, and male dominated—she coped and created. Writing with understanding for and about Ozark men, women, and children, she dispelled the hillbilly caricature of their culture and allowed readers to see its dignity and value.

Many noted people braved the backwoods roads to become her friends. For many years she participated in a networking of intellectual people in Taney County and carried on extensive correspondence with people in Missouri, Arkansas, and elsewhere. Folklorist Vance Randolph wrote to her in a letter, October 21, 1943, "I think you know more about dialect and superstitions and old customs than anyone in this country."

After reading Mary Elizabeth's "In the Hills" column in the Springfield paper, May Kennedy McCord, of Springfield, Missouri, radio station KWTO fame, traveled to the Mahnkey store in Oasis to meet her. McCord wrote in *Missouri Magazine* about their first meeting: "We came away silent and admiring, withal a bit subdued, but with no words to describe this woman with the light in her face from the candle within her soul."

Mary Elizabeth's inner light brightened the lives of all who knew her or read her writings. My purpose in this biography is to share her soft flame and to help today's readers to appreciate and understand life in the Ozark hills as she experienced it.

I'm not the only one recognizing her as an original writer and recorder of the culture of the Ozarks. Posthumous honors are still coming. In 1988 she was one of the 600 writers listed on "A Literary Map of Missouri," compiled by McReynolds and Patterson at Central Missouri State University at Warrensburg. Her biography was included in *Show Me Missouri Women, Vol. I*, edited by Mary K. Dains, Jefferson University Press in 1989.

In 1975 Mary Elizabeth was one of the first six people recognized in the Greater Ozarks Hall of Fame at the Ralph Foster Museum at the College of the Ozarks at Point Lookout, Missouri. The other initial honorees were Rose O'Neill,

Foreword

Thomas Hart Benton, Harold Bell Wright, May Kennedy McCord, and Vance Randolph. Although much has been written about the other five, Mary Elizabeth's story is almost unknown.

I have included some of her writings. All reported incidents, dialogues, and activities are gleaned from her published writings, her private journals, notes and letters, her interviews with journalist Marguerite Lyon, and from my visits with her family and friends.

Her story covers many years and places. Except for the first chapter, her award-winning trip to New York City, the book is chronological. The beginning of each chapter gives the location (or subject) and the dates covered.

I believe you will enjoy meeting Mary Elizabeth (Prather) Mahnkey, who continually turned and patched her life's fabric to show its brighter side. The light in her face from the candle within her soul rarely dimmed.

Mary Elizabeth Mahnkey, Oasis, 1930s

Chapter 1

FAR FROM A MOUNTAIN TRAIL
Award Trip to New York: July 19-29, 1935

What shall I do in the city
I with my mountain tread
With arms that are bramble-torn
And hands that are coarse and red?

Lost without my apron
And familiar old milk pail,
Bewildered, frightened, homesick
Far from a mountain trail.

Give me thy strength, O City,
That I may walk at ease
Among the throngs of strangers
As I do 'mid friendly trees.

Give me thy secret, O City,
To carry home with me
That I may bring my neighbors
A taste of this ecstasy.
                    (July 15, 1935)

"Mrs. Mahnkey, what do you think about Franklin Roosevelt and the New Deal?" the stylish reporter for the *New York Sun* asked the white-haired woman seated across the crowded hotel suite.

Mary Elizabeth Mahnkey paused briefly to think about her answer as she had often done during this interview. For over an hour more than a dozen big-city reporters had been firing questions at her. When asked a difficult question, she moved her head rapidly from side to side as lines appeared in her face. "I promised not to talk about the President or politics. I'm a staunch Republican."

"What about the people back in your Ozark hills?" the young woman persisted. "Do they have confidence in the Roosevelt administration?"

"Those who are on relief do," she retorted. All the reporters chuckled as they scribbled in their note pads.

"But don't you admit that his policies are bringing more prosperity?" a man asked.

"The people in my section of the country look to God, and not the administration, for prosperity. Out our way prosperity means do we have rain or don't we have rain. If we have rain, we are prosperous." Mary Elizabeth's soft voice quieted everyone.

The interview in the Chatham Hotel on Vanderbilt Avenue and 48th Street in New York City, July 21, 1935, was only minutes old when the reporters discovered that this simply dressed woman who sat up straight and greeted each one with a friendly smile was different from any celebrity they had ever talked with. They had not known what to expect from this woman from the hills, winner of the Crowell Publishing Company's widely publicized contest for country correspondents from the United States and Canada.

To these big-time journalists, working for a weekly country newspaper was the bottom step of journalism. *Time* magazine called the rural journalists the "nation's most obscure reporters"—the voluntary contributors like Mary Elizabeth Mahnkey, who sent in neighborhood news once a week. This woman had no journalistic training, little more than a grade school education, and hailed from a crossroads village that was not on most maps. She came from a backward county in a state little known to New Yorkers—Missouri.

No doubt the reporters from the *New York Times* or *World-Telegram* expected from this assignment only one short article in the back sections.

But even before they noticed the plump lady in a navy blue crepe dress sitting in the arm chair in the corner of her hotel suite reception room, latecomers recognized by the excitement in the room that this was *good* copy. Everyone was here—the Associated Press, all the bigwigs of Crowell Publishing Company, including its president Thomas Beck, Gertrude Lane of *Woman's Home Companion*, and even reporters from many out-of-town papers like Boston, Washington, D.C., and Montreal, Canada.

Though she was trembling slightly, Mary Elizabeth Mahnkey's grace, friendliness, wit, perfect English, and wide fund of knowledge quickly dispelled any notions of a stereotyped, backwoodsy character. She turned the interview into a friendly chat. Soon most of the reporters began relating to her as a fellow reporter who understood their assignment and was interested in them individually. She asked them questions while answering theirs and occasionally jotted down notes on pieces of paper and tucked them away. The reporters were "kind and considerate," she wrote later, "and I felt like I was visiting with a group of lively youngsters from back home."

If the reporters were surprised to find themselves assigned to cover a country correspondent, how much more surprised and amazed was Mary Elizabeth to find herself the center of nationwide publicity in New York City. "I realized exactly how Cinderella must have felt," she later wrote in her column. Since she had left home two days ago, cameras clicked and reporters asked questions every place she went. Friday, July 19, 1935, was the day she boarded the train in Branson, Missouri, for this trip to New York and Washington, D.C.—all part of her award for being judged by *The Country Home* as having written the best selections out of 1,581 sent in by country correspondents.

Like the New York reporters, modest Mary Elizabeth did not consider that she had done anything remarkable, even though she had been writing her column for forty-four years and was the one selected to represent the best of probably 100,000 rural correspondents. She told the reporters that there were only twenty-seven people in Oasis, the isolated crossroads village on Long Creek in western Taney County where, until recently, she and her husband had operated the store, post office, and gristmill. The newspaper she wrote for, the *Taney County Republican*, was published in Forsyth, the county seat.

"What news is there to write about with only twenty-seven people in your town?" a woman asked.

Mary Elizabeth laughed. "Sometimes I don't have enough. I jot down ideas all week while I'm tending the store or at home. When someone comes to the store, I visit with them and write down notes on sugar sacks or any bits of paper."

"But what about real news? How many robberies or murders would there be?"

"If any exciting crime or anything not exactly right happened in Oasis, I just let it go and didn't write it up." Mary Elizabeth patiently explained her method of news-reporting. "Those sorts of things happen in any place and there's not much of that anyway." She paused as her bewildered listeners took notes. "Everybody knows about those things, anyway."

"Well, what do you write about?" the reporter insisted.

"If any stranger came in," she said, "or anybody moved or a baby was born or somebody got married or died, then that was news. And when kinfolks came from a long way off, I'd mention all their names. If something I could write would brighten up the columns or make some one laugh or please some little child or some old, old person, I'd try to do that."

"Then you'd just write stuff like, 'Tom Smith drove his truck to town Saturday?'" a man asked. "Who'd want to read that?"

"He would and his family would," Mary Elizabeth retorted quickly, and then smiled. "But I wouldn't write just that. I'd write why he went. First, for example, I'd tell about Willie Knowlton's three little girls. They picked sixty gallons of huckleberries. Think of that! And then in his little old Ford truck he carried the berries all the way to Springfield on mighty crooked, rough roads, and sold them for fifty cents a gallon. That's what I call news. Huckleberries are awfully little."

"That isn't really news. It's just simple, commonplace items."

"Simple? Commonplace? Yes, of course they are. But there is beauty in simple things. I wonder sometimes if He, who walked by blue Galilee and who spoke always of simple things and loved to walk and talk with simple people, would be remembered at all if He had discussed nothing but relativity and the thusness of the thisness?"

The reporters were silent for a few seconds. "I understand that Oasis may be flooded if the proposed Table Rock Dam is built," said a reporter who had done his home work. "Do you write about that?"

"Only now and then," she said. "There's been speculation on the dam for years, and it will be a long time off before it is built, years probably. But my husband and I realize that Oasis will be gone some day. Already the town is being abandoned. We sold our store and moved into Forsyth."

"Do you ever run out of things to write?"

"When news is scarce, I fill the column with my poems."

Shyly Mary Elizabeth showed them *Ozark Lyrics*, her little book of poems, and passed around a scrapbook full of her clippings. After repeated urgings, she read in dialect:

Ridge Runner

If I could live on White Oak Ridge
It seems to me I'd ruther,
These river fields so rich and green
They cling, an' clutch, an' smother.

I love to feel a clean high wind
That whips the leaves together,
An' watch the lights in far off homes
Dance through the rainy weather.

What little breeze comes in this way
Is hot from heavy tillage.
How cool the shady door yards
In my little old home village.

This stiflin' corn shets off my breath
I'm tired of rakin', mowin'.
I'd ruther ramble down the ridge
See huckleberries growin'.

She looked up. "We in the Ozarks get mad when outsiders call us hillbillies. I can call myself that or we can call each other hillbillies, but others can't. Ridge runner is all right."

"Can you sum up your writing experience for us?" a reporter asked.

Mary Elizabeth passed her hand over her white hair, studying carefully before answering. "After forty-four years of writing for the paper, I can sum up my ideas in a few words. To tell the truth kindly, to remember that mankind's chief interest is man, and to read over my copy and scratch out most of the adjectives. As for my poetry, I really can't tell how I do it. It just comes to me so mysteriously that I have become quite reverent and solemn about it."

When at last the ordeal with the reporters was over, Wheeler McMillen, editor of *The Country Home*, took her for a walk. Later she wrote, "I thought that was the nicest thing. He just seemed to know what a country woman would like. It rested me so much."

That night after her first day in New York, she was too excited, too tired to sleep. The three days since she left home had been filled with new experiences. Now she needed to think back about how this all started and to organize her impressions in her mind. She needed to find the words to help share with her readers back home "A taste of this ecstasy."

First there was W. E. Freeland, the editor of the *Taney County Republican*. He had encouraged her to enter the contest because he admired her ability to write with a human touch that reached the heart. But she hadn't wanted to enter because she never had any luck in contests. Though judges admired her diction, phrasing, and ability to catch human emotion, "technical errors in meter" kept her poems from first place.

Sensitive and easily hurt, Mary Elizabeth had agreed to enter only if Freeland would pick out the columns. She mailed in his choices and then forgot about the contest during the busy time of selling the store and moving.

Actually, the original idea for the contest was Mary Elizabeth's. She had written several times to Russell Lord, one of *The Country Home* editors, submitting letters and poems for his section of the magazine, a readers' column called "The Forum." In one letter she suggested that some recognition be given country correspondents. A former reporter on a country paper himself, Mr. Lord thought that would be a worthwhile project for his magazine.

It was Russell Lord's task to narrow down the hundreds of entries to the few to be presented to the panel of judges. When he came across Mary Elizabeth's entry, he remembered her. Though he was certain that her work was the best, he removed the names and locations of all contestants from their entries and said nothing about any of the writers as he gave the submissions to the judges. The judges' decision agreed with his. They chose Mary Elizabeth unanimously.

She first received a telegram from editor Wheeler. McMillen notifying her she had won and then a letter inviting her to New York. Though greatly honored, she did not want to go to New York to receive the award.

"Anything I wanted less in my life than a trip to New York, I don't know what it would have been, unless maybe the smallpox!" she said. But her son Douglas and her friends insisted.

She had a busy time getting ready. Many friends offered help. One made two dresses for her and another brought her silk nightgowns and underwear. "The first silk pants I ever owned. My, I felt dressed up with all those nice things!" Mary Elizabeth wrote. The total for all her purchases for the trip was $12.67—a hat, hose, and material for two dresses and a slip.

Her author friend, Rose Wilder Lane, daughter of Laura Ingalls Wilder, brought her a black velvet dress and an evening wrap, saying that even if Mary Elizabeth spilled gravy or anything on the dress it would be all right. But it was too fancy for Mary Elizabeth; she didn't bring it. Lane did lend her two leather bags. The Taneyhills Study Club, the group that had published her book of verses, presented her with a handbag. Luggage was a problem, since she had never gone any place where she needed more than a basket.

Not all her friends' help was in the form of material things. Just before she left home, a neighbor told Mary Elizabeth about overhearing her mother praying more loudly and more fervently than she ever prayed before. When the mother came out of the next room wiping her eyes, she gave a long drawn sigh, like one who was relieved after a terrible strain. "Well," she said, "Mamie will be all right even though they are taking her on that awful trip to New York. I've just been praying for her."

Mary Elizabeth was pleased to hear her youthful nickname. She was Mother, Nanny, or Mrs. Mahnkey now. Her husband, Pres, rarely used any name other than Old Lady. In her journal she wondered if it was a sign of increasing age? She'd soon be fifty-eight. Or maybe finally she was being recognized as a person in her own right, separate from her family. She thought it was strange, for when she first tried sending pieces and poems for publications, other than the weekly column in the county paper, she had success only when she used her full name, Mary Elizabeth Mahnkey.

But not everyone had been excited about her winning entry. Mary Elizabeth remembered what one old woman said, "I never could see nothin' in ol' Miz Mahnkey's writings to make them win such honor."

Mary Elizabeth agreed. She'd been writing her column since she was fourteen—when her father had given her his job of writing community news for the county paper because his election to the Missouri Legislature kept him away from home for a few months of the year. She had written over 2,200 such items, rarely missing a week; she had become so accustomed to writing that she thought nothing of it. She also had done the family washing that many times, but that was not grounds for a trip to New York.

All ready to leave, with friends waiting to drive her to the train station, she admitted to her husband that she worried about how she should act. Pres had said, "Well, Old Lady, just be yourself." She hated leaving him standing alone at the gate, as she had never been away from him for so long on a purely pleasure trip. Nervous and frightened from the moment she left home, she had controlled her feelings and braced herself for whatever she must do.

Now, three days later, nine stories up in the middle of metropolitan New York, she appreciated her neighbors' concern for her going so far away. Her home, her hills, and the people in her real world were quite a contrast to this glamorous, flower-filled hotel parlor recently crowded with city reporters. Her suite had two bedrooms, which together were about the size of the little house she and Pres had just moved into after selling their country store at Oasis.

She was so filled with impressions she hardly knew which to record for her readers back home. She'd ridden trains before, but not in a Pullman berth. "I never got used to it. A woman that's lulled to sleep all summer by the rustling of leaves just outside her window will find no comfort in a Pullman berth. It's too artificial. I felt like a bird in a cage. I got out and sat by the window all night."

Even more confining than a Pullman was the subway. Declaring it an underground trap, she refused to ride one.

But she had climbed too many trees and mountains to let something like the Empire State Building inhibit her. In contrast to the subways and the crowded streets, high places were open and free. From up there the New York skyscrapers looked like poplar trees in a mist.

Coming from a self-sufficient lifestyle, she was impressed by this different way of life. She wrote:

> Here they are, seven million human souls, and they don't produce an egg, a chicken, a beef, a hog. They don't grow a tomato, a potato, a cabbage head, or a grain of wheat or oats or anything they eat. There isn't one of them can go out to the barn in the morning and bring in a half dozen freshly laid eggs for breakfast. There isn't a smokehouse in the whole place where a woman can go and cut off a slice or two of ham for dinner. There isn't a garden where she can go to pick a mess of lettuce or dig a boiling of new potatoes.

She couldn't understand how people would choose to be so dependent. "I'd rather live in the Ozarks where I can raise my own garden truck, hogs, and chickens, and when we want fish, all we have to do is walk down a few rods to White River and put out a throw line and get a mess of fish. I wouldn't trade my little old farm for all New York."

Another contrast that struck her was the crowds of people. In her country store at home on slow days, maybe only a dozen people would stop by. "New York is so large, the buildings so tall, the rivers of humanity so endless in its streets that I feel crushed and oppressed by the weight of it every minute. It is so unreal to me, brought up among the hills; New York is so wildly alert and energetic, so restless that it all seems to me as a bad dream. I feel like I imagine Jack felt when he climbed the bean stalk and got to the land of the giants, where everything was so big that it set his head awhirl. That's New York, a big, unnatural giant, with little pygmies of humans streaming through the canyons between its mighty cliffs, and at night disappearing into its caves to crawl out again next morning to stream ceaselessly through its canyons again."

The next two days in New York were a whirl of places and people. Mary Elizabeth smiled at everyone and began calling the women reporters "honey." She enjoyed getting to know the men on *The Country Home* staff, especially Russell Lord. She was escorted around New York, steeling herself to get through the difficult times, such as the radio interview, but enjoying the sightseeing and other experiences.

She did not appear nervous as she chatted with James W. Barrett, editor of the Press Radio Bureau at Radio City on NBC-WEAF national radio. "Ever since I can remember I wanted to write," she spoke into the microphone. "When I was a little girl, I told my parents I was sure I was going to grow up to be an old maid and a famous writer. I wrote one novel after another but always burned them up after I wrote them."

She was nervous about meeting Al Smith and Mayor Fiorella H. LaGuardia, but both quickly put her at ease. She thought Al Smith looked old and tired, and although she had voted against him in the 1928 presidential election because he was a Democrat, she admired him. "He was good to his mother and grandmother. He is rich in humanness."

Mayor LaGuardia won her heart by presenting her with a ship-in-a-bottle, something she had always wanted. It was a three masted topsail schooner in full sail inside a pint whiskey bottle with the sides pinched in.

"What kind of ship is it?" Mary Elizabeth asked.

The mayor laughed, "I don't know what kind of ship it is, but I sure know what kind of a bottle it's in!"

While drinking lemonade and chatting, Mary Elizabeth admitted her weakness was writing.

"My weakness is talking too much, I'm afraid," the mayor said.

In spite of her fatigue and nervousness from the activities and the pressure of reporters, Mary Elizabeth did not miss a thing. When asked if she would like to visit the Stork Club, a fashionable night club, she said, "Yes, I want to do it up right because I'll never be back anymore."

"Will you wear an evening dress, Mrs. Mahnkey?"

"No ma'am!" she returned emphatically. Her best Sunday dress was quite sufficient for any occasion.

She had never seen such dancing and singing as in Cole Porter's musical, *Anything Goes*. "The seats were three dollars and five dollars, and I couldn't understand why anyone would pay so much to see such a silly thing," she said. "But I'm an old-fashioned woman and I'll never get used to naked women." When corrected that they were not naked, she answered, "Those on the stage didn't have on enough clothes to wad a shotgun."

Of more interest to her were the big newspapers. Their size amazed her. Reporters carried the bulky papers around under their arms and then tossed them away carelessly. Though she stacked them up to read at night after she got to her room, most of the time she was too tired. And the next day there would be another stack. She thought of how her family loved their daily newspaper from Springfield and would give it to someone else to read after they finished it.

One of the reporters told her that the famous columnist, Haywood Broun, president of the American Newspaper Guild, wrote about her in his column. He had read that the prize-winning rural correspondent did not write about crime and, pointing out that her pay consisted only of a subscription to the paper and writing paper and stamps, he intimated that she was not a real newspaper woman.

"Is that so!" Mary Elizabeth declared. "Well, if this Mr. Broun lived in a place of twenty-seven people and was married to the proprietor of the general store, maybe he wouldn't be so quick to send in stories that reflected on the residents."

After justifying herself to the amusement of the reporters around her, she added a more serious tone, "New Yorkers seem to be like the folks back home in one respect—they seem to be surprised and amazed at my winning this prize. Some of them can't understand how a woman should have won the prize when there were so many men writers trying for it. But out our way women do everything. Our banker, who accompanied me on my trip east, is a woman, Mrs. Ella McHaffie. The taxicab that took me to the Missouri Pacific Railroad station when I left home was driven by a woman, who owns and runs it."

New York offered Mary Elizabeth other experiences which moved her to express indignation or tears.

Just after driving through Chinatown, she saw long lines of men inching along in bread lines. She wrote, "Just think of that! Those poor fellows! They couldn't have been very well filled up after they got to the Salvation Army, for there were so many of them. Then in the Park I saw great big strapping fellows, handsome and smart-looking, lying on park benches with their knees all drawn up and newspapers over them. I asked why those big fellows weren't out working, and Mr. Lord said they would be mighty happy if they could be working. Of course, fellows don't work all the time in the hills, but they don't lie down out in public like that. They would be around the barn or on a creek bank some place."

But usually she enjoyed the crowds and the eager young reporters who were around her most of the time. "I like to be where there's something going on," she said.

But she admitted she did not think she could write much

in New York. "I'd be sort of out of tune with things, some way."

After visiting Washington, D.C., another long train ride awaited her. At every change of trains on her trip home there were reporters. In St. Louis reporters from the *Globe Democrat* and *Post Dispatch* met her at the station. As she changed trains in Carthage, Missouri, local reporters and one from the *Kansas City Star* interviewed her.

But there were no reporters at her home depot in Branson. She stepped gladly out of the cool coach into the Missouri heat where she could see the blue Ozark hills. No one was there, not even her son Doug to greet her. She paid the taxi driver two dollars to drive her the last few miles to her home in Forsyth where she surprised her husband and Doug's family, who were expecting her train two hours later.

Doug and Merle and their children were cooking a big dinner for her return. Grandchildren Pat and Mary Jo flew to greet her. Pres stood by grinning, happy to have her back. A few minutes later her daughter's children, Leon and Winnie Bee, burst in, followed by their parents, Bertie and Roy Jones. Awaiting her return were cheerful notes of congratulations from her second son and his wife, Reggie and Bertha, who lived in North Dakota.

She was home where she belonged. Her family, her neighbors, the Ozark land—from these she gathered her strength, her inspiration.

In the days that followed she relived her trip, reflecting on her experiences and the contrasts she saw between her life in the isolated hills and that of people in the eastern metropolitan areas. How different her life would be if her parents' families had remained in the East.

With leisure to think about it, she knew that more than the public recognition of her work, more than meeting the famous people in New York and touring the Library of Congress in Washington, D.C., the high points of her trip may have been seeing the areas where her parents and grandparents once lived. Traveling through the regions she had heard her mother and father talk about helped her to understand her background and her family's migration to the Ozarks.

The train trip had taken her through upper New York state, former home of her mother's family, the McMillans. Then the train stopped in Cincinnati, where her parents, Lieutenant and Mrs. Alonzo Prather, had spent their honeymoon while he was on convalescent furlough during the Civil War.

Through the moving window she had glimpsed the station sign, "North Vernon," the Indiana town where her mother and father met, lived for a few years before and after their marriage, and where her three older brothers were born.

As she crossed Missouri she rode through or near many of the places she herself had lived, rekindling old memories and stories. The journey helped her review the times and places important to her as well as affirm her love of her hills and people.

Now it was Mary Elizabeth's turn to be the storyteller, and like her family, the Prathers and McMillans, she moved many times. "I think the Prathers should be classified among the nomad tribes," Mary Elizabeth had written in her journal as early as January 22, 1902. She did not know then at the beginning of her marriage that she and Pres would rarely stay long in one location. Constantly searching for something better, time after time they packed up for new locations, new opportunities, or new experiences.

Her grandparents, her parents, and now she and her husband, were all restless. Though she had lost count of her parents' moves, she kept a running list of those she and Pres had made in their married life together. Counting their present home in the little house near Forsyth, there were thirty.

Chapter 2

SHE MADE LIFE SWEET
Ancestry and Early Childhood—
Indiana, Arkansas, and Kansas
1857-1880

When they talk of praying mothers
My thoughts go back to mine.
I do not remember prosy prayers
But a love almost divine.

How patiently she worked for us
And made life sweet and gay
As she whistled at her daily tasks
Or helped us in our play.

Nellie Gray, or Red Wing
Or He Leads Me by the Hand,
And I know that mother talked with God
When she whistled Beulah Land.

Though moving was not new to the Prather family when they came to north central Arkansas in 1869 eight years before Mary Elizabeth was born, neither was it the end of their search for better opportunities.

One of Mary Elizabeth's earliest memories was the

move her family made in 1878 from Harrison, Arkansas, to south central Kansas near the present town of Mulvane when she was barely two years old.

One day during the long and tedious journey west, Colonel Alonzo Prather and his wife, Betsy, were sitting on the high front seat of the covered wagon, Betsy holding in her arms baby Joe, who was born just before leaving Harrison. In the bed of the wagon, with all their belongings, rode the four boys and little sister. Betsy had given the boys strict orders to watch out for Mamie, as her family called Mary Elizabeth. There was not much to do, and it was raining. The noise of water hitting the canvas cover was so loud the children could hardly hear one another.

Little Mary Elizabeth's inquisitive hand was about to touch the canvas wagon cover where, full of water, it had sunk in momentarily. Her brother Ben grabbed her hand. The boys all understood that one never broke the magic spell of the canvas in rain by touching it or it would let the water stream through.

The child pulled her hand back promptly. Anything these big brothers did or said was law to her. She adored these four big brothers—the oldest, thoughtful and kind Bob, dashing Ben and Frank, and stylish, elegant Dick.

Mary Elizabeth remembered that Frank was stretched out across the opening at the back of the wagon, probably thinking to keep his active little sister corralled. But the rocking of the wagon, the monotonous sounds of the horses' feet, and the beating of the rain lulled him to sleep. The other three boys were playing a game in which she was too small to join. They forgot about her as they soon tired of the game and likewise fell asleep.

Not so little Mary Elizabeth. Wide awake, she crawled over Frank to peer out the side where the canvas was looped up to let in air. Even as a toddler, she expressed her love of nature and beauty. Perhaps the inner light of her candle began with this early memory. Fascinated with the wet, dripping countryside disappearing behind the wagon, she leaned over the side. Not content with merely seeing, she stretched out her arms to feel the warm rain and perhaps catch a pretty leaf as the wagon rumbled by.

Mary Elizabeth Prather, circa 1880

Suddenly a front wheel struck a rock; the wagon lurched violently and threw Mary Elizabeth out. Just as her head hit a big rock, the rear wagon wheel ran over her hand. Unconscious she lay there in the rain in the track of the wagon wheel.

When the wagon jolted, the team jumped. Cursing, the colonel fought to control the horses, while his wife beside him tightened her grasp on the baby as she held on to the iron railing of the seat to prevent being thrown forward under the horses' feet. The boys barely stirred, so used were they to the wagon's rough motion.

Behind them, her golden curls and full-skirted, long-sleeved, woolen dress becoming wet with rain, Mary Elizabeth lay unconscious in the trail. The wagon traveled about two miles before her mother turned to check on the children.

It was too quiet back there. She spied the four sleeping boys but could not see Mary Elizabeth.

The family searched frantically, finally realizing she must have fallen out when the wagon struck the big rock. Alonzo quickly turned the horses around; Betsy handed the sleeping baby to brother Ben, parents and brothers all straining to see a tiny girl in a dark dress. She would be almost impossible to discern in the rain.

When was the last time anyone remembered seeing her? How far had they come? Was she hurt? Did she walk off in the woods looking for a pretty flower or leaf? Even at that young age she was known to wander off, losing herself fondling and picking flowers. Did someone find her and take her away? No, they hadn't met any wagons. What about wild animals? These and many other fears and possibilities went through their minds as the wagon backtracked.

The worry of the parents as they raced the tired horses back was increased when they thought of the two baby girls they had already lost.

Suddenly around a bend they saw the child, still unconscious, lying limp and sodden beside the rock. Alonzo pulled the horses to a stop, jumped out, and picked her up tenderly. He stood there for a few seconds without speaking.

He examined her quickly, experienced by his years on the battlefield. He found a big bump on her head and a crushed right hand.

While her mother held her, Alonzo hurried the horses back over the trail to the little town they passed through that morning.

There the doctor examined the child. "No bones are broken except this right hand. These two fingers are crushed. He held the small mangled hand in his big one, carefully cleaning the mud from it. He moved and examined the fingers.

"I'm afraid we'll have to cut off these two fingers."

As he and the anxious parents bent over the hand, Mary Elizabeth stirred. Without opening her eyes she whispered, "Don't cut off Mamie's fingers."

The doctor did not cut them off. All her life those two fingers were never quite as agile as the others, and during cold weather they ached a little, but otherwise Mary Elizabeth suffered no harmful effects from her tumble out of the wagon.

This move to Kansas was only one in a long series for her family, the McMillans and the Prathers. Like thousands of other early American families, each generation made at least one move, often many moves. The McMillans, originally from Londonderry, Ireland, settled in Oneida County, New York. Ephriam McMillan, Mary Elizabeth's grandfather, died there of tuberculosis when her mother was small. The youngest boy, Jarius B. McMillan, settled in North Vernon in southeastern Indiana, and in 1857 sent for his mother and three younger sisters, fixing up a house for them.

One of the sisters was Mary Elizabeth's mother, Ada Maria (the early spelling, Adah Mariah, shows how it was pronounced). When thirteen-year-old Ada, usually called Betsy, started to the new school in the Indiana town, a tall boy in one of the upper grades, Alonzo Prather, looked scornfully at her and said, "Well, a little blue-bellied Yankee has come to town."

The Prather family had been in America since 1622 when Thomas Prater (original spelling) ran away from his home in England. He stowed away on the ship *Marie Providence* and settled in Virginia. In the next four generations, Mary Elizabeth's branch of the Prather family moved from Virginia to Maryland, to North Carolina, and then to Indiana. Hiram Prather, Mary Elizabeth's grandfather, helped found North Vernon, Indiana.

When Fort Sumter fell April 13, 1861, Hiram Prather and his seven sons all volunteered for Lincoln's army. Hiram and three sons, including Alonzo, served in the 6th Regiment of Indiana Volunteers, which was organized September 20, 1861. Hiram was a lieutenant colonel and fought in the Battle of Shiloh. All seven brothers had honorable records, all becoming officers. Alonzo Prather, Mary Elizabeth's father, fought at Shiloh, was wounded at Chickamauga on September 20, 1863, went home to recover, and then, rejoining the army, marched with Sherman to the sea.

Enlisting as a sergeant, Alonzo achieved the rank of second lieutenant. Given the honorary title of Lieutenant Colonel, in later years he was always addressed as Colonel Prather.

While Alonzo Prather was home convalescing from the wound received at Chickamauga, he looked upon little Betsy McMillan differently from the way he did when she first moved into the town as a child. Though still small in build, she was grown up and pretty. They married. Mary Elizabeth wrote that though her mother was "meek, gentle, and dove-like, she had a steely tenacity," a quality she needed during the many hardships ahead of her in Arkansas, Kansas, and Missouri.

After the war the couple lived in North Vernon for a few years. Three little boys, Frank, Ben, and Bob, arrived one after the other. Alonzo continued his interrupted college work in law. He did some farming and served as doorkeeper in the House of the Indiana legislature.

Restless after his army service, seeking better opportunities for his growing family, and wanting to heal the breach and help the people of the Confederacy to regain their place in the Union, Alonzo Prather accepted a government position in Arkansas.

Later Colonel Prather was appointed Superintendent of

Public Instruction of a district in north Arkansas embracing nine present day counties. He was chairman of the Building Committee of the Arkansas Industrial University at Fayetteville, now the University of Arkansas.

After the move to Arkansas the fourth son, Dick, was born, followed by two daughters who died. Gracie reached ten months of age; the other was still-born. Mary Elizabeth was born August 16, 1877, in Harrison, Arkansas, where her father was Receiver for the Land Office.

After spending several years in Arkansas, Colonel Prather wanted some land and a home for his family. He bought the section of land in Kansas.

Mary Elizabeth believed her tumble from the wagon on the move there foretold that the Kansas migration would fail. Her mother hated Kansas and to the end of her ninety-five years spoke with horror of their experience there. First, though they obtained a section of land, cultivating it was unlike any farming they had known in Indiana or Arkansas. The land was different; the thick virgin prairie sod had to be broken before they could plant.

The horses that brought them from Arkansas were not equal to the job. Colonel Prather traded them for two wiry mules, which were hardly sufficient, either. The sharp prairie grasses cut the mules' legs until they bled. The Prathers loved animals and could not bear to see them suffer. Though they had very little bedding or any fabric furnishings other than what they had brought in the wagon, Betsy got out her counterpanes—fine, handwoven bedspreads that were mainly decorative. Without a qualm she tore the beautiful spreads into strips which the men bound around the legs of the mules each morning before they were hitched to the plow.

Probably most of all Betsy hated the incessant wind, which, according to Mary Elizabeth, literally "blew the hems out of her sheets when she hung them on the clothesline." The wind blew her bonnet off and tugged at her long skirts until she could hardly walk for clutching them to keep them down. It tore at the garden plants. The hot wind dried out everyone's skin and wore out the animals and people as they continually fought their way against it.

The Indians were also a problem. Betsy was halfway afraid of them. "Real blanket Indians," she said. "They would come right into the house, without knocking or invitation, and let it be known they wanted food."

The Prathers rarely had much extra food, but since the Indians demanded it, Betsy fed them. One time when Alonzo and the boys were gone, some Indians barged in. Betsy had just dumped out of the pans the complete bi-weekly baking of brown-crusted, fragrant bread. The Indians filled the kitchen, jabbering and laughing about the hot loaves on the table. They ate every crumb.

Betsy was incensed at the Indians' behavior but knew to remain quiet and not to interfere since she was alone in the house. Little Mamie watched them curiously as they broke the bread into chunks and wolfed it down. Her mother had just changed her dress and combed out her curls which hung in golden ringlets. Though she was not quite three years old, she remembered clearly their leaving after they had eaten all the bread and drunk from the water pail. One tall Indian turned back, picked her up, and joined the others in the yard. With no fear at all, the child peered curiously into the Indian's face, even smiling shyly when the Indian and his companions amused themselves by pulling out the tight curls as far as they could go and letting them bounce back in place. The Indians laughed at the fair child who was so different from their children.

Horrified, Betsy stood silent with clasped hands as she

watched the big Indian run through the gate carrying her little girl. Betsy was probably praying, though when she told the story years after, she never said so. "She was always awfully quiet about things like that," Mary Elizabeth wrote.

Just beyond the gate, all of the Indians were talking, gesticulating, and pointing back to the house. The other Indians seemed to be arguing with the one carrying the child. Then the big Indian ran back and gently set the little girl over the fence. Without a backward glance he ran to rejoin his companions.

Many years later Mary Elizabeth told the story to her wide-eyed grandchildren gathered around her kitchen writing table. Little Pat looked at her, not knowing if this was a true tale or one of her "ha'nt" stories. "How come they brought you back?" he asked.

"You see, children," she answered, "the other Indians made the kidnapper bring me back because they had broken bread in our house. Wasn't it lucky for me that Mother had let them eat that bread?"

She let the information sink in and ended gaily, "And that's how the Indians almost got your granny!"

Chapter 3

I HAD THE FUN
Childhood: 1880 - 1890

We went a-fishing,
My brother and I;
He watched the stream
I watched the sky.
He had a fight
With a wild black bass,
I smiled to see
A blue crane pass.
He did the work
I had the fun—
And yet that night
When the fish were done
Crispy and brown
With hot cornbread—
"You seem to like 'em,"
My brother said.

After the unsuccessful year in Kansas, the Prathers moved back to the hills, this time selecting Taney County in the Missouri Ozarks. Restless as many soldiers were after the war, Alonzo uprooted the family many times, seeking better opportunities and dealing in land sales. He sold or traded property as readily as he sold his livestock. During these years, the family grew. Adelia (Deal) was born in 1883 and Margaret (Mag) in 1886. The big brothers grew up and began leaving home. When the family moved back to Missouri from Kansas, they lived at first in several places near Kirbyville, a thriving village in the bald knob country of southern Taney County. Later they moved to a big farm in St. Clair County, and then into Appleton City. They lived in Ponce de Leon for a short time, in the town of Ozark two different times, and at least twice on a big farm just south of Springfield on Finley River.

The endless moving of the Prathers, and later of Mary Elizabeth and her husband, was not typical of hill families. Most people stayed, once they moved to the area and owned their farm. In fact, the population of the Ozarks has been traditionally stable, continuing to this day having less out-migration than most areas in the United States.

Each time the Prather family moved, if the distance was a short one, it would be an exciting event for the children. With the help of the almost grown older boys, the Prathers loaded four or five wagons with furniture, canned fruits, hay, and grain. The horses and cattle brought up the rear. The boys drove some of the wagons, and neighbors went along to drive others.

On the move from Appleton City back to Taney County, the Colonel did not have much help as the two oldest boys did not move with them that time. The oldest son, Frank, was in the printing business in Appleton City, and Bob stayed to finish his education. Mary Elizabeth remembered the move as an adventure for her and her younger brother, Joe. They loved the beautiful countryside and thought fording the sparkling rivers and creeks was fun. Since it was warm weather, the children waded in the creeks.

The procession was exciting because the Colonel had

bought some quality horses and cattle, including a good shorthorn bull. Traveling slowly because of the cattle, they camped along the way at night. On the trail the Colonel prepared most of the meals, expertly starting a fire. In a little black kettle, he cooked potatoes in their jackets, sometimes adding eggs to the boiling water. He would go to nearby farm houses for apples and peaches.

"This is a picture of me taken when I was thirteen years old and Deal was nine." Mamie Prather.

Alonzo and the boys slept under the wagon with tarpaulins draped around the sides to make an impromptu tent. Betsy, Mary Elizabeth, and little sister Deal slept inside the covered wagon on a mattress and springs that were fitted on the sides of the wagon bed.

Inside a grown person had to stoop to move around, but the little girls could stand upright under the bows which held up the canvas covers. At night Betsy and the girls changed into their nightgowns and nightcaps. Though little girls all had to wear a nightcap to protect their hair, Mary Elizabeth didn't like hers because it was hot and difficult to iron.

Nearly always when the family camped near a house, men joined them to visit with the travelers by the fire. Women did not come. "In the hills, the old-time mountain women were pretty backward. They kept out of sight when anyone came," Mary Elizabeth said during her long interviews with Marguerite Lyon in 1946.

One night a man said to Alonzo, "You ain't a-goin' to let them young'uns sleep under that wagon? Why jis' t'other day I killed a great big rattlesnake right about here." The possibility of snakes pleased Joe. After that he thought that it was a great adventure to sleep under the wagon. "He probably hoped he'd wake up with a rattler in each pocket," Mary Elizabeth said.

When the family reached the town of Ozark, Alonzo traded a family ring for a farm. Mary Elizabeth said, "Sometimes I believe a love of land can be as great a curse as love of gambling or any other vice."

The heavy ring had a bright, pretty colored stone set in it. "Dad had all of us look at it--sort of a farewell ceremony, perhaps," Mary Elizabeth said. "It was farewell to more than that. Dad had started out with such high ambitions, and there he was, beginning to let loose of little things that he cherished." Years later when the Colonel saw the man again he recognized the ring on his hand.

Mary Elizabeth thought it was strange that soldiers returning from the war had to do so much floating around before they could settle down. Though her father had a large family, he sold their home, traded off family treasures, took his children out of school, and moved on.

It seems a paradox that being educated himself, working hard for public elementary education in Arkansas, and helping found the University of Arkansas, Colonel Prather neglected the education of his own younger children. In her childhood years Mary Elizabeth did not attend formal school more than a total of twenty or twenty-five months—a short session in Appleton City when she was seven, two three-month terms at Oak Grove, part of a term in Ozark when she was twelve, and some scattered schooling later in Kirbyville and Forsyth.

But lack of formal schooling did not mean she was un-educated. She learned from her family. Her parents were well educated for the times, and her older brothers, growing up in the more stable Arkansas days, had received regular school-ing. And no matter how crowded the wagon in moving, the family took their library; no matter how crimped financially, a big-city newspaper came regularly to their current address.

"Read, read, read," Colonel Prather used to say. "That's the way to learn."

Mary Elizabeth learned to read before she attended school. Dick, the youngest of the four older brothers and six years older than she, taught her to read one winter by reading the newspapers covering the walls of their farmhouse. Some of the newspapers were pasted upside down. "We nearly broke our necks reading those," Mary Elizabeth said.

After they were settled on the Oak Grove farm back in the bald knobs, she attended only two terms of school al-though the family lived there four years. The school term was just three months, September, October, and November. In later years Mary Elizabeth was a little ashamed of her lack of education. Even though self-educated beyond many, and proud of her ability, she indicated that her lack of formal edu-cation probably contributed to her life-long shyness around important people and her sensitivity to social or literary criti-cism.

Just before her first day at the Oak Grove School, Colo-nel Prather brought home from Kirbyville a first reader. Mary Elizabeth sat down and read it aloud from cover to cover to her little brother and sister.

"Can you read?" the cross old teacher with bushy eyebrows asked her the next morning.

"Yes, I can read," she said proudly. "I've read *The Vicar of Wakefield*, *Pilgrim's Progress*, and lots of others."

The teacher gave her a strange look and said curtly, "Sit down and read in your first reader."

In the one-room school building, Dick heard the conversation. That night at home he told the family, "The little fool said she had read Oliver Goldsmith's *The Vicar of Wakefield*, and the teacher had never heard of it!" Everyone laughed because of the teacher's ignorance. But Mary Elizabeth thought Dick was making fun of her.

"Dick was so superior and I was awfully afraid of him," Mary Elizabeth said. "He had a kind of ridiculing manner. Probably he didn't mean it at all, but he was just born with extra talent and he was big and wonderful looking. My inferiority complex grew by the hour when he was around."

The one-room log schoolhouse was very crude. The children hung their wraps on smoothly whittled pegs that were driven into holes bored in the log walls. There was a row of pegs on each side of the door. There were no desks, only hard uncomfortable benches so high that the smaller children had to swing their feet all day. Since there was no place to lay their books, pupils had to hold them.

The teacher's discipline was strict and cruel. The slightest whisper brought punishment. One day someone rode a horse up to the schoolhouse. Without thinking Mary Elizabeth whispered to her seat mate, "Who is that?"

Etta didn't answer. She just shook her head. The teacher, walking around the room carrying a big pointed iron bar used in mining, thought Etta was whispering. He struck her twice across her knees and her hand as hard as he could. Big tears rolled down Etta's cheeks, but she took the whipping without a word. She did not tell him that Mary Elizabeth whispered to her. For years afterward, Mary Elizabeth worried about causing her friend to get a whipping.

One day the schoolhouse roof caught fire from the stove-pipe that ran up through the ceiling. Since there was no other way of extinguishing the flames—the only water was the spring quite a distance away—the big boys climbed up on the roof and tore the shingles off with their bare hands.

"Quick now, ever'body," the teacher shouted over the excited cries of the children and the noise of the boys on the roof, "Quick, git your books and git outside!"

Mary Elizabeth thought only of her two books, her McGuffey's Reader and the blue-backed spelling book. Her friend staggered out with a big load, her own and the books belonging to the boys fighting the fire. She looked at Mary Elizabeth's load, "Is that all you brung?"

The second teacher at Oak Grove was quite a contrast to the first. Rose DeLong was refined and loving to the children. Mary Elizabeth loved her. She lived near the Prathers, riding to school on a large gray horse called Shiloh.

Rose had a small, hairless Mexican dog named Gyp that she would bring to school. Since he was always cold, she let the little girls hold him during lessons. He loved Mary Elizabeth. Once when a girl tried to take him away from her, the dog howled like he was being killed. Rose laughed. Instead of whipping the girls as the other teacher would have done, Rose let Mary Elizabeth keep Gyp until he was ready to go to someone else.

Mary Elizabeth loved school, even the walk there every day. She, Dick, and Joe met the three neighbor children and walked the mile and a half to school around the bald knob. The top of the knob was covered with bluestem prairie grass which came up to the children's necks. If they fell down as they played games in the grass, they would be out of sight.

Even in winter the grass was beautiful when ice formed on it in feathery crystals. Since a clump of frosted grass looked like a rabbit sitting up, they called it rabbit ice.

There were many children at the school, as many as forty and fifty, some coming as far as five miles. One group came on horseback from the White River, bringing into the schoolhouse their dinner buckets, their saddles, and the sacks of corn to feed their horses at noon.

Quite a contrast to the Oak Grove School was the private school in Appleton City run by a woman of culture and refinement. Mary Elizabeth was happy in the school and enjoyed the other families she knew and associated with. "It seems to me that was the only chance I ever had for any sort of gracious living—at least in my childhood--and it seemed so pleasant and happy."

Mary Elizabeth was twelve before she had any arithmetic teaching other than simple addition and subtraction on the slates she had at home. In 1889 Colonel Prather moved his family first to Ponce de Leon and then to Ozark, where he bought a store. When Mary Elizabeth attended school in Ozark, the first lesson was long division. She was ashamed of her ignorance. One of the girls felt sorry for her and tried to help her. Mary Elizabeth wrote in her journal, "When the teacher saw that I knew no mathematics, she jumped in and helped me, and by early spring, I was in simple fractions."

Though she was never very good with figures, Mary Elizabeth excelled in reading and composition. Penmanship, however was difficult for her to learn. During the severe winter of 1888, when the family was snowbound for many days, Dick taught her to write. The writing instructions were worse for her than the reading lessons had been. Often Dick slapped her hands, shouting at her to quit cramping her fingers, to stop holding the pen like it was a hammer. What she hated most was his making her hold her right hand level to write so smoothly that a dime would stay on the back of her wrist. That was stupid, she thought.

When still a child Mary Elizabeth began writing stories, a natural act for her as she often saw her mother writing in her journals and writing lengthy letters to her family back East. Her father, Dick, and Frank all wrote for or edited newspapers at various times.

Mary Elizabeth and Joe made their own pens and ink to write down their adventures. They fashioned pens from chicken feathers. For ink they extracted a purplish juice from small marble-like growths they found on blackjack oak sprouts.

Reading, either alone or listening to a family member, was another treasured activity. On cold nights by the fireplace, after Betsy Prather prepared supper for her family, one of the older brothers would read aloud a long serial story from a weekly newspaper.

Nothing was more precious to Mary Elizabeth than a book. "When I was a girl," she wrote in *The Country Home*, April 8, 1933, "books were scarce, but I grew up with the tattered remains of a grand old library that toured the Ozark hills with us. So I revered a book and would walk miles to where folks lived who had books, thinking they would loan me one. But one unseeing soul gave me a cabbage to carry home instead of a 'blame book.' I never did like her."

Just twenty-three months younger, the sibling nearest Mary Elizabeth's age was Joe. In *Missouri Magazine*, October 1930, Mary Elizabeth described their fun-filled, carefree days. "Warmly dressed we played outdoors all winter. Always I wore little waterproof flannel dresses, checked aprons, and flannel bloomers. Brother wore a little round hat and I had a little blue hood. Both of us wore copper-toed shoes. My, how often I moistened my fingers in my mouth and then with much labor rubbed those copper toes until they turned to glistening yellow gold. How often since those halcyon days, by using plenty of elbow grease and imagination have I transformed the commonest of commonplace things into silver and gold."

The children made dolls of corn cobs, using the bright golden corn silk for hair and smuggling out scraps of their mother's quilt patches for clothing.

The imaginative children even used nails for dolls. Like most people in the hills, the Prather parents saved anything that could have a future use, pieces of fabric for quilts, or old nails. Colonel Prather kept used nails in an old tin can. When he passed a board with a nail in it, he pulled it out, carefully straightened it, and added it to his collection.

One time he brought home from Forsyth a package of new slim nails unlike the square homemade nails they were used to. These shiny, slim and tapering nails were irresistible to the children. Mary Elizabeth confiscated a few to make dolls of them. She wrapped them in bits of bright calico and with care got them to stand upright. She loved her new and beautiful family of dolls. "Then Father missed them and anxiously inquired who had been using his new nails," she wrote in her "In the Hills" column. "Fearsomely, tearfully, I produced my little dolls. He laughed and let me keep three."

Nearly always brother and sister played well together, sometimes with dolls, sometimes with stick horses. When it was dolls, Joe would be a poor Indian who had to take care of the papoose because the mother had been killed. When they played with stick horses, Mary Elizabeth was always a rich young lady riding the finest of saddle stock.

Although they sometimes fought, their fights never lasted long. They could always depend on each other, especially if either one was sick. One summer when cherries were ripe, Mary Elizabeth almost died of pneumonia. Joe was always with her. While sitting by her bed one day, he was eating some ripe cherries. She begged for one, but the parents said emphatically no. One bite, they said, and she might die at once! Ignoring them, she ate all the cherries Joe could sneak into her room. Years later she said, "I can still taste that heavenly tart sweetness, so cooling and cleansing to that fever-parched mouth. Perhaps the cherries saved my life."

The next summer when Joe's eyes became sore and he had to stay in a dark room, Mary Elizabeth played under the window so he could join in. The doctor said the best medicine for Joe's eyes was a liquid made by soaking the pith of sassafras branches in rain water. Mary Elizabeth ran to the field for sassafras limbs to make the solution. While there she found some sheep sorrel which they both loved to eat.

Even insects were playthings for the children. They chased lightning bugs to fill a bottle. Catching a granddaddy long legs, they sang over and over, "Granddaddy Long Legs which-a-way are the cows?" Eventually the insect pointed a quivering leg off in one direction or the other.

They called up doodle bugs by chanting, "Doodle bug, doodle bug, tell me are you home?"

Joe, less squeamish than his sister, would clutch a grasshopper. Staring it in the face he would demand, "Now spit tobacco juice and I'll turn you loose."

They knew that if they laid their hands against a big tree where the katydids were singing, the insects would hush as if by magic. They built a miniature cellar, covered it over with earth, and then caught some locusts (cicadas). They poked them into the cellar, made a door of sticks and more dirt, and then sat down to enjoy the strange music that soon began underground.

There was also the bee they called the news bee; it resembled a yellow jacket, only longer. When one flew into the house (there were no screens on the doors or windows in the Ozarks in the 1880s) the children knew that they would soon hear about something that had just happened.

Loving nature, Mary Elizabeth found solitary pleasure outside. The summer her family lived in Ponce de Leon she discovered a spring. She did not tell anyone; it was her private place. Like a fountain, the water bubbled up from its natural stone basin. Though she did not know it, the spring had a local reputation for its healing properties. One morning when she came to drink from its cold, clear water, she surprised an old man bathing his loathsome-looking, cancerous arm in the spring. She never returned.

Sometimes interesting discoveries came from unpleasant experiences. When they lived in the big house in Appleton City, Betsy Prather punished the children by putting them in a dark closet off the front hall. Mary Elizabeth would have preferred a hard whipping to that closed-up blackness. She always believed that her fear of the dark probably originated from that closet. She screamed and kicked the door the whole time. She wasn't angry, but terrified of the sensations that washed over her. Dick, thinking it strange that she should make such a fuss at being shut up, wondered if maybe there was something there to cause her fear. Examining the closet one day, he discovered an old door behind some built-in shelves. He tore out the shelves, opened the door, and found it led to a secret stairway that went down into a cellar.

Everyone wondered what the cellar had been used for. Probably not for moonshining because Mary Elizabeth said, "Whiskey was as free as water in those days." She thought it might have been a hiding place in the underground railroad during slave times. Whatever its use, it seemed pervaded by something evil, for she sensed terror every minute she was locked in the closet.

Chapter 4

IN SABLE HOOD AND CLOAK
The Bald Knobber Era,
Taney County Missouri: 1883 - 1889

Dave King, the unafraid,
And my dad the same,
Found evil crime and trouble
When to these hills they came.
Grim, and sad, and resolute
Through glad or stormy weather
Vigilant and valiant
Rode these two together.
Oath-bound to service
Cold blue steel in leather,
Out to the distant signal fire
Light as a gray hawk's feather
Rode Dave King and my dad
Quietly together.

Dave King and my dad
They helped to bring
Peace into these mountains
My dad and old Dave King.

During her childhood Mary Elizabeth experienced other
frightening events, which exposed her to the darker side of

humanity. Interspersed with pleasant times were periods of danger and violence caused by the lawlessness in the county when they first moved back from Kansas in the early 1880s, and the ensuing troubles stemming from the Bald Knobber movement.

During the Civil War the hilly border counties of Missouri and Arkansas had suffered greatly. All able-bodied men left to join either the North or the South. Both armies swept the countryside, burning and pillaging. The Taney County courthouse, like many in southern Missouri, was burned in 1863.

But even worse than the raids of the armies through the country were the criminal activity of bushwhackers and other outlaws, such as Alf Bolin, who terrorized the populace, murdering and stealing at will. Many people abandoned their homes and evacuated the region.

The end of the war, however, did not stop the carnage in Taney County. Discharged soldiers and returning families found the land desolated and the weak government controlled by the lawless element. The reign of terror continued into the early 1880s when the Prather family moved to the area. And, since her own father and older brothers became involved, these historical events were part of Mary Elizabeth's growing up.

Because of Alonzo Prather's legal background, army experience, and general stature in the county, he was active in most community activities. A large, strong man with military bearing, penetrating blue eyes, white hair and beard, he commanded attention in any group.

But it was "Captain" Nat Kinney, their neighbor, who dominated the men at the Oak Grove Sunday School, which he had organized. An experienced leader, this six-foot-six, fair-skinned charismatic man often urged his listeners to do something to restore law and order. For years there had been talk with no action.

Mary Elizabeth and Joe loved Kinney. He told them stories and often let them ride behind him on his big horse to Sunday School. But on some Sunday mornings when the family arrived, the anger among the men in the yard was so great that Betsy Prather would not let the children go to Kinney.

In spite of her mother's warnings to stay away from the angry groups of men, Mary Elizabeth couldn't help but hear their talk about the inability of elected officials to control the continuing violence in the county. Since the end of the Civil War, thirty men had been shot to death, and not one of those responsible was punished. Either they were never caught, or if arrested, they were soon released. Everyone agreed that something had to be done. But what? Sensitive to others' emotions and a careful observer even then, Mary Elizabeth noticed that the men listened more to Kinney's radical ideas than to her father's more moderate suggestions.

The situation was brought to a head by the shooting of Jim Everett, a well-liked general store merchant in Forsyth. During the drought of 1882, Everett had extended credit to many families. But the man who shot him, Al Layton, was tried and released on a plea of self-defense. News of the acquittal, which seemed to them a travesty of justice, caused angry citizens to gather around Captain Kinney at the Oak Grove schoolhouse.

Aroused to action, thirteen prominent Taney County citizens, including Alonzo Prather and Nat Kinney, met in the back room of Jim Everett's store to organize a citizens' vigilante group, the League of Law and Order. One hundred selected men took an oath to "assist in the enforcement of the law; to report all lawbreakers; to assist one another," all under penalty of death. Kinney was elected leader.

As the organization grew rapidly, Kinney organized the men into companies, each with group leaders like army captains. All reported to Kinney. The groups met on the tops of the hills, or knobs, near Kirbyville. These hills were not high, but stood alone above the surrounding land. They were locally called "balds" because on top there were natural open grassy glades. Kinney selected the balds as meeting places because of the lookout advantages and because sentries could detect unauthorized men who might sneak up on the meetings. Members of the League soon became known as Bald Knobbers.

Colonel Prather and the older Prather boys were involved at the beginning, not only as neighbors of Captain Kinney, but also because they thought that the purpose of the organization was noble and patriotic. At the meetings on the knobs the leaders would prop up the flag in a pile of rocks.

The poem heading this chapter, "The Bald Knobber," illustrates Mary Elizabeth's pride in the original intent of the movement and her father's participation.

Mary Elizabeth remembered one particular time when "my father and the Van Zandt boys and my oldest brother went out one night with their guns. Probably they had joined a band of Bald Knobbers for I learned, in the way children learn things, that they had retrieved four wagon loads of hogs that had been stolen by some no-good trash and were being rushed to market. They caught up with them at Harrison [Arkansas]."

The meetings were held to initiate new members and to decide the punishment of law breakers. League members then warned or whipped offenders. A lazy man who wouldn't support his family might be visited at night and warned of his duty by a bundle of switches thrown at his feet by masked riders. People deemed undesirable had only until the next night to leave the area. For the first time law breakers feared getting caught.

Unfortunately, as the membership spread, unscrupulous men joined, enjoyed their power and the excitement of the night rides, and went too far, often becoming violent themselves. The group became political, causing the county politics to split into two factions, the Bald Knobbers and the Anti-Bald Knobbers. For two elections, 1884 and 1886, candidates favoring the Bald Knobbers won.

Though at first Prather and his older sons were part of the movement, the colonel avoided much active participation, often serving as moderator, or, when things got dangerous, moving his family out of the county for periods of time.

Years afterwards in her journal Mary Elizabeth summarized the movement's downfall. "Later, when Captain Kinney was running for the office of state representative, he wanted votes. I reckon he figured that all the Bald Knobbers would vote for him, so the ranks were thrown open to all who wanted to join. Naturally a lawless element crept in, and it was this element that had terrorized the community. They did such dreadful acts of violence. It was said they poisoned springs— anything to force people to do their bidding. One man had a fine bull that he thought so much of. One morning he found the bull dead from a miserable death. It had been tied to the fence, castrated, and its tongue cut out. Oh, they would stoop to anything."

Though Captain Kinney was a favorite with the Prather children and always welcomed in their house, Mary Elizabeth believed that her father did not like him. Kinney might have been too extreme for the colonel, too anxious to take the law into his own hands. Mary Elizabeth remembered a time in their home when the two big men quarreled. They were shouting and beginning to get physical. Although Betsy Prather was a tiny woman, barely five feet tall with delicate features and bones, she stepped between the two bearded giants and pushed them apart. "You stop this, you two gray-headed old fools," she scolded.

It was not long before the hill people feared the Bald Knobbers as much as they had feared the earlier bushwhackers. Eventually, at the order of Governor John C. Marmaduke and through the intermediary of Colonel Prather, the group led by Captain Kinney publicly disbanded in April 1886. Summarized, the group's resolutions stated that they would uphold the legal officers of the county; they expressed belief that authorities could handle criminal elements without organized militia; and they denounced any organized citizen militia.

As far as Colonel Prather and many other citizens were concerned, this ended the League of Law and Order, or the Bald Knobbers. Unfortunately this official end of the league did not end the trouble. Though there is no evidence that Kinney ever led the Bald Knobbers again, some men continued to ride in Taney County and neighboring Christian and Douglas counties. Many Taney County citizens believed Kinney still led the groups which continued to use the disguise of cloaks and black-hooded masks. For many years after the dissolution of the League, the resentment and antagonism of many Anti-Bald Knobbers continued.

In the summer of 1888, Captain Kinney was killed while invoicing the goods of a bankrupt Forsyth merchant, J. S. Berry. Because of Berry's threat that he would kill anyone who came to serve the papers, the circuit judge had appointed Kinney, the only person willing to act as receiver. Berry and the local Miles brothers were friends; all held some animosity toward Kinney. It was Billy Miles who shot him.

Kinney's death deeply affected the Prather family. The day was still fresh in Mary Elizabeth's mind fifty-six years later in 1946 when she told Marguerite Lyon, "One day Father came home riding his gray mare fast. The boys went out to put her away, and Father came into the house terribly excited and angry.

"He said to Mother, 'Well, they got ol' Captain Kinney a while ago. I heard them say the ol' colonel will be next! So I just walked up and down the street but they didn't do anything.' Mother was so frightened. The tragedy touched us too, because brother Bob had married the captain's step-daughter, Gertrude DeLong."

It was feared that Kinney's death would set off another reign of terror and violence because, though arrested for the murder, Miles was released with a plea of self-defense. But the friends of the captain abided by their resolution to let the officials handle problems of law and order.

"After that," Mary Elizabeth said, "the community lived in fear and trembling, wondering who would be next. Captain Kinney's grave was never marked. Father often wanted to

The Prather girls, Mag, Mary Elizabeth, and Deal

send away and get a stone like they put up for old soldiers, but he was afraid to do it—afraid he might offend someone."

After Kinney's death, Betsy Prather was so worried about her husband's safety that the family moved into Kirbyville. The summer of 1889, Mary Elizabeth remembered was "quiet, uneventful. Then came the Fourth of July Picnic. It was a great day. All the country people from miles around came into town to eat ice cream, dance, and shoot firecrackers. We noticed that the sheriff had a stranger with him, a handsome young fellow. In a matter of minutes everyone knew he was a United States marshall."

The stranger, Edward Funk, was not an officer, and there was no warrant. It seems that Sheriff G.E. (Gabe) Branson and Funk were out to kill Billy Miles. They had been elsewhere in the county looking for him, reaching the Kirbyville picnic late in the afternoon. The Miles brothers, Billy, Jim, and Manuel, were at the spring below the picnic ground when Branson and Funk caught up with them.

In the ensuing gunfire Jim Miles shot Funk. Either Billy or Manuel shot Branson. Both Funk and Branson lay dead and Jim Miles was wounded.

Meanwhile, at the nearby picnic grounds twelve-year-old Mary Elizabeth was lined up with other children by the ice cream freezers when two sharp reports rang out.

"Shots!" someone yelled.

"Oh, just cannon firecrackers," said someone else.

But Mary Elizabeth knew they were shots. "I left the ice cream," she said, "and ran down toward the spring where everybody seemed to be running. There was Aunt Addie Anderson lifting up someone's head in her arms and wiping the blood off his face. It was Sheriff Gabe Branson. A little way from him lay the young stranger, also dead. I could smell the smoke from the guns for it was still hanging in the hot still air."

No one panicked or screamed. All seemed to know what had happened; they believed that the killers were the three Miles brothers. Billy hadn't been convicted for killing Captain Kinney. He had killed again, everyone said.

"Of course, Mother was terribly excited when the killing happened," Mary Elizabeth continued with her account. "Fortunately, Bob and Gertrude [Mary Elizabeth's brother and his wife, step-daughter of Kinney] had driven in, in a big wagon, to attend the picnic with us. Gertrude was wonderful. She helped Mother get us children home. Then she ran back with sheets on which they laid the dead men out in front of the speaker's stand. Someone took a buggy—there weren't many buggies in those days—and went out in the country and brought in Betsy Branson, Gabe's wife. It was sundown before they could complete the trip. Then in the blue twilight, when fireflies had begun to flicker in the hot still evening air, I could hear her screaming clear from the edge of town as they brought her to the speaker's stand where the two dead men lay on our best sheets."

Two Miles brothers, Billy and Jim, were brought to trial, but were found not guilty on a plea of self-defense. Their brother Manuel was not charged.

After this double death, the residents of Taney County saw no more lawlessness than any county in the Ozarks. Bitter feelings and hatred engendered during that time continued for many years, but did not erupt into violence. The reign was over.

Growing up in this violent period did not seem to affect Mary Elizabeth as much as one might think. When she and her little brother played scary games, instead of fearing an old witch or the bogeyman, they pretended the Bald Knobbers got them. But they felt safe with their strong father and four big brothers. The violent episodes which intruded into their lives were months apart. Normal life continued in the Prather household, the children catching only whispered messages between their parents that there was trouble.

These childhood experiences showing the violent side of humanity probably influenced Mary Elizabeth's writings. She did not restrict her writing to beauty and the best qualities of the hill people. In some narrative poems she described occasional violence with an objectivity which is not present in her poetry about the horrors of war. She recorded the way people are, good and bad.

Chapter 5

RAPTURE YET TO BE
Adolescence: 1890 - 1894

What if some evening when the stars were shining
And wind-blown clouds were floating, cold and thin,
I'd come for you as in the distant days, dear,
With trembling fingers would you let me in?
Abashed, amazed, to see the old love glowing,
The years of glory, rapture yet to be—
Would you cast his garments down that you were mending
And close his cabin door to go with me?

By the end of the 1880s, life in the Prather family had both stabilized and changed. Much of the Bald Knobber trouble was over. Although feelings still ran high, the Prathers could live in Taney County again. Most of the time they lived either near Kirbyville, which was the social and educational center of the county at that time, or on the farm Colonel Prather bought on Swan Creek near the present town of Taneyville, north and east of Forsyth.

Alonzo had his hand in a variety of farming and business activities. He dealt in real estate, speculating in buying and selling land. In Taney County alone at least twenty of his land transactions were recorded between 1886 and 1909, plus much buying and selling of lots in Taneyville, Kirbyville, and Branson.

He was elected to the state legislature for five different non-consecutive, two-year terms between 1888 and 1910. His connections from his army days and his growing influence in the Missouri Republican Party also obtained for him several appointments to short-term positions, which necessitated his traveling and being away from home a great deal.

There were no more children in the Prather family after Mag in 1886, but by the 1890s the older boys were grown. Joe soon left, leaving at home only Mary Elizabeth and her two younger sisters.

Mary Elizabeth's adolescent years were similar to those of most girls in the hills—helping her mother at home, caring for and playing with her little sisters, becoming interested in boys, dating, and eventually marrying. However, her teen years also were different from those of most girls in Taney County at that time. She began writing for the county paper, she attended short terms at three higher educational institutes, and she taught three terms of school.

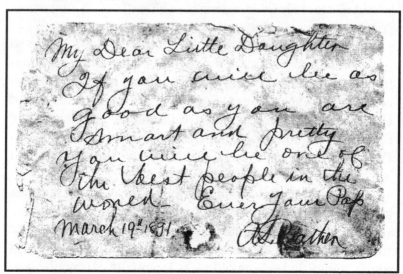

An original letter to Mary Elizabeth from her father, Alonzo S. Prather.

Like most girls, she enjoyed parties and gatherings in her home communities. Even though her family sometimes lived in isolated and backward conditions, when she was a child she was exposed to social life. Her brother Dick, five years older, went to many parties. When he learned to dance and attended play parties, he came home singing the words of the play party tunes. He'd grab Mary Elizabeth as his partner as he danced around the house. Although some people considered dancing wicked because of the rowdiness often associated with public square dances and live music, no one objected to play parties which did not use musical instruments. At play parties the couples danced through the figures to their own singing. Some of the ones Dick taught his sister were "Weevily Wheat," "Miller Boy," "Old Dan Tucker," "Skip to My Lou," and "Marching Around the Levee."

"John Jones's Peach Tree" was Dick's favorite because he got to kiss the girls. The young people played it at every party. Using an old hat and a broom for props, they danced while acting out the words of the song, such as shooting a gun, putting on a hat, stepping over a broomstick, and of course, kissing.

Though the play parties were fun, the young people preferred dances that used instruments—a fiddle with organ, guitar, or banjo second. Mary Elizabeth learned to dance when she was twelve. She said, "That had seemed just part of life, for dancing was as natural as riding horseback to hill youngsters. It had no implications of romance." In their home her mother would sit on the edge of the table smiling, swinging her feet and clapping her hands in time to the music when Dick and his friends included Mary Elizabeth in their dances.

If any one event marked her growing up, it was probably her first real party. A refined neighbor in Kirbyville whom Mary Elizabeth admired was Edna Layton, daughter in one of the leading families. She loved to visit the Laytons because of the books the family owned. Books overflowed the book case. They lay on the floor, on window ledges, on tables, everywhere. When Mary Elizabeth walked by the big home on the main street, she enjoyed the sound of Miss Edna's voice as she accompanied herself on the cottage organ.

One May morning when Mary Elizabeth passed the Layton house on her way to the store to trade eggs for brown sugar, Arbuckle coffee, a package of envelopes, and writing paper, Miss Edna hurried out to the fence.

"Mamie, wait a minute," she called. She handed Mary Elizabeth a red rose and an invitation. She said that her cousin was at her grandfather Layton's. "I'm going to give her a party tomorrow night and I want you to be sure and come."

Mary Elizabeth ran home with the red rose thrust into the packages in her basket. Her mother was almost as thrilled as she while they remodeled her party dress, letting it out and adding a blue silk sash from the old trunk.

Even seeing the fashionable new dress of her girl friend, Bertie Kintrea, did not spoil her delight with her remodeled dress. Mary Elizabeth was pleased with herself. The Layton house was rearranged for the party with the organ moved to the dining room to accompany the three fiddles, the guitar, and the banjo.

Though beautiful in a stylish dress that was a marvel to the hill girls, the guest of honor, Vinnie Ream Clarke, was ill at ease as the center of attention. There was an awkward moment as she stood alone in silence after introductions, the boys too shy to begin the dance, the girls not sure of the proper behavior for a fancy party.

Then, always confident, Dick Prather asked Vinnie Ream to dance. The tension disappeared. Boys chose their partners. To her surprise Mary Elizabeth was included in the first set.

The caller began:

> Lady 'round lady,
> Gent don't go
> Lady 'round lady,
> Gent so-low.
> Chase that rabbit,
> Chase that coon
> Chase that purty gal
> 'Round the moon.

The steady beat of the organ and the wail of the strings created dance music that no one could resist. Dick especially was in his element. Teasing, he bowed low to his sister when they met. Sometimes he would caution her, "Mamie, quit that jigging! Stop that hopping!"

After the dance, Vinnie Ream singled out Mary Elizabeth to join her in the back bedroom while she powdered her nose. The girls talked and confided in an intimacy that began a friendship that endured for forty-one years.

Another friend entered her life about this time. She met Pres Mahnkey. In the autumn of 1890, the

Mary Elizabeth Prather circa 1890

Prathers lived just south of Kirbyville on the old Springfield-Harrison Road. The road, which passed between their house and barn, was the main thoroughfare for overland travel from Springfield into northern Arkansas. Men on horseback, in wagons, and wagon trains passed daily. Mary Elizabeth was especially interested one day in three covered wagons creeping southward. Behind the wagons was a herd of cattle and merino sheep driven by two boys. The oldest, a dark-haired, blue-eyed boy of fifteen, handled the stock easily.

Hearing the wagons approach, the Prather boys stopped working to watch. Colonel Prather, walking out to the road, raised his hand in greeting. The caravan stopped while the colonel talked with the head of the family. There were two big girls and one grown boy, several younger boys and a small girl. Resting her folded arms on top of the gate, Mary Elizabeth listened to the conversation from behind the yard fence.

The stranger, a muscular, rather heavy set man about five feet six inches tall with red whiskers and a big black hat, introduced himself as Charles Mahnkey from St. Louis County. Desirous of more land to provide a better living for his family, he had moved first to Cedar County. Now, nearing the end of his trip south, he planned to buy a place near Pine Mountain where he could graze his sheep and cattle on the bluestem grass that covered the bald knobs in the free range country of Taney County.

Mary Elizabeth's casual curiosity about the travelers became excited interest. They would be neighbors. The quiet boy minding the sheep boldly stared back at her when she glanced his way.

The colonel and Mr. Mahnkey visited several minutes, her father giving some friendly advice about local conditions. The men shook hands in parting. As he stepped back, the colonel tipped his hat to Mrs. Mahnkey, who was holding a baby boy, and to the two almost grown daughters. The caravan moved slowly on. Last to pass the gate was young Pres Mahnkey who had expertly prodded the sheep back to their feet and now herded them and the cattle through the dust raised by the last wagon. As he passed Mary Elizabeth at the yard gate, he turned to her and smiled.

This meeting when Mary Elizabeth and Pres were thirteen and fifteen began a lifelong friendship between the two families. The Mahnkeys bought the farm at Free Jack Spring, just two miles south of the Prathers. Mary Elizabeth and Pres grew up neighbors. They sometimes attended elementary school together at Kirbyville. Though Pres was two years older, he seemed younger. Since he had even fewer educational opportunities than Mary Elizabeth, at school he usually sat with Joe instead of with the older boys.

The three often walked to school together. Mary Elizabeth always liked Pres. There was a tie between them; during his frequent absences from school when he was needed to work at home, Mary Elizabeth missed him.

Once on the trail to school Pres told her, "You are my girl and someday I'll marry you." Mary Elizabeth liked the attention, but did not take his words seriously. Marriage was a long time off.

They both enjoyed the social events that all the young people attended—square dances, candy-breakings, play parties, and spelling bees—but they never went as a couple, nor did Mary Elizabeth think of him as more than a good friend.

She explained their friendship, "One time when Father had sent me for the mail, I came past a picnic where a group of young folks were dancing. I just rode my pony down to watch them for a moment. I dismounted, and stood there in that long black riding skirt over my dress, holding the pony's reins in my hand. Pres was among the dancers. When he saw

me, he yelled, 'Take off that skirt and come dance with me.' ·
I protested that I had Father's mail and he wanted it. He
hollered again, 'You heard what I said. Take off that skirt and
come dance with me.' And that's just what I did, meek as
could be. Another time, when I hadn't seen him for a long
time, he came up to me at church and we spoke to each other.
Then he sat down beside me and just sat with my hand in his.
But we had never been sweethearts. Even that night it was just
the same. We were just glad to see each other."

At least once a week someone would give a dance. In the
close community there were no invitations sent out. "Everybody was welcome and everybody went. Unless he was too
religious!" Mary Elizabeth said. "If the house where the dance
was being held was too small for the crowd, the beds were
taken out to make room. We danced the old square dances
with the calls."

One of the best dancers and callers was Pres Mahnkey,

Kirbyville, Missouri (date unkonwn, probably early 1900's)

though he could not go to all the dances because he and his brothers had to work. "Their father was an old type German who believed his boys should start to do a man's work early in life, and it didn't leave much time for fun," she said. "But Pres and his brothers had that inborn feeling for music and dancing so many Germans had in the good old days when they could think of such things."

Another favorite pastime of the young people was horse-back riding. In 1893 when she was sixteen, in a period between terms at the state legislature, her father took the opportunity to work as a guard at the Columbia Exposition at the Chicago World's Fair. Lonesome for some of his family, he sent Mary Elizabeth thirty dollars to join him. She didn't want to spend the money "on anything as silly and useless as a trip to Chicago." This was her opportunity to buy Kit, the mare she had long wanted.

Her friend and companion for several years, Kit was a western pony owned by Hiram Bryan, one of the young men in her crowd. Kit was a smooth riding, golden sorrel, with a flax mane and tail. "She was smart, too." Mary Elizabeth said. "When we asked her how old she was, she would paw the ground three times. She still stuck to three, even when she was ten or twelve years old. She liked to hear me whistle as we rode along, and at certain songs she would put her ears back and listen, just as though she enjoyed those tunes more than others."

The Prather girls frequently rode over to visit neighboring girls. Mary Elizabeth recorded one occasion years later in *Hill and Holler News*, White River Valley Electric Cooperative's publication:

> One August day, when the threshers were at Captain Van Zandt's place, the next farm to ours, little sister and I asked

Mother if we could go over there to see the marvelous machinery in action. Grandmother Van Zandt was rearing two little granddaughters whose mother had died, and there was always a number of little girl cousins, so when we all got together to go out to the field, we were a merry group. But when Grandma saw where we were headed, she stopped her stirring, mixing, beating, and oven door slamming to say sternly, "No. You'll not go a-near, for they say they're all working with their shirt tails out." Shocking! We were overcome with embarrassment and did not go.

Mary Elizabeth's first love began when she was fourteen. He was Dick's friend, Paul Kinney, son of Captain Kinney. She had known Paul ever since the Kinneys moved to Taney County in 1883 and they both attended Oak Grove School.

"It was in school," she said, "when I learned the misery and exultation of love. To me it was the real thing as I sat there worshipping Paul Kinney. Paul had shining black hair and dark eyes, while we had blue eyes and fair hair. He was alert and dashing and bright—undoubtedly the sort to set any girl's heart a-pounding in any time."

When she was older, Paul came to see her often, sometimes on pre-arranged dates, sometimes just dropping in.

"We always had good times when he came over," she said. "It seemed easy to talk in those days. We would talk about the last party and the happenings of the neighborhood. We looked at the stereopticon pictures, too. That was a popular form of entertainment when the boys and girls got together. Perhaps it was just a sort of hero worship, but I was almost engaged to him."

In 1946 and 1947 Mary Elizabeth told the story of her life to Marguerite Lyon, a journalist/author from Chicago who moved to the Ozarks. Much of the information recorded here

Mary Elizabeth wrote in her "In the Hills" column during the 1930s and 1940s. But more revealing of her youthful years than either of these sources are those accounts she wrote when she was a girl.

Compared to the obligations, work, and hardships of most of her adult life, her adolescent years were happy, carefree times as evidenced by "My Journel" [sic] which she wrote from March 10 to April 23, 1892, when she was not quite fifteen. Her entries indicate that she already wanted to be a writer—that she was writing for an audience. She described the novels she read. She wrote of her friends, both girls and boys, and the outings and parties they had. She slept late in the morning, responsible for only a few chores, such as milking their cow and helping her mother with the housework. She stopped school "cause I am not learning," meaning that she knew more than the teacher.

During these months her father was in the Oklahoma Territory, waiting for the announcement of opening day when the government would open additional lands for homesteading. He, some of his sons, and other young men Mary Elizabeth knew from Taney County wanted to claim some land. She and her mother and younger sisters were "running the ranch" themselves.

In this early journal, characteristics of her later writing are apparent, such as her interest in flowers and the beauty of nature. "I start this Journal with the intention of 'sticking to it.' There is a regular 'March wind' blowing today. I am almost afraid to step out of the house cause its blowing so." Five days later she wrote, "There was snow four inches deep on the ground this morning—and is there yet. Oh, how dreary and white everything looked today and I couldn't help thinking 'how cold these poor little buttercups must be, under all this snow.'"

March 19: "Today was Saturday, my 'busy day' but I have not been very busy like I was a week ago today. The snow is melting away fast. I guess the buttercups are sorry they bloomed. I know I am for this snow may kill them."

Most of her entries were about boys. "I am going to Mr. McKnight's Exhibition tomorrow night with Paul Kinney. I expect to have a nice time."

And she did. "I got to go to the Exhibition and with Paul. There was a hack-load of Forsyth young folks out. I sat with Paul and Nellie Hilsabeck and had—oh! a splendid time. The moon shone so pretty and bright tonight."

But Paul wasn't her only interest. "Hiram Bryan came early this morning to see about the dance. Mama told him she guessed we would have it. I earnestly hope we will. I know I will enjoy myself. I had a letter from Nora Crouch today and in it she called me the 'Belle of Kirbyville.' Dear me—ought'ent I to feel proud?"

The next day: "We had the dance and such a dance! I danced 11 sets. Paul was not here. I guess he thought it was too bad weather to have the party. I danced three sets with Arthur Bedford. There was lots of candy here tonight and a great many sly flirtations going on considering the scarceness of girls. I wish old Paul had been here. Just think! Paul not at his own dance. Every girl here tonight was sorry because he was not here."

Apparently so was Paul when he heard about the dance from several friends. He stopped by to see Mary Elizabeth several times in the next week. On March 25: "Oh! what a pretty day it was. I'll never forget it if I live to be as old as Noah of the Ark. After dinner Paul and I went walking up on the Bald. We found a good seat and sat down and talked a long time. Paul found some pretty flowers—I found a few. Today was the happiest day of my life for Paul asked me to marry

60

him and in two years I will. I am awfully young—but love him dearly. Paul staid a little while and then told me goodby and went away. It was all I could do to keep back the tears. Paul is going to start in the morning. I hate to see him go. He is going to 'Brake.' [Work as brakeman on the railroad. But first he went to Oklahoma to try for land.] I am so miserable. Tears *keep* coming to my eyes all the time I am writing this. I hope Paul will write soon. I will be very lonesome when he is gone. I don't know what I will do."

What she did was have another party. "Hiram came again this afternoon to see if we could have the candy pull. It was just a nice time to have it cause it was cold and candy always pulls good in cold weather. Mama said yes—so Hiram said he would come back after while. Then we hurried and got supper—washed the dishes and I dressed. I had only to take off my gingham apron and put on my white one and tie a red ribbon round my neck. I wore my blue calico dress that I wore at our dance that night. I pinned a bunch of violets on and that was all.

"Pretty soon the company came. We talked a little while then I got out a game of mine called 'Peter Coddles Adventures in New York' and we played it. It was awfully funny. Then the candy was ready and we pulled. It was splendid candy although it stuck a little at first. After the candy was pulled we all went into the room 'cross the hall and played 'Blind Man's Bluff.' Then 'Puss in a Corner.' Dr. Smith played as wild as any of us and I think he looks better with his dignity off. Hiram is nice—so's Dr. Smith—so's Bobby but 'My Paul' is 'The greatest roman of them all.' None can come up with him."

On April 14 she lost another friend. "Hiram went to Oklahoma this morning. He came in and told us goodby. I liked to have cried but I'll bite my tongue in two before I'll ever cry. I hated to tell Hiram goodby but not as bad as I did Paul. I will always think of him as a good Comrad—one I had lots of fun with."

Even then Mary Elizabeth was writing for an audience. She continued, "I 'spect people in coming ages who read this will think it was a bad case of crush? But Hiram and I are too wise for such folly—and besides I love Sweetheart Paul with my whole heart and soul and I am 'true blue.' Bertie [her girl friend] is struck on Hiram but he is a confirmed woman hater, I do believe. His eyes will never gaze with favor at anything but his money, cattle, and little pony Kit. I've come to the end of my Ledger and will have to get another one. Goodby old Journel."

Mary Elizabeth bought Hiram's pony Kit when he left to join the other men in the Oklahoma Territory.

Nothing came of the land venture into Oklahoma for her father or the other men in Mary Elizabeth's life. Paul did not return to Taney County to live. He worked for the Union Pacific Railroad first as brakeman, progressing to conductor, assistant trainmaster, trainmaster, then to assistant superintendent of the road in Denver. He and Mary Elizabeth wrote to each other for a time. "He was busy carving out a career for himself," Mary Elizabeth said.

Chapter 6

I SNATCHED A ROSE
Writing, Schooling, and Teaching: 1892 - 1899

> I snatched a rose
> How glad am I.
> I snatched the rose
> As I came by,
> For its silky fragrance
> Filled the day
> And no more grew
> Along my way.

During the years 1892 and 1893, Mary Elizabeth began the youthful experiences which were not typical of most hill girls. Instead of marrying in her late teens, or staying at home until marriage, the expected role for girls, she began two other careers—writing and teaching.

Before tying herself down with a family and responsibilities, she took this opportunity to be independent, to "snatch the rose," by developing some talents she would improve throughout her life. She wrote for the county paper, and she attended three institutions of higher education to enable her to teach school.

Writing for publication was a natural step for her. She had always loved to write, spending many hours writing letters and making up stories just for the love of seeing the words on the paper. Many of the Prathers wrote, both privately and publicly. Her sisters wrote poetry. Her mother kept journals and carried on extensive correspondence with family and friends. Two brothers, Dick and Frank, did newspaper work. For years the colonel had an interest in the local paper and sent in community news. Since he was away from home so much, he gave his job as rural correspondent to Mary Elizabeth.

The news about the affairs in Kirbyville were her first published writings. Starting when she was fourteen and to the end of her life, she continued sending in weekly news from wherever she lived.

The spring of 1893, when she was sixteen, began her advanced education and school teaching. Colonel Prather finally recognized his daughter's need of education and made it possible for her to attend a teacher education school, then called a Normal School.

In the town of Bradleyville in the extreme northeastern corner of Taney County, there was founded in 1891 the Bradleyville Normal School. Established especially for teachers and students of the county, the school was housed in a two-story building constructed by the citizens of Bradleyville.

The term lasted from March to June at a cost of $1.50 per month. The studies were mainly eighth grade level arithmetic, English, physiology, geography, history, and political science.

Even though Mary Elizabeth was hungry for knowledge, what impressed her more than the classes were the experiences of being away from home for the first time, participating in the Literary Society and the activities of the other young people at the school, and enjoying the daily association with the lady where she boarded. Many of her acquaintances became subjects of her later writings which showed her admiration for strong, independent women.

She stayed with Aunt Martha Groves, an imposing widow in her seventies. She was no relation to Mary Elizabeth. The "aunt" or "uncle" before an older person's name was one of respect. Tall, lithe, and active, Aunt Martha worked quickly and efficiently, equally at ease in her kitchen, in her garden, or in the barn lot. Completely unafraid, she walked with long easy steps into a lot full of young horses and mules. She would order, "Stand back there!" to a wild-eyed filly that started to bolt. The filly would obey.

There were no dormitories at the school; students boarded in private homes like Aunt Martha's. For $1.50 a week Mary Elizabeth had her own room with a soft feather bed and white, handspun and handwoven wool blankets.

The table groaned under Aunt Martha's spread of food. Mary Elizabeth said, "There were stored vegetables from the tater hole, cabbage pit, and the mounds of turnips and carrots in the garden, along with every kind of a pickle that could be made from a bean, cucumber, cabbage, onion, or pepper pod—and every kind of jam, jelly, preserve, or fruit butter. For bread, we had biscuits or corn cakes (fried cornbread) to eat along with the best milk and butter and bitterly strong coffee. Everything was seasoned and flavored as I have never found elsewhere. From Aunt Martha I learned how to make corn cakes and just how to cook a chicken with dumplings."

With the arrival of the first spring day, Mary Elizabeth went hunting for wild greens with Aunt Martha. In 1935 Mary Elizabeth wrote in the Wastebasket column of the Springfield paper.

She scooped out dozens of wild herbs with her worn black-handled knife. I remember the names but could never find them again. But I really believe if I could race again, up and down those plushy, green banks and braes, in and out of those tropical little jungles of pawpaw and buckeye with their fantastic greenery, I know I could find "Ladies Finger," "Spotted Britches," "Greasy heel," "Carpenter Square," and, then on around the fence and out in the pasture "Old Field Salet." I might even find a little spring branch that trickled in to the old swimming hole in Beaver, that was a strip of floating verdure, watercress, that added its peppery twang to our first mess of wild greens, boiled with hog-jowl or ham bone.

Mary Elizabeth met another unusual woman at Bradleyville—a gypsy who lived alone in a cabin on the mountain. Throughout her life, in oral and written stories, Mary Elizabeth recounted tales of supernatural, or "ha'nt" stories. She also described some unexplainable happenings she experienced.

She described the gypsy as big and dark with a barbaric beauty made more striking by a red silken scarf around her head. Though friendly with the gypsy, she was fearful when she heard her sarcastic laughter or felt the woman's black eyes on her.

The gypsy often followed Mary Elizabeth as she helped Aunt Martha do her evening chores. Looking for eggs one evening, Mary Elizabeth climbed an old ladder of an abandoned cotton gin to the unfloored loft. She balanced herself on the rickety beam, found the eggs, ran back across the beam and down the ladder. When she reached the floor, the young gypsy woman grabbed her shoulder, shook her roughly, and said in a shaking voice, "Don't ever do that again! You must never run along a beam like that. I am a gypsy and know things you don't. You are marked for accident."

Many years later Mary Elizabeth said, "Of course, I wasn't marked for accident, and I've always been glad I could prove that she was mistaken."

Aunt Martha had no patience with the gypsy's powers, especially with the gypsy's spirit companion called Kate. One day there was a muffled, but distinct tapping on the roof.

"Ask me anything you want to know," the gypsy said, "for Kate has come."

Aunt Martha promptly replied, "I already know two things. It is beginning to rain, and we better go out and drive in the little turkeys before they drown!"

Mary Elizabeth's superstitious streak suggested to her that perhaps the gypsy did have some powers. Once she and some friends climbed the rocky trail to the gypsy's cabin. The hill, white with blossoms of wild plums and "sarvus" berry trees, was in stark contrast to the dark, shut-up cabin with a thin rope of smoke wavering over it. To imaginative Mary Elizabeth, the smoke seemed as if it were a chained, unclean spirit. The gypsy woman sat by the fire.

During their visit, as the gypsy bent over a worn deck of cards telling the boys' fortunes, Mary Elizabeth heard a muffled tapping. She turned cold with fear, thinking it must be Kate, the gypsy's friend from another sphere.

As if she knew what Mary Elizabeth was thinking, the gypsy said, "Don't be frightened, little girl. That is only my pet crippled chicken." Out from under the bed hopped a one-legged white pullet.

She told one boy, "You've lost something on the way up the trail, but you'll find it on the way down."

Mary Elizabeth didn't want her fortune told when it was her turn. "It's a good thing," the gypsy said, "for it is not to be as you think."

As the young people ran down the mountain, the boy who had lost something found the handkerchief he had dropped on the way up but had not missed.

Between the outings and visits, Mary Elizabeth finished

the course at Bradleyville. She then took a teachers' examination to try for a teaching certificate. She made ninety-nine per cent in history and sixty-three per cent in arithmetic. Because of her scores on the examination, she received a certificate on June 29, 1894, to teach for one year. The subjects she was qualified to teach were written in the handwriting of the clerk of her first school as (sic) "Arithmetic, language lessons, english grammar, geography, spelling, reading, writing, united States history, civil government including state government, physiology and school management."

On September 3, 1894, two weeks after her seventeenth birthday, Mary Elizabeth began her first school in what later became the Melva-Ridgedale district on Turkey Creek. It was south of Hollister about three miles from the Arkansas border. Though her formal education had been spotty, she was still one of the best educated of the county rural teachers. Very few had any Normal school training.

The first day of school she was shy and frightened. That first autumn morning in the makeshift classroom, she copied down on a sheet of tablet paper the names of all the children. She hung the big gold watch her father lent her on the log wall.

The morning dragged by. Ill at ease, she hardly heard the music of Turkey Creek outside the door or the calls of the blue jays in the tall trees for the loud ticking of her father's watch. It seemed to be saying, "Courage, courage, courage."

At last it was recess time. Of the seventeen children, there were seven from the Youngblood family, the family Mary Elizabeth boarded with. The oldest Youngblood boy spent the recess time scraping the beggar lice off his pants legs with a long-bladed knife. Just when he had them all off, his little brother sat down in them, and then jumped up dismayed. As he twisted around trying to get them off, everyone laughed. The restraint was broken. The rest of the day, teacher and students exchanged amused glances whenever the little boy wiggled.

At noon everyone went to the creek to eat lunch. In Mary Elizabeth's new dinner pail that Mrs. Youngblood packed for her, she was happy to find candied sweet potatoes, fried squirrel, and a glass mug filled with butter and honey.

The teaching facilities were very poor, according to her term report filed with the clerk of the school district on November 23, 1894, and from the monthly minutes of school directors' meetings in September, October, and November. School was held during the first two weeks, until the log schoolhouse was finished, in an old building on J.H. Whorton's farm. There were no charts, no maps, no globes, no blackboards, no desks not defaced with cutting or writing, no library, and no books added during the term. There was one dictionary, and the school did use textbooks adopted by the county commission of education. Total value of school property was two dollars.

Before 1892 in that whole township there had been no schools, as the wooded, mountainous area was almost uninhabited. When the school was organized in 1892, there were thirty-two children between six and nineteen years of age, though not all attended. In the third term of the school, the one Mary Elizabeth taught, only twenty per cent of the enumeration were enrolled. There were five boys and nine girls under sixteen, and two girls and one boy over sixteen, for a total of seventeen students. Even those enrolled did not attend regularly. The average number of pupils who attended each day was twenty-seven percent. There were ninety-eight cases of tardiness.

The school term was three months, sixty school days, for which Mary Elizabeth received twenty dollars a month.

The children accepted Mary Elizabeth. Not a rigid disciplinarian like many teachers at the time who switched students at any sign of inattention, she kept order by loving and respecting her students. Even when they yawned or went to sleep, Miss Mamie did not scold them. Instead, she often made a pallet for the little ones in the corner, even shooing away the flies with a limb. At the end of the term, she reported no truancies and no corporal punishment.

Everyone was glad to move into the new schoolhouse with a tiny box stove and four small windows. Before cold weather, a school director came one afternoon to chink the big cracks between the logs with wedges of wood and then daub them with soft mud. Before the mud dried, the children decorated the strips with rows of red haw (berries from a deciduous holly often known as possum haw). They filled the one-room building with wild flowers and colored autumn leaves.

"Perhaps I laughed too much for a very good teacher," Mary Elizabeth said, "But we all learned fast." Her work was a joy as the children quickly learned their lessons. Years later one of her students remembered how much emphasis Mary Elizabeth put on reading. Most children enjoyed spelling, one of the teacher's favorite subjects. Her students never forgot her pleasant bearing, her understanding, and her commitment to learning.

Since there was no firewood for the school, the first cool days found the teacher and children carrying in dead limbs and pine knots from the hillsides. On one foraging trip, Mary Elizabeth saw something wavering near one of her barefooted girls. She thought it was a dead crooked stick the child had stepped on. Instead it was a coiled rattler, blind with the cold, but still venomous. Mary Elizabeth quickly killed the snake with a club before it could strike. The boys stripped off the rattlers, which she displayed for years above her writing table.

The long walk home up the mountain with the Youngblood children was always pleasant. "John Youngblood was a true woodsman, son of a mighty huntsman, he was,"

Mary Elizabeth said. "He told me that he could get out on a lonely mountain point and imitate a wolf call until one would answer him. He brought his hounds to school with him. One time he disputed Father's watch, for he said old Ranger had howled, and he always howled at four, for he knew it was feeding time."

One of the advantages of teaching a rural school was that the teacher could interrupt lessons when she wanted. One chilly October afternoon there was a funeral at the burial ground just by the school. Since several students were related to the deceased, Mary Elizabeth dismissed, and they all walked over. One little boy said with pride as if he were preparing his teacher for a great performance, "Granny'll shout. Granny's nigh ninety, but she'll shout."

Granny did shout. Mary Elizabeth was affected by the old woman's constant reiteration, "Oh, she's gone on to glory, and we'll all meet her there."

Because Betsy Prather thought the long walk up the mountain each evening with the Youngblood children was too hard on her daughter, after the first two weeks Mary Elizabeth stayed with another family nearer the school. But when Mary Elizabeth rode Kit back up a grassy trail to the Youngbloods to get her things, there was a fire in the woods so heavy with smoke that she could not see the skyline. Though the fire was close, some places burning right on the trail, she was not worried because ground fires, which were deliberately set to kill the ticks and clear the woods for spring grass, were common occurrences. She urged Kit through the burning woods.

Suddenly there was a roar and a thump. The fire had burned through the trunk of a dead tree which fell just behind them. The sound reverberated through the canyon frightening both Mary Elizabeth and Kit. The pony needed no urging to race to the Youngblood clearing with Mary Elizabeth hanging onto the old, flat sidesaddle.

Teaching and living away from home also had its social side. One night after school a big fellow rode up to Mary Elizabeth's boarding place on a mule.

"I've come to take Teacher to a housewarming."

Thrilled, Mary Elizabeth ran out to catch Kit. The pony would not be caught.

"You'll jes' have to ride behind me on my mule," the young man said. He kicked and spurred the mule to an old stone wall so that she could climb on.

Dressed up in a skirt, shirtwaist, and a jacket with big sleeves, Mary Elizabeth sat sideways without a blanket between her and the mule's rump. But when she got on, the mule sat down. It took some urging and pulling to get the animal up, but mulelike, in his own time, he got up and ambled to the party while Mary Elizabeth clutched the young man's waist to keep her seat.

As they approached the new house, dance music filled the clearing. Children ran out excitedly calling, "Teacher's comin', Teacher's comin'!" They clustered around her chatting and laughing, pulling her inside the clean-smelling house made of new pine lumber.

The second place she boarded that term was with Jim and Vina Fox, who lived on Turkey Creek. Vina's little sister Millie was one of Mary Elizabeth's pupils. The quiet child and teacher were drawn together. Millie was more like an old lady than a girl of ten because of her superstitions and old wise sayings. The child and young teacher were irresistibly drawn to the waters of the creek, often sitting on the roots of a sycamore that clutched the bank. One November night while sitting there, the dark water gurgling under them and the black hills projecting into the sky, Mary Elizabeth talked about the brightness of the stars.

I Snatched a Rose

"Oh, look, Millie! Aren't they beautiful?"

Child and young woman seemed to exemplify the contrasts in Mary Elizabeth's life. The darkness of night and light of stars, nearness of tree and water and unimaginable distance of the stars, close companionship of the two and utter emptiness of space.

"Let's see how many stars we can count," Mary Elizabeth suggested pointing to the North Star and the Big Dipper showing close to the horizon above the mountain. "One, two..."

Millie caught her hand. "O, Teacher! *Never, never* count the stars. That's awful bad luck!"

Years later Mary Elizabeth often wondered if, as a young school teacher on Turkey Creek, there had been some foreboding of tragedy. Often as she and Millie sat there watching colored leaves dance by in the bright waters, or as on the night she counted the stars, she was sad enough to weep.

"Was this prescience?" Mary Elizabeth asked when telling about it. "Many, many years later, only a little farther down, the muddy waters of this same stream brought me my greatest sorrow. But when I was a young teacher, I thought my unrest was due to the mystic old legends that I heard in that region, for somehow I felt the unhappiness still about me."

Some changes in the Prather family situation prevented Mary Elizabeth from teaching the next year.

First, her brother Bob became ill with tuberculosis. Before he died, Betsy Prather traded houses with him so he would be in a warmer home. Mary Elizabeth was needed at home as her mother and sisters Deal and Mag were alone then; the colonel was away at the legislature or on other assignments much of the time.

This first death of an immediate family member kept the family in sorrow for many months. A few days after Bob's burial, Betsy Prather said in her soft voice, "I felt a little bad

73

all summer, for did any of you notice the morning glories and the touch-me-nots and the petunias all bloomed white?"

Next, the family moved to Swan Creek. Of all the farms and other property Colonel Prather purchased and traded, the one he loved best was the farm on Swan Creek north of Forsyth. He built a new house for his family on a high point overlooking a big horseshoe bend in the creek which enclosed many rich acres of open bottom land. It was about two miles west of the newly settled crossroads village of Taney City, now Taneyville.

After the unsettled year of Bob's death and building the Swan Creek house, Mary Elizabeth was not needed at home and was ready to teach again, especially since brother Frank stayed with the family for a few months helping build a hen house. (Later he married and lived in Springfield where he and Dick published the newspaper, *The Republican*, a predecessor to the *News-Leader*.)

Her next school was Brushy Creek School, also called Union Flat, just south of Bradleyville. With one school teaching experience behind her, Mary Elizabeth was not so frightened this time. She worked with the youngsters, enjoyed the friendship of the lady she boarded with, and, as always, entered into the community social life.

One special student was a large boy much behind the other children his age. An orphan who had to work from early childhood, he had very little opportunity to go to school. Especially fond of boys, Mary Elizabeth felt drawn to him. Knowing the man-sized boy would not stay long in a class of children, Mary Elizabeth worked hard with him, taking advantage of the time he was in school. She struggled to teach him some standard English such as the proper use of "was" and "were," as well as the rudiments of arithmetic. Before the term was over, the boy could add, multiply, and figure faster than his teacher.

Years later while Mary Elizabeth's son Douglas was running for public office, a big man brought the large sack of ballots from his precinct to the courthouse to be tallied. He walked over to Doug, shook hands, identified himself as his mother's former student, and said, "When I found you was Mamie Prather's son, I got out and beat the bushes for you. She is one of the sweetest persons that ever lived."

Since school terms usually lasted only three months, there was plenty of time left in the year for a teacher to do other things. In the summer of 1896, a chain of events led Mary Elizabeth to Springfield to take a business college course, her second experience with higher education.

Colonel Prather was gone that summer with the State Department of Agriculture instructing farmers. Mary Elizabeth said, "Of course, Father was no great shakes as a farmer, but he preached the need of ponds, cisterns, and tree preservation." While Alonzo was away lecturing and also making the campaign tour to get back in the legislature again after being out two terms, Ben Prather came home to make the crop. Again, Mary Elizabeth was not needed at home.

Then Dick, as editor of a newspaper in Ozark, received a scholarship from the business college in payment for an advertisement he ran in the paper. He gave the scholarship to Mary Elizabeth, who supported herself in Springfield with a part-time job.

Though Mary Elizabeth made two friends at the business college, rural students like herself, she felt out of place among the sophisticated city girls and boys. When she discovered that the whole school went on a picnic without including her, she quit. At home she was always included in everything.

Her brief stay in Springfield was important, not for any business training she received, but because this was the first time she deliberately returned to the hills. She could have stayed, completed the course, and worked in the city. Instead, she returned home, smarting from her first real experience of prejudice against her people and her hills.

The snub left its mark. All her life she avoided women's social groups, especially society women, much preferring the company of working people. They were the subjects of her writing; they were her readers.

However, the city was not the only place she felt the pain of snubs and ridicule. Even at home there were those who made her feel inferior.

Each season the Prather girls received a box of almost new clothes from their cousin in New York. For years these clothes had enabled Mary Elizabeth to dress better than would have been possible otherwise. But sometimes the clothes were too fancy for the hills, especially as the cousin grew up. In one box there was a beautiful long plume. To brighten up her black felt hat, and her own spirits, during the long winter after brother Bob's death, she sewed it to her hat. Pleased with her appearance, she wore the decorated hat to church. Riding her pony seven miles to church with a sweeping plume hanging from her hat was an accomplishment in itself.

When she walked proudly into the church, she heard a girl say, "Well, she must have killed the old rooster before she came to church."

Several of her poems deal with her feelings about such slights. In 1940 she wrote:

> With fang and claw he fought the other males
> For love of her, his wounds gaped deep and red.
> No fangs, no claws were used on me today
> The weapon used, sharp, cruel ridicule instead.

After the business college, her last formal educational venture was the four-week teachers' institute in 1898 at Protem in southeastern Taney County. In 1891, in order to improve the qualifications of teachers in Missouri, the state legislature passed the Teacher's Institute Law. This law provided for short courses in rural communities and set up standard examinations to qualify teachers. Depending on their grade on the examination, each teacher received graded certificates—first grade (good for three years), second grade (two years), or third grade (one year). These institutes were held in different parts of the county in different years. Qualified instructors came from area colleges to teach.

Mary Elizabeth and sister Deal both attended the institute at Protem. Mary Elizabeth enjoyed this session much more than the business college. Courses in history and English literature were much more to her liking than accounting and shorthand. And her fellow students were like her, local men and women wanting to teach in the rural schools. She was included in all social activities.

Though Deal did not pass the teachers' examination, Mary Elizabeth received a second grade certificate and obtained the old Branson School up Roark Creek from the Branson postoffice and store. Her contract was for six months with the best pay of any—thirty dollars a month.

The school on Roark Creek was more difficult to teach than the others. Mary Elizabeth had more pupils and had to work harder to keep ahead of them. One student in particular caused her to work many extra hours. This student quickly discovered that she was better than the teacher in mathematics. Mary Elizabeth's self respect could not tolerate that. One night, after the girl had pointed out the teacher's ignorance of ratios, Mary Elizabeth complained to the lady she was boarding with. Her friend urged her to omit that particular recitation class for a few days, and study the key to the textbook.

Though there were no teacher's editions or guidebooks for teaching the textbooks at that time, there were special answer keys for the math books. A friend from the institute at Protem had sent her the key. With the answer to the problem, she could work backwards, figuring out the steps of the solutions. Unsure of herself, she worked many hours, but managed to stay one step ahead of her brightest student.

At the end of the term, Mary Elizabeth was pleased with herself in general. She had handled a difficult job. She was living away from home, enjoying teaching school, and earning her own money. She was acquainted with people all over Taney County from her teaching, but especially through her Kirbyville column in the paper. She was a mature woman, twenty-one years old. Now was the time for the next step. She was ready to get more from life than teaching a different school for a few months a year and boarding at first one place then another.

Roark Creek School, 1898. Seated on the second row, third from the left, Mary Elizabeth is wearing the fancy hat. Her sister Mag is fourth from the left on the back row.

Chapter 7

THANKS FOR OAKEN ROOF AND GRAY HEARTHSTONE
Courtship and Marriage:
Fall 1898 - October 1900

A dress and apron hanging on the wall,
A little blue sunbonnet, that is all;
And she who dreamed of scarlet lace and scarlet shawl
Gives thanks for oaken roof and gray hearthstone,
Forgetting dreams she dreamed when all alone
Before this little cabin was her own.

One Friday night in the fall of 1898, riding home for the weekend from teaching Roark school, Mary Elizabeth was so tired that she almost didn't get off her pony while crossing the White River on the Boston Ferry. Most people stayed on their horses or in their wagons as the crossing was usually smooth and did not take many minutes. But since Mary Elizabeth was never sure of Kit on the ferry, she always dismounted. On the home side of the river after she had mounted and was riding up the bank, she spotted her sister Deal galloping up on her pony.

"Hurry up! Let's get home so you can get dressed. There's a dance at Mahnkeys' tonight!"

Deal always looked forward to a dance, but that night she was more excited than usual. The infrequent dances at the Mahnkeys' were the best as the five Mahnkeys boys were all good dancers and callers.

Mary Elizabeth was so worn out from the week's teaching she did not want to go. Deal insisted. Although Mary Elizabeth thought they shouldn't go because they had no escort, their mother said it would be all right for the two girls to ride their ponies to the dance. Mary Elizabeth quickly changed into a red wool shirtwaist with fancy buttons up the front and a blue skirt. Over that she wore a black wool riding skirt. However, by that time, young women often left off the riding skirts. Sometimes when out of sight of their mother, the girls would even ride astride. Deal was the first girl to ride astride openly in that neighborhood. They heard talk about her; some called her "that wild girl of Prathers." Though Deal did not care, such gossip would have devastated Mary Elizabeth.

When the girls reached the Mahnkey home, the music was already playing. Mary Elizabeth had to primp a little, but Deal was ready the minute she got off her horse, not a bit embarrassed to be walking in without an escort. The girls left their wraps in the front room, spoke to members of the family, and went to the door leading to the dancing. Mary Elizabeth was ill at ease, weary from the long horseback rides, and unhappy about arriving unescorted. If someone didn't ask her to dance, she felt she would die from shame.

She needn't have worried. As she paused in the door, Pres Mahnkey stepped up to her. She was very glad since she hadn't seen him during the year he had been working in Kansas.

He stood there, five feet six, lean, and muscular. "Hello, Mamie. Will you dance with me?" His smiling blue eyes seemed even bluer in contrast to his dark hair and tanned face.

Of course she would dance with him, an old friend and

probably the best dancer there. Mary Elizabeth also had quite a reputation as a dancer. They danced together several times during the night that turned out to be wonderful. All memory of her weariness disappeared under the spell of the organ, banjo, and guitar, and the fiddle music of Little Jack Van Zandt. The young people danced squares and waltzes, polkas, and schottisches.

She enjoyed the feel of Pres's strong hands and arms as he swung her possessively when they met in the square dance figures. Every time she looked his way, his intense eyes were watching her.

Pres seemed different that night from the good friend and neighbor he had been all the years she had known him. He had grown up. So had Mary Elizabeth. They were twenty-three and twenty-one. As always they were glad to be together, and Pres held her hand as he used to do many times, but this time it was more than friendship. There was a mature desire and longing quite different from the other times in boyhood when he held her hand on the way to school and called her his girl. This time his touch kindled feelings which made Mary Elizabeth giddy. She found herself watching him to the exclusion of all the other young men there. The memory of the girlish interest in Paul Kinney faded in this powerful attraction. Pres and Mary Elizabeth both knew before the dance was over that whatever their future would be, it would be together.

But the Prathers were not happy with her growing attachment for young Mahnkey. Though hard-working, honest, and well respected in the Kirbyville community, Pres may not have measured up to the expectations of the Prathers for their eldest daughter. Colonel Prather was a somebody—a college graduate, an officer in the Union Army, a governmental official in Arkansas for several years, and always a leading figure in Taney County whether in law and order, newspaper work, agriculture, or politics. Now he was state representative. Young Pres Mahnkey, grandson of a German immigrant, had nothing but himself—no education, no money, no property.

It is also possible that the Prathers, recognizing their daughter's talents, may have wanted more opportunities for her than as a married farm woman in the hills. When Mary Elizabeth's school term ended, and her father returned to Jefferson City to the legislature, he wanted her to accompany him and find a job there where some women were beginning to have careers apart from marriage. But after her short experience in Springfield, she had no interest in her father's plans for her. For the second time she decided to remain in the hills.

Having already dismissed her wish to be a novelist as girlish fantasy, she became caught up in society's plan that women should find a man. She found one. Pres's qualifications suited her.

By December the young couple decided to marry. Among Mary Elizabeth's keepsakes is a yellowed letter from Pres written December 19, 1898. She wrote on the envelope, "My most precious letter."

>At home
>Dear Girl
>This has bin the longest day to me I ever have seen I think. Don't know how it has seemed to you. I hope you have enjoyed the day better than I have. There hasant bin a secant but what I have thought of you.
>Well, I don't know now when I will get to see you as I habe to go to Hairson Ark. tomorrow. Don't know when I can get back. I am going down thare to see about som cattle but I guess I will get back in 3 days.
>I wont get to ask your Pa for you but he surley knows I want you. Tell him he has got all of my best wishes. O yes

I'll tell you what ma told me today. She said she hoped we wouldant have quite so many kids to take care of as she did. She said she ust to wash with one hand and rock the cradle with the other.

From your Press

They married on January 18, 1899. Mary Elizabeth later described the day: "The family had moved to Kirbyville from Oak Grove and that night a group of young people walked with Pres and me to the Reverend James Van Zandt's to see us get married—Deal and her boy friend, Mag, Little Jack Van Zandt, and a whole crowd of boys and other girls. It was the most beautiful night I have ever seen—as bright as day with a big silvery moon shining down on us. We walked down the road to the next farm, just a little way out of Kirbyville. But there was something odd about that walk. We didn't sing and laugh and holler as we always did when a group of us went walking like that. This was a serious occasion. Mamie was doing something she had never done before. She was going away to get married."

The ceremony was in the Van Zandts' large front room, warmed by a fire in a big fireplace and lit with several lamps. With dignity, the former Civil War captain told Pres and Mary Elizabeth to join hands. He didn't have them repeat anything, but he had each of them say, "I do." Then he said, "I pronounce you man and wife."

They had no ring, for rings were not easy to get and it wasn't customary to have a ring in a country wedding.

The best man was Black Jim Van Zandt. Mary Elizabeth explained, "There were so many of the Van Zandts, often with the same name, that they had to use adjectives to sort them out. For instance, there were Black Jim, Long Jim, and Crazy Jim in our community. Then there were Big Jack and Little

Jack Van Zandt. Black Jim had helped with all the details and had gone with Pres to get the license."

Mary Elizabeth and Pres both understood the solemnity and permanence of holy wedlock. They gave serious attention to the Reverend Van Zandt's good advice not to both get mad at the same time.

After the ceremony all the young people walked back to the Prather home, where they ate the cakes Betsy baked. She hadn't let Mary Elizabeth help her. "It was bad luck for a bride to help with her own wedding feast." The group played cards and visited.

That night their friends gave them an unusual shivaree. It was customary that on the wedding night or some night later, friends and neighbors would meet someplace near the newlyweds' house. With noise makers they would sneak up to the house and at a signal, everyone would shout, blow fox horns, bang on tubs, and otherwise make all the noise possible to surprise the couple in bed. The couple must then treat the people. If caught unprepared with treats, usually cigars and candy, the crowd would do something to the groom such as roll him in a snow bank, carry him into the woods and turn him loose barefooted, or throw him into a creek or pond.

Since the colonel was away at the legislature and Pres was afraid a shivaree would make Betsy Prather nervous, he bribed the boys with a jug of whiskey not to make noise in the middle of the night. His friends kept their word, but after sampling the whiskey, they came back and marched around the house singing:

> There were three crows sat on a tree
> And they were black as crows could be
> And one of these crows said to his mate
> What will we do for grub to ate.

> There is a horse on yonder plain
> We'll eat him up, both tail and mane
> We'll light upon his breastbone
> And pick his eyes out one by one.

Mary Elizabeth said, "It was a pretty doleful song for a wedding song, but then, I suppose it was the only one they all knew. Or maybe they thought marriage was a doleful occasion!"

The day after the wedding was the infare, a dinner at the home of the groom. Traditionally it was as merry as the wedding itself. Pres on his gray saddle horse and Mary Elizabeth on Kit rode over to the elder Mahnkeys' home. "It was a beautiful day, the sun shining bright, and the ride was just like we were in another world. We had a magnificent dinner, too, turkey, pies, cakes, canned fruit, and everything a farm dinner could be," said Mary Elizabeth.

The newlyweds stayed a day and night at the Mahnkeys before going to the home of Pres's sister, Emma, and her husband, Sol Wheeler, spending a typical country honeymoon with relatives before moving into their own home.

When Mary Elizabeth and Pres moved into the place he had rented, they were proud and excited. They were on their own. They had made the holy commitment to each other; now they could begin a new life in their own home separate from their families. Pres was anxious to begin farming for himself and his new wife. He had dreamed of marrying Mary Elizabeth ever since boyhood when he saw her watching his family trek by on that journey from Cedar County almost ten years earlier.

Though Pres was fully aware of Mary Elizabeth's good looks, her intelligence, and other talents, he rarely told her so or praised her as she bragged about him. He assumed she knew all that. There was much work to do. Full of youthful confidence that he could succeed and sure of her life-long commitment, he expressed his love by working hard.

Mary Elizabeth shared his enthusiasm. At last she had a home all her own with a hard-working, steady man. It never occurred to her that he thought she was quite a catch. She knew she would not have to worry about his running around or drinking. Nor would she be left alone for weeks at a time, as her mother had been for years while her man worked away from home. Though Mary Elizabeth admired her busy and important father, she appreciated Pres's home-oriented qualities. As partners they would work together.

However, in the hills at the beginning of the twentieth century, women were more accurately sub-partners, often with no voice in decisions. The man was the head of the family. To live in any sort of harmony, no woman forgot that, not even Mary Elizabeth, who had been independent for a few years. Headstrong, impulsive, and perhaps spoiled and indulged by her father and brothers, Mary Elizabeth had some difficult adjustments to make with this stolid, quiet-spoken man. Many times she retreated to private tears of frustration and resentment; sometimes in the early years there was open confrontation, but always she recognized her secondary place. She had promised to obey. She would learn patience to wait and hope eventually to get her way.

But those adjustments were yet to come as the enthusiastic young couple set up housekeeping. Neither was dismayed by the cold, open old cabin which was not much more than a hen house or that they had very little furniture. Pres was handy with tools; he would make anything they needed and fix up the house. Mary Elizabeth was imaginative and artistic, creating beauty wherever she was. The ugly cabin was a challenge. Certainly she had helped her own mother make beautiful and comfortable surroundings in the dozens of places the Prathers had lived in her memory. Come spring she would plant some flowers—hollyhocks, marigolds, and asters.

Pres and Mary Elizabeth appreciated the good points of the farm, especially the cleared ground for crops and garden. Since this was before the laws requiring fencing of livestock, they had the use of the native bluestem grass on the free range. And perhaps best of all, the farm was close to Pres's parents and not far from the Prather family in Kirbyville.

It did not take the young couple long to move in their scanty furniture. Pres bought some handmade chairs. Betsy Prather gave them two rocking chairs and the usual gift for a new couple, two straw ticks, a feather bed, four feather pillows, and some quilts.

Together they fixed up their belongings, beginning the sharing of work that continued the rest of their lives together. Pres was careful and clever in many things. Though manly and tough (neighboring men had learned long ago not to get at cross purposes with the Mahnkey boys) he also never hesitated to help with household tasks even though housekeeping was not a man's job. One of their first shared tasks was filling the new straw ticks to put on the rope slats of their bed as a foundation for the feather bed mattress.

Mary Elizabeth and Pres carried their new ticks to the Mahnkeys' straw stack. Raking off the top weathered layer, they pulled out armloads of the clean, yellow straw. While one of them held the tick open, the other stuffed in the slick, sweet-smelling straw, making a tight, full tick before Mary Elizabeth sewed up the opening.

Pres was methodical in everything he did, even in picking up handfuls of straw to be sure nothing but good fresh straw went in. He would never do anything as careless as Mary Elizabeth and Deal did one time when they refilled their straw tick and accidentally put in a lizard.

While Mary Elizabeth had finished her term at Roark Creek School, Pres prepared the house and farm for them to move in. He added to the cows he already owned and traded off an old pistol for some chickens. On the farm was a good barn for their team and Kit. He butchered his own meat and rendered out the lard. They had a heating stove, a cook stove, and plenty of wood. There was nothing covering the wooden floor, not even a handmade rug, but that did not concern them since very few country homes had anything on the floor. Pres scrubbed it shiny clean. Together they papered the walls with newspapers. Pres built a corner shelf for Mary Elizabeth's books and trinkets. Though they had very few things that could be called pretty, Mary Elizabeth did her best to make their home attractive.

Her eye for beauty even included the kerosene lamps. It was customary to put a cloth down in the oil of the lamp to absorb the sediment. Some women used red flannel to add some color, but Mary Elizabeth did more. She crocheted little red and yellow flowers with green leaves. When she carried the lamps from room to room and the flowers would wave in the oil as though the wind were blowing through them, she liked to imagine that they were dancing in a summer breeze.

Pres was not alone in doing chores carefully and thoroughly. Mary Elizabeth, though quicker and more impulsive, worked diligently at every job. Since the whole responsibility of cooking was now hers, she wanted to become an excellent cook. She had helped her mother in the kitchen, but not as much as most farm girls did. Her mother did the main cooking, and as a former New Yorker, her dishes and menus were different from those of the hill people. Mary Elizabeth wanted to cook what Pres liked. She got recipes from her mother-in-law.

On the farm most of the food was home produced.

Though the young Mahnkeys had to wait until spring to begin their first garden, they had their own meat, milk, and eggs. They bought other staples such as coffee, flour, cornmeal, soda, salt. To satisfy their sweet tooth they bought sorghum molasses from a neighbor at twenty-five cents a gallon. Molasses meant pies, cakes, and cookies. Mary Elizabeth quickly mastered vinegar pie, a dessert substitute when fruit was scarce, made by cooking vinegar, butter, and sugar to a thick mixture and adding thin strips of dumplings.

After this success, she hunted up recipes for other desserts. As with most novice cooks, some of her early attempts were disasters, such as her first cookies. When she took the inedible panful from the oven, she wadded up the rest of the dough, not sure what to do with the gooey mess. If she didn't destroy the evidence, she would never hear the last of it. It wouldn't burn. No use throwing it out or burying it, for the dog might bring it right to the kitchen door. Then she noticed a loose floor board in the kitchen that she often tripped over. Raising up that board, she stuck the rest of the dough under it.

Pres loved pancakes or, as he called them, flapjacks. Mary Elizabeth learned from her mother-in-law how to mix the pancakes just right to be light and tender, and how to make cornbread more tasty by using buttermilk. With considerable practice, she mastered both sourdough and yeast bread. These breads, spread with homemade butter and sorghum, became staples in their diets through all their years.

The first winter of their marriage was a cold one. The huge pile of wood Pres had cut was soon gone. Together they went to the timber to cut more, Pres on one end of the cross-cut saw and Mary Elizabeth on the other. Pres easily loaded the heavy pieces into the wagon, while Mary Elizabeth handled the smaller ones. One of Pres's nightly chores was to split some of the wood into heating stove size, and to fill the wood box with a day's supply split into smaller cook stove thickness.

They could not keep the drafty cabin warm. Continual exposure to the moist cold caused Mary Elizabeth to develop chilblains in her feet which bothered her for years afterward. Though the young couple suffered only minor health problems, the Charles Mahnkey household had a long siege of sickness that winter. First Pres's brothers Andrew and George and then his mother became sick with typhoid. Neighbors flocked in to help. Since Mary Elizabeth and Pres lived close, they fed the visitors, grinding a pound of Arbuckle coffee every day for the people who sat up to tend the sick ones. It kept two men busy cutting wood to feed the fires.

When the sick ones got well, the young Mahnkey couple could again devote their time to their own place. As woman of the house, it was Mary Elizabeth's job to care for the chickens and garden. She enjoyed working outside and had an affinity for growing things. Throughout her life in all the places they lived she always kept chickens.

She also took great pride in her garden. Pres plowed the ground and carefully worked down the seed bed. Together they planted the greens, onions, and potatoes as early in the spring as weather permitted, and according to the correct planting time in the almanac from the signs of the zodiac. Then Mary Elizabeth took over most of the responsibility for tending and harvesting the garden, Pres helping when another hand was needed. His greatest help was plowing through the potatoes a couple of times with a walking plow behind one of his horses. After the frozen winter, Mary Elizabeth rejoiced as the garden prospered. Then, just when the vegetables were ready to produce, the cow got through the rail fence and ate everything.

While they lived near the elder Mahnkeys, Mary Elizabeth also learned how to get along with her in-laws even though they were different from her family. She admitted she never seemed to fit in with the Mahnkeys. They never stopped working from early in the morning. Mary Elizabeth said, "They were the workingest people I had ever known. Always in approaching their place, one was struck by the busy, stirring, teeming life—little mule colts, half grown mules, sheep and lambs, and calves." The Prathers took things easier.

On the elder Mahnkey farm on the Harrison Road was a good spring called the Free Jack Spring, named after a black man who, freed by his owner, Harrison Snapp, built a log cabin at the edge of the grasslands.

Charles Mahnkey saw the advantages of the watering place for the many freighters on the busy road to Arkansas. He built a camp house and a big barn that became a popular stopping place. Many times there would be as many as twenty wagons at a time in the campground yard.

The camp house, with its roaring fire in the big box stove, was like a club house on winter nights. Mr. Mahnkey and others would tell jokes and stories and listen to the music of a banjoist or two in the crowd of drivers.

Pres's mother, Mattie Mahnkey, was descended from the St. Louis French. Her cooking and baking had a special difference from the usual hill cooking. Mary Elizabeth said it had a "delicacy of texture in pastry and a blending of flavors and seasoning that was highly individual." Taking advantage of the camp house situation, Pres's mother made extra income by cooking "biskit bread" at ten cents a dozen for the freighters.

Mattie Mahnkey and her daughters worked as hard as the men, putting up hundreds of cans of fruit, vegetables, pickles, and jams. Mary Elizabeth was in awe of their productivity, their accomplishments, and their almost instinctive knowledge of how to handle any household contingency.

While developing the camp house and prospering with

their farming and stock enterprises, Pres's parents had painted the box house on their farm a shiny white trimmed in yellow. Mary Elizabeth especially loved the yellow climbing rose and the trumpet vine with its red-orange blossoms growing in front of the house.

During her first two years of marriage, Mary Elizabeth experienced many things which seemed to set a pattern of action for her life. It was a time of learning and achievement and maturing. It was a time of great fulfillment and shared happiness in discovering her womanhood and new family relationships. She never ceased her devotion to her own family and to Pres's family. It was also the beginning of a new cycle of incessant moving. Pres had not thought of getting a contract on their rental farm. Their first little log home was sold out from under them. After a year of living briefly on two other farms, they moved in January 1900 to another rented place west of Mincy on Pine Hill.

Mary Elizabeth enjoyed their stay there. They liked being close to Emma and Sol Wheeler, Pres's sister and brother-in-law. Compared to the small farm they first rented, they prospered on the "ranch" as she called it, an almost untouched area with big pine trees. She felt secure in the love of her husband, the companionship of congenial neighbors, the peace of the wild beauty everywhere she looked, and the beginning of financial success with the increase of their stock.

But getting married didn't lessen Mary Elizabeth's love of writing. Besides continuing with the weekly news items to the county paper, she jotted down her thoughts and impressions whenever she had time. Foremost in her personal writing is her appreciation of natural beauty.

> This is such a perfect morning if midsummer mornings ever reach perfection; there is no dew, no fresh grass, the

vegetation is burned and sere. But the cool little morning breeze is fresh from the distant river hills and tried in vain to woo some life into the dead stalks. The golden rod, merely faint hints of yellow on long pale-green stems, waves obedient to the wind, patiently awaiting its time of bloom. The woodchucks and jaybirds, the only birds August has in her train down here, are noisily reveling in the dead treetops. The shadow of our little house is long and dark and cool, the slant of the roof reaching far into the pine woods. It is early yet. I hear Emma just now calling the calves and Pres singing in the distant fields as he binds up the fodder. There is a faint haze over the blue down in the southwest and today may bring the longed for rain. The cows are retreating into the cool woodsiness of the hills, giving back a scarcely audible low to the plaint of their calves left in the pasture. Duckie, I hear plainer than any. She has such a stentorian voice for a cow-lady.
August 20, 1900

Mary Elizabeth knew that greater happiness was to come. She was going to have a child. The anticipation of this child was the ultimate fulfilling of her new life as a married woman.

Working for herself and Pres was greatly rewarding. The hardships were temporary conditions necessary for future abundance. Together they made a home of the cabin they had to live in. They put out a crop. The cow had a calf, the sow had pigs, the mare had a colt. They had each other. And now there would be three of them. All their efforts were for the new child.

However, a premonition of coming trouble oppressed her. One day she was sitting in the yard making a dress for the baby. She remembered, "It was such a beautiful place that I should have been happy, for I so loved beauty. As I sat there,

I finished the little dress and spread it out over my lap to look at it. And all at once, such a feeling of sadness came over me that I began to cry. Somehow, the little sleeves looked so pathetic. I folded the dress and put it away with the most heart broken feeling I had ever experienced."

On an October evening Mary Elizabeth saddled Kit to go get the cows. In the rough, free range land surrounding their house, the cows would sometimes stray quite a distance. Since horseback was the only transportation, country women thought nothing of riding horses even when they were well along in their pregnancy. The chores had to be done and women could not be coddled, nor did they want to be. Most young married women in the hills were carrying a baby, either unborn or in their arms.

When Kit came to a log in the woods, she jumped it just as she always did. This time, however, the jar to Mary Elizabeth was harder than usual. Though she did not lose her seat in the saddle because her left leg was clamped securely around the horn of her side saddle and her right foot supported in the one stirrup, she lurched dangerously. With Mary Elizabeth's shift in weight, high spirited Kit began loping through the woods.

Though doubled over in pain, she checked Kit's flight. In premature labor, she managed to ride through the uninhabited woods to their cabin.

That night, October 6, 1900, the baby was born. In the hills at that time, seven-month babies had little chance to live. In just a few days, sister-in-law Emma brought the baby girl to her bedside, dressed in the white dress which had warned Mary Elizabeth of some sadness. The baby was dead. Her parents buried her in Van Zandt Cemetery.

Grief over the loss of her baby almost incapacitated Mary Elizabeth. She lost her vitality, her ever-ready smile, her interest in her home. For the next year, minor irritations became magnified so that she questioned her family's love, even Pres's. Nine months later, August 10, 1901, she wrote in her journal, "O God, my wasted, ruined life. Whose fault is it? Why is it that nothing I desire comes to pass? I have wanted a home of my own. We have moved six times in 2 1/2 years. I wanted little ones of my own—Baby lived nine days. As a girl I prayed for an education, for pretty clothes, for a nice home."

One day Deal told her to pull herself together. "Forget it," she said. "You still have Pres. You'll have other babies." Knowing Deal was right, Mary Elizabeth buried the grief inside her.

After this loss, she rarely displayed openly her grief or unhappiness. Showing a cheerful front, she shed her tears only when alone. She expressed her loss in her journals and in her poetry.

This death was perhaps the first major tear in the fabric of her life. She mended it, as well as later tragedies and misfortunes, by putting on a bold, smiling front. Her family and friends did not suspect that the mending only covered the sadness, and perhaps some bitterness, that always remained.

During the first two years of marriage she learned the joys and the griefs of what was expected of a woman.

> I hunted a place where I could cry
> Far removed from mortal eye
> But Duty said, "You must not weep
> Go on back home, and dust and sweep.
> No one cries, and no one sobs
> They're all too busy hunting jobs.
> Dry your eyes, make lemon pies
> Stick to your job
> If you are wise.

Chapter 8

I QUIT MY DANCIN' AN' SETTLED DOWN
Farming at the Homestead and Swan Creek:
November 1900-1903

He quit his fiddlin'
An' settled down
On a rocky farm
Far away from town.

He learned haymaking
Castration of pigs
But still he'd whistle
His wild Irish jigs.

He learned patience
To doctor a cow
To build rail fences
To mend a plow.

I quit my dancin'
An' settled down
But I dreamed at night
Of the little town.

An' makin' jelly
Or makin' soap
There is always a sly
Little whisperin' hope

That some day he'll fiddle
An' I'll fly aroun'
Just as we did
In our little town.

Even before the baby's death, Pres and Mary Elizabeth did not want to stay longer in the pine hills. They wanted their own place. Without money to buy land, their solution was to get a government claim. Pres bought the homestead relinquishment rights from a man who "cash entered" on the land but had made no improvements. On September 18, 1900, Pres paid the seven dollar fee to file for the homestead.

Even as late as 1900 there was still government land in Taney County open to the Homestead Law of 1862. In his name only, Pres filed for eighty acres in the rugged hill land north of Colonel Prather's Swan Creek farm. It was just two miles south of the Christian County border in an unpopulated region. For years big cattlemen had grazed their stock on the free range. Pres's claim was a rocky ridge near the foot of a mountain. (Though technically not mountains, in south Missouri these lone elevations were called mountains because they were higher than the surrounding hilly land.)

When his debts were paid, Pres had no money to live on. Grubbing an existence from the rocky glade, besides being arduous, would be unprofitable. The land was too thin to produce. Thinking he could get a job during the winter to get a stake for next year, Pres took Mary Elizabeth to St. Louis barely a month after the baby's death. Construction for the St. Louis exhibition of 1904 was beginning. Dick Prather told

Pres that he could get a good job. But the only job Pres could find was driving a team of mules on a street building job. Mary Elizabeth and Pres both knew that they should not stay in the city. Once again she returned to the hills.

Before leaving Taney County, Pres had taken his team and good Springfield wagon to his mother to sell for them. Alone in the city, Mary Elizabeth realized that Pres could not return to farming without them. Without Pres knowing it, she wrote to his mother not to sell them. Mrs. Mahnkey read Mary Elizabeth's letter that the mail hack left just before hurrying across the road to the camp house where a man was looking at Pres's team. She shouted to her husband, who was about to close the deal, "Don't sell Pres's team! He's a-comin' back!"

Mary Elizabeth came home two weeks before Pres. They had never been apart, but she could stay no longer. In 1900 there was no railroad in Taney County. The nearest station was at Chadwick, north of Forsyth in Christian County. From there she took the mail hack to Taneyville to spend the night with her brother Ben and Janie, his wife. Then she and Janie rode horseback to the Swan Creek farm where the Prathers were living.

Her family was surprised and overjoyed to see her, though sorry the excursion to the city turned out badly. For a few days her mother spoiled her, and she had fun fishing and riding horseback with Deal and Mag. It was nice to be a girl at home again, even for a short time.

When Pres returned, they moved to the homestead. Fixing a home and living on this land was difficult and primitive beyond anything either Pres or Mary Elizabeth ever experienced. Pres cut logs to build a makeshift cabin. There was no spring on the flinty glade. Their only water was what ran off the roof into a rain barrel. They would drink it even though it was stagnant and green with algae, and they had to strain it to get out the wiggletails. But neither complained of the work or difficulties. This was *their* land. They would own it by cultivating and improving it.

Pres spent the winter clearing a little patch of land to put out a crop. The couple had no money. In order to get the seed, Pres needed credit. A young man starting out, he could not get credit at any of the stores in Taneyville unless his father-in-law signed for it. The colonel hadn't wanted Mary Elizabeth to marry Pres; the hardships of their first months of marriage seemed to justify the colonel's disapproval. Young Pres Mahnkey was a proud man who could not ask for credit on those terms. He did not want anyone to stand good for his debts. Just as Mary Elizabeth never felt a part of the Mahnkey family, neither did Pres feel comfortable with the Prathers, especially the colonel. Ben Prather was the only one of the Prather boys Pres really liked; Dick was too high-minded and fancy for him.

Finally, L.L. Morrow extended credit in his store to young Mahnkey, (actually only a few dollars) to put in the crop. Pres paid that debt and every other debt during his life quickly and promptly. His motto was, "Always do what you promise, but be careful what you promise." Many years later during the hard times of the great Depression when Pres was the storekeeper himself, he surely remembered this man's faith in him when he first needed financing because Pres, in his turn, extended credit to many farmers who might otherwise have faced ruin.

The young couple did not live on the homestead very long before the colonel and Mrs. Prather and the girls, Deal and Mag, moved to Taneyville. They offered to let them live on the Swan Creek farm. Pres continued to improve the homestead, both he and Mary Elizabeth going up there occasionally to spend some days in order to prove his claim.

I Quit My Dancin' An' Settled Down

The Swan Creek farm was lovely, the house comfortable and full of books and keepsakes dear to Mary Elizabeth. They both put all their efforts into their work. Mary Elizabeth continued recording their daily life in her journal, finding adventure and pathos in common occurrences.

April 5, 1901, Friday morn
It is 20 minutes past 8. I have done all the housework, churned, slopped the hogs and am now waiting for my irons to heat for I have a pretty big ironing. I washed yesterday. Then in the evening took the dogs and went down to where Pres was at work. The blue pup is growing into a big footed long-legged ugly dog. Pres plowed up a tiny young rabbit. As it scampered down the furrow, the puppy discovered it and wildly gave chase. He caught it, shook it, and laid it down. It did not stir or run any more. It was dead. He had killed it. He patted it gently with one foot. Still it did not move. Then he turned his head heavenward and uttered a plaintive heart-rending howl. He carried it tenderly away and buried it in plowed ground. But alas for his pretended sorrow. I saw him in 15 minutes or more, stealthily slip back, disinter it and eat it all up. A long time afterwards when Booze came up to us, tired and weary from hunting big rabbits in the hazel brush, the puppy did not deign to notice him or fawn upon him as was his wont. He retained a majestic reserve and dignity. Booze scented the blood of the adventure, for excitedly he smelled of the pup's nose and paws. Puppy cast a sly glance at me and licked his chops with reflective complacency.

April 8, 1901, Monday
O! my—something awful has happened. Poor puppy went mad and is now dead. Pres shot him. O how I miss him and how nervous I am, for I was here all alone when it happened, busy washing dishes and heard him howling on the

front porch. I opened the door and looked out at him and he was having a fit, frothing at the mouth and biting at himself. Then I slammed the door and nearly fainted. I watched out of the window—he jumped up and ran staggering out to the gate, ran into the fence like he was blind, and ran all over the yard that way, finally taking after the chickens frothing at the mouth all the time. O! I did not know what to do. I thought of ringing the bell so Pres would come to the house, then thought the pup would maybe bite him, him having no weapon, nor not knowing he was mad. So nerving myself, I took the gun, slipped out the back door, ran down, and got over the fence by the chicken house, so afraid he would run after me for he follows me everywhere. But he did not see me. My! how I flew down that path to the field, and how frightened Pres was when he saw me all breathless and scared to death. I told him between gasps, he jerked the harness off old Ben, jumped on, took the gun and galloped away. Then I collapsed. I weakly climbed up on the fence and sat there till I heard the gun. Then I started slowly up to the house, met Pres and he told me puppy was dead, poor little fellow.

That spring, 1901, Pres put out oats and corn in the rich creek bottom field of Swan Creek. Mary Elizabeth planted a big garden, each spring hopeful, each spring a new start.

The early peas and a few green onions marked the end of that garden. One good rain in May made the oat crop in the creek bottom, but it beat the ground down around the corn. The corn barely made fodder, for there was no more moisture until the winter snows. For many years, actually until the drought years of 1934 and 1936, old-timers called 1901 The Dry Year.

It was a difficult time, for no one had any money or much food. Though money was always scarce in the hills, every family could usually depend on a garden and their own meat.

With gardens and pastures drying up, people were forced to sell their animals. When that money was gone, there was nothing.

The drought, however, was not the hardest thing for Mary Elizabeth and Pres to deal with. They had come to the farm broke and, in their eyes, failures. The death of the baby weighed heavily on both. What was hardest of all was Colonel Prather's open disapproval of Pres. The young couple felt trapped on the farm because before he let them move to the farm, the colonel insisted they mortgage their team for a hundred dollars to buy some of the Prather stock. Nothing Pres did satisfied the colonel.

Mary Elizabeth's journal of that year is full of their problems. "July 9, Thursday: I dread the winter. Verily the lot of the farmer is hard. Buyers say the bottom has fallen out of the market. I don't know what to do. Seems like which ever way we raise our heads, something awful smites us down."

Pres sometimes added entries in her journal. Added to the above he wrote, "Dry and no corn. I will haft to get out of this place shure and hunt me a job or starve."

On July 29, Pres wrote, "Mamie has gone to town. I am waiting for her to come back. I had ought to of went but was afraid I would have a little hell with Prathers so I dident go. We are going to have rosten ears for diner. I am going to have diner reddy when my little wife gets back for she will be tired. We have had a little rain and I look for more. Hope it will rain so we will have fodder anyway. I am here all alone. My I miss my little wife but she is not gone for good but when she is I hope I will not last any longer."

The next day Mary Elizabeth wrote, "I had to stay to dinner yesterday at pa's, an hour or two of torture because he and mother are always abusing Pres so, and he one of the noblest men that ever lived. I just told them he was better to me than anyone else had ever been. But they are so obtuse. I came home sick and cross. I am not going out there any more. I guess we will try to get credit at Forsyth and go to trading there."

In spite of these difficulties, the young Mahnkeys fared better during the drought than most of their neighbors. Mary Elizabeth was not the only one learning and maturing in these first years of marriage. Pres had learned to manage. With an established credit rating, in the fall he took a long chance by borrowing a hundred dollars. A few dollars he spent for flour and some other staples. The main part of the money went for chopped wheat to fatten hogs. When cold weather came, he sold some of the hogs and butchered enough for their own meat. Mary Elizabeth sold eggs at ten cents a dozen and butter for fifteen cents a pound. In late summer Pres gathered sacks of peaches from an abandoned farm where the trees had managed to survive the drought. Together he and Mary Elizabeth canned and dried them for the winter. With Pres's foresight, they came through the drought better off than the previous year after returning broke from St. Louis.

The young Mahnkeys and their neighbors could not continually worry about the weather or their problems. Life continued and they tried to enjoy themselves. When one family had a party, Deal and Mag came to go with Mary Elizabeth and Pres. Mary Elizabeth was excited, and with her sisters' help, tried to fix herself up. Living as she had for the past few years, she had got out of the habit of dressing up. She did not use any of the helps women did at that time for cosmetics, and she never considered herself attractive, though she was probably one of the prettiest girls in the community. But this time she thought she would feel better if she dressed up.

She succeeded. Though as usual Pres did not say anything about her appearance, there was pride in his eyes. But being a married woman at a party was not like being a single girl. She danced one set with Pres and then sat with the matrons because "an old married woman" was not supposed to dance any more. None of the men talked with her or asked her to dance, and Pres, as was the custom, deserted her to talk business and trading and swap fishing stories with his buddies. Mary Elizabeth spent the evening watching her popular sisters fly around the dance floor excited, flushed and happy, while she listened to the women's endless chatter about cooking, canning, and children. That was their life. There was no talk about current affairs, except the drought. Nothing about books or literature or beauty.

Mary Elizabeth did not lose her interest in the world outside her valley. She continued to treasure newspapers, magazines, and books, reading everything she could lay her hands on. She especially enjoyed her sisters' company that long hot summer. Tomboyish Deal was energetic, riding horses and fishing. Mag, more the lady, would stay with Mary Elizabeth, helping her with her work. As the continued hot and dry days shortened into October, Mag's visits helped her even more, for Mary Elizabeth knew she was going to have another child.

This time the knowledge worried her, for she was afraid the outcome would be like the first. She dared not get excited or anticipate the baby's coming too much. By attempting a sort of inoculation against grief, she tried to avoid another traumatic aftermath if it turned out badly again. But this time she had good clothes for the baby because her cousin back East, whose clothes fit her so well, had a baby and sent Mary Elizabeth the complete outfit. She also did some sewing herself. She sold some hens and bought a piece of red and green plaid woolen material which she stitched up with red thread.

The baby was due in June. The winter following the drought was just as icy and cold as the summer had been dry and hot. People and animals had difficulty getting around on the ice. Mary Elizabeth's mother coined two words to describe the time—tumblesome and wobblesome. Many animals were crippled trying to get to water. Pres chopped blocks of packed snow and melted them in kettles to save some stock that strayed onto his place. He chopped a path from the barn to let his animals out. Once again Pres showed his managerial skills. When some farmers sold their stock that had survived the drought, Pres traded for them, acquiring some good heifers and cows. All winter he worked outside preparing for spring, fixing fences, preparing his tools and equipment, caring for the stock, and spreading manure.

That spring, since Mary Elizabeth was expecting a baby, and they were both more careful this time, Pres put out the garden. It flourished. During the summer Mary Elizabeth proudly sent her mother sacks of cabbage, cucumbers, and tomatoes. It was quite an achievement for her to be able to help her family at last.

Pres planted his crops with good seeds and no debt. As state representative, Colonel Prather worked to get the government to furnish seeds to farmers who were burned out by the drought. Pres shared in that program.

Then as hard evidence that their luck was changing, their second child was born June 18, 1902, Charles Douglas Mahnkey.

After the baby's birth Mary Elizabeth did not spring back as she wished, not regaining her usual robustness for several months. The baby was also sickly. In those days Ozark women did not know much about infant nutrition. Since the baby had nothing but his mother's milk, if she was sick, or did not have enough milk, the baby suffered. Even if mothers tried feeding cow's milk to babies, they did not know to sterilize the equipment, to dilute the milk, or to sweeten it to more nearly equal mother's milk. They would not give a baby any water. When Douglas was born, he was licking his lips. The women who attended Mary Elizabeth jokingly asked her what she was craving, because that was what the baby was wanting, too. Mary Elizabeth answered, "If the baby wants anything, it is a good cold drink of water."

"Oh my!" they said. "That will never do. Never give water to a baby."

Each new visitor told Mary Elizabeth something different to do for the baby. She tried everything anyone suggested. Later she wondered if trying all those remedies was what was the matter with him.

One time, however, the home remedy seemed to work. When the baby's kidneys would not function, an old lady told her to gather cobwebs to put in the child's groins. The lady prepared the cobwebs and put them on the baby. He recovered within hours.

Even when she weaned him she had problems because, like her, he did not like milk. The only way she could make him drink it was to put a little coffee in the milk. The neighbor women were horrified.

By the end of the summer both Mary Elizabeth and infant Doug were better. Perhaps the effects of the drought and the hard winter of the year before were finally wearing off. She resumed her interest in their farm.

Mary Elizabeth loved her chickens and cattle, rejoicing over new chicks and calves. The purpose of their labor and crops was to feed the stock, the source of their livelihood, not only for their eggs, milk, butter, and meat, but for their monetary value which could be turned quickly into cash or traded for profit. Pres was becoming adept at trading, juggling their small inventory of stock around to come out better. It was therefore inevitable that while she was gone one afternoon, he would get an offer he could not resist to sell Kit, Mary Elizabeth's mare.

On March 23, 1903, she wrote in her journal, "Pres traded Kit for a nice black mare and $55. Well, 'tis no use to grieve. Pres does the very best he can, and we all act blindly, but we shall never forget the 'filly.' She helped haul our first housekeeping things to the English place [their first home]. And Pres has sold two mule colts of hers for $45. He will invest the remaining $50 in a good milk cow the very next thing he does, for we're clear out of milk, and it's pretty tough living."

Though she justified Pres's actions, years later when she wrote this poem she wasn't as forgiving.

MY BARNEY

When he swapped my Barney for a cow, I cried.
For Barney was a saddler, with limber, swinging stride.
"Now Barney's gettin' old," he said. "We better
   let him go
And a cow is worth more money, on the farm, you know."

And now, I ride no more in woodsy vale
But bend my head above the foaming pail.
Wickedly, I hate the milk and cream
And long for Barney and that amber stream
Where he would pause to drink in shadows dark and still
And I would dream of beauty I would find yon side
   the hill.
Or wildly we would dash against the March wind's wall
Or madly race with golden leaves from maples in the fall.

When he swapped my Barney for a cow, I cried
And now, these jewel dreams of mine, I slip away
   and hide.

Mary Elizabeth was learning to accept her inferior partnership.

Chapter 9

JUST A LITTLE HOUSE
Adjustments:
Omaha, Arkansas, and the Stout Farm
Fall 1903 - February 1905

Just a little house, O God
At the edge of thy kingdom divine.
A wee little house, a little white house
With a morning glory vine.

A little white house with a picket fence
And a little pink-blossom peach tree
And this, O God, is all I ask
For this will be Heaven for me.

The success of the two years on Swan Creek allowed the Mahnkeys to buy their first real farm when Pres sold all the young stock that had grown well during the summer. It was difficult for Mary Elizabeth to see them all go, for she loved and named every one. Though they were not able to make complete payment for the new farm, they now owned their own place, eighty acres known as the John Stout place about two miles west of the Prathers' Swan Creek farm. Pres said it was ideal for cattle; he planned to expand it into a cattle ranch.

Not wild like their homestead, the Stout place was already improved and cleared with level fields and lots of fruit trees. Mary Elizabeth's aesthetic nature loved the pleasant three-room box house with its fresh, clean porch surrounded by flowering lilacs and rose of Sharon bushes.

Being a good wife and mother was her goal now, as Pres's goal, then and always, was to make for his family the best living possible. Acquiring this good farm was the first major step forward for both.

But they wanted to pay it out in full. In rural areas in the early 1900s there were very few jobs one could get during slack farming seasons. Therefore, it was good fortune for the young Mahnkeys when in late summer and early fall of 1903, Pres obtained a job as a driller on a railroad tunnel just across the Arkansas border at Omaha. They postponed moving to the Stout farm; the money he earned would pay off the farm.

The first railroad into Taney County, the Missouri Pacific and Iron Mountain Railroad, was building its White River Line from east-central Arkansas to Carthage, Missouri, through the developing Taney County towns of Hollister and Branson. Reaching both towns in 1905, the railroad encouraged growth even before the White River bridge joined the two lines in early 1906. Branson soon surpassed Hollister, Kirbyville, and Forsyth as the largest and foremost town in the county.

But the development of Branson and Hollister and the effect of a railroad in Taney County were still in the future in the late summer of 1903 when Pres left Mary Elizabeth and fourteen-month-old Douglas at the Swan Creek farm (the Prathers had moved back) and crossed the border into Arkansas to work on Tunnel C. He began work at $1.75 a day, and soon drew $2.00.

He had worked there only a short time when he wrote

Mary Elizabeth on August 12 to arrange to cut their corn and dig their potatoes for "fifty cents a day, if possible, or even seventy-five cents if necessary. Say, I want you to come just as soon as you can. I don't think I can stay without you and the boy. We had just as well be together. Lord how I do miss you."

At first the family lived in a tent where many others were camping out for the duration of the work. More fortunate than some workers, Pres soon rented a room in an abandoned log house two miles from the camp.

Though primitive, living there was better than camping out, and Mary Elizabeth could make things comfortable for her family. She had brought some chickens and a cow from their farm. Since food from the camp commissary was cheap, she prepared good meals and made the rooms pleasant.

She used a little wagon to pull Doug and haul home her groceries from the commissary. Many of the workers were foreigners, all called dagoes, though they were not all Italian. Mother and son would pass the big camp of the dark-skinned workers, going by the large oven where the men were often cooking. They never glanced her way when she was alone, but on Sunday, when Pres was with them, the men crowded around to see the child. Doug's blond curly hair and home-made green and red plaid coat with matching red shoes and cap must have looked novel to them.

Though the railroad camp was an interesting place, Mary Elizabeth knew it held as many dangers for Pres as did the mountain that might fall in on him while he was working inside it with the pneumatic drill. There were killings and lawlessness. To keep Pres home after working hours, she used her ingenuity however she could. Since he had a quick temper and was ready to fight when angry, she constantly worried that he would get drunk like many of the men did and get into brawls.

On Christmas Day she was sick with longing for home

and family and worry about Pres. That frosty morning a friend from their home neighborhood came by to take Pres to the notorious Old State Line Saloon. If Pres went, it would mean a long, lonely, anxious day for Mary Elizabeth. Thinking quickly, she invited the friend to their Christmas dinner, first telling him to go get what liquor he wanted.

With Pres's help she quickly prepared a good dinner. She even helped her guest mix fancy drinks using techniques she learned from her mother, an expert at making eggnog and apple toddy. In the coals of the fireplace, she roasted apples wrapped in brown paper. She carefully unwrapped them and, placing a steaming, fluffy apple in a glass, covered it with sugar before pouring in hot water and brandy.

Pres and his friend had a great time; they ate, drank, told stories, and cracked hickory nuts that Mary Elizabeth had gathered out on the ridge. She was pleased when the friend told her as he left that night that he had never passed a more pleasant Christmas.

When the tunnel was finished, before moving to the Stout place, the Mahnkeys returned to the Prathers' Swan Creek farm to collect their belongings and their stock, which the colonel and the girls had fed for them. Relations between Pres and Alonzo improved. Pres had paid off his obligations to the colonel and now owned debt-free a good farm; he was proving worthy.

Though the family has no records to document it, Pres probably sold or traded off the homestead farm sometime after moving to the Stout farm.

Early in January of 1904, Pres and Mary Elizabeth, full of hope and anticipation in the first real place of their own, moved to their new farm in the highlands. Moving was no problem for Mary Elizabeth. She knew from childhood just how to pack and where to put things in the wagon. The young

Mahnkeys had not acquired too many belongings; one wagon held them all. Most precious of all was the little son Mary Elizabeth carried as she walked behind the wagon.

Up on the wagon seat Pres drove the team over the slick roads. Without noticing the danger, he urged the team up an icy slope. Part way up, the horses began slipping and sliding back, unable to hold their ground. The wagon was headed toward a precipice when Mary Elizabeth saw the danger. She quickly shoved Doug to a safe place on a ledge, snatched a pick ax from the back of the wagon, and frantically pounded and chopped the ice on the road. When the team slipped backward to the chopped spot, they found a foot hold. Encouraged by Pres's firm hands on the reins and his calm voice, the horses leaned against the neck yoke on the wagon tongue, holding their ground.

Spring came and the yearly cycle repeated. As always they were hopeful. The poor rocky ridge farm could become a cattle ranch, even though they had sold most of their animals. But they still had the breeding stock, the old sows, and the cows. They had the chickens, and they had each other. Anything was possible. Pres was ever an optimist, trading, gambling—not with money, for he rarely had much, but gambling with his livelihood, as farmers do. An accomplished farm wife by now, Mary Elizabeth was also hopeful for better times.

Pres increased his stock and improved their place. Thanks to the money earned in Arkansas, their immediate financial worry was over. When Colonel Prather became very ill, Pres and Mary Elizabeth were with him most of the time. After he recovered they turned their attention to their farm. Besides its isolation, its biggest drawback was the shallow well which went dry, necessitating their hauling water from the creek. They had good luck raising chickens, but out in the wild, there were as many foxes as chickens. Many hens disappeared.

The pretty farmstead and their satisfaction with the stock were not the only things making their life pleasant. Little Douglas grew fat and sturdy. His parents raised a crop of peanuts that summer and stored them in the shed. Doug loved them. Old-timers said peanuts would kill him, but Mary Elizabeth looked at the handsome, active two-year-old child and laughed, "He doesn't look much like he's dying."

In fact Doug was so active she had to watch him continually. One evening he was playing near his father when the neighbor came over to have Pres shoe his horses. Mary Elizabeth was in the house getting supper. She never completely trusted her husband with the boy, for Pres concentrated so intently on what he was doing at the time that nothing else crossed his mind. Some premonition that all was not well caused her to look out the window. "Where's the baby?" she cried when she did not see him.

"Oh, he's around here." Bending over nearly double, Pres had his leg hooked over the horse's hind leg as he drove in the last nails. He did not look up.

"Oh, no, he isn't!" she cried. Dropping her biscuit dough and wiping her hands on her apron, she ran out to look for him. When she got no answer to her calls, the men also became frightened. They spread out to search. Just before dark, about a quarter of a mile from the house in the direction of the creek, they saw the farm dog running back and forth as if trying to herd something. There was little Doug trudging on.

Doug was good company to Mary Elizabeth on their isolated farm, very early becoming his mother's helper, admirer, and good friend. The two formed a close companionship that lasted all her life. Both parents were always busy, but it was Mary Elizabeth who found time to play with him, talk with him, and teach him.

Besides little Douglas, there were other things in her life to offset the hardships. Her weekly writing and the companionship of her special friends were antidotes to disappointments and grief, as well as to routine housework and isolated farm life.

By this time Mary Elizabeth had been writing her weekly news to the county paper for thirteen years. Having lived in several communities, she knew many people and enjoyed a following of readers. She developed her style of telling the good news, the achievements, with sometimes sad and amusing anecdotes. She did not yet put in her philosophies and interpretations, nor add little poems to her column. It was still mainly a news item, but one that earned her a place among the best country correspondents.

Country correspondents of the time were held in high regard as newspapers were the main means of knowing about community, county, or national news. Many people took the county weekly, or if they could not afford it, read their neighbor's paper. Over half of the paper was devoted to the rural correspondents' news. Since they read everything in the paper, not just sections of special interest, people all over the county read Mary Elizabeth's column in the *Taney County Republican*. Residents knew everyone through the correspondents' columns. When people met in Forsyth, Taneyville, or Kirbyville, they already knew of one another, or at least knew of a relative. It did not take long for them to become acquainted.

The columns contained more than news. Personalities and philosophies emerged. Correspondents wrote to one another through their columns, commenting on the other writers' news or viewpoints. The editor also wrote comments. The effect was similar to a modern television talk show except taking several weeks to get other viewpoints. The avidly read columns kept people abreast of local activities. Each correspondent inspired others.

During her busy early years, Mary Elizabeth wrote her column almost any place, in the quiet of her bedroom or in the noisy clamor of a front room filled with Prathers or Mahnkeys. Sometimes she took her notebook and pencil out by the spring or under a flaming autumn tree. She even wrote while jogging along a country road on her pony. She wrote for the joy of seeing words come out of her mind and lie flat on paper. She would write human interest news such as this:

> Seven charming geese have taken up their abode in this neighborhood, undecided which is their happy home, at Uncle Jim Parnell's or at Pres Mahnkey's. Unless called for soon Uncle Jim says he intends to try some gander-steak while Pres says he will make goose-dumplings.

Mary Elizabeth also wrote for herself in her private notebooks and journals, in which she expressed her hopes and her hidden feelings. There she sorted out her priorities and compensated for disappointments and unfulfilled dreams of her girlhood.

A Simple Biography

Mamie Prather was a maiden who imagined the angel of Fame was holding his trumpet purposely low for her to toot upon. But she soon became convinced of her error and found it to be a dinner horn for a farmer husband; she makes the welkin ring and the creek bluffs echo. She is proud of the served repast, consisting of vegetables and cornbread and milk, and as Mamie Mahnkey is a much healthier and happier and better creature.1901

The hardest part of life is to force oneself down to the commonplace reality of living. And when one has renounced dreams and lost all power of hoping or believing or expecting to live, then life itself is over.
January 22, 1902

She too will learn that all distant hills are not blue, nor all domes gilded. When one finally reaches them, they are only mountains that one must climb very painfully and laboriously, and only very commonplace houses, where one must live a very commonplace life, and eat and sleep and work.

I might have made an indifferent writer. I have made a home and one man happy which is better than tons and tons of mediocre poetry and flimsy fiction. It is well that I can console myself. For the renunciation of the *trying* was hard. But who could ask for paper and ink and postage stamps when shoes and bread and hame-strings and plow points were necessary propositions?

Mary Elizabeth wrote this last when she was twenty-five years old. Was she giving in to what society expected, denying her dream? At this point her writing, both public and private, though not the novels that she once envisioned, was a major source of comfort for her. The weekly columns were her voluntary service to fill her neighbors' need for news; her private writing helped release her frustrations and understand what was important to her. The general tone of her journals during this time was recognizing what was most important to her and convincing herself that she was contented.

Her journals were not hidden away in a drawer, but left out for family members to read if they wanted to. Occasionally Pres, her sisters, and later her children wrote in them.

The candle within Mary Elizabeth's soul was already lighting the lives of others. One friend's daughter remembered how precious to her mother were Mary Elizabeth's columns in the paper. Her friend cut them out and pasted them on the wall of her log house in Swan, a store and post office directly north of Taneyville and near the Stout Farm.

When she came to visit or trade at the store, Mary Elizabeth rode her horse down the trail over the south hill behind the house and store. She rode sidesaddle with a basket of eggs in her lap, a couple of chickens to trade hanging by their legs from the saddle strings, and little Douglas sitting behind her. Sometimes she would put her hand behind her to hold on to the child when the horse started down a steep slope. With one leg hooked over the horn and the other solidly in the one stirrup, she could grasp the basket of eggs or sweet butter resting in the fullness of her skirt with her legs, while one hand steadied the child and the other neck-reined the horse.

An outfit she wore during this period included a white bonnet with lace around the face and hairline. A pretty apron covered a two piece dress—a full skirt to her ankles and a blouse called a dressing sack, which, gathered at the waist with a pull string, hung four or five inches below the waist.

The summer and fall of 1904 brought more family illnesses. Pres had a big abscess, or carbuncle, on his hip which made him feverish and thirsty all the time. Since their well was dry, Mary Elizabeth rode astride in Pres's saddle to Stout Creek with a big brown jug to get him the cold water from Dripping Spring. With no way to keep the water cold, sometimes she had to make two or three trips a day.

Pres's father, Charles Mahnkey, was ill at the same time. He was in his final illness when he asked to see little Doug. Though Mr. Mahnkey had other grandchildren, Doug was a favorite, the first grandchild with the Mahnkey name.

One evening just before sunset as she was preparing supper in front of her kitchen window, Mary Elizabeth looked up. She later described what she saw. "There, just as plain as could be, a white horse with a strange rider in old-fashioned clothes, was riding across the field—across the field, where no road or trail could be! I knew it was a sign and I flew into Pres's room. He was just the same as he had been, no better, but no worse. Then in an hour we had word that Pres's father had died. It was the second time I had seen that vision, so I was quite prepared."

The end of the winter of 1905 brought new happiness, but for a few harrowing hours, Mary Elizabeth was in serious danger. She was in labor alone at home on February 21 while Pres was riding through snow knee-deep to his horse to fetch old Granny Hull. Beside himself with worry and frustration on a trail he did not know, he finally found the house of the granny woman, or midwife. Together they hurried their horses back through the drifts as quickly as possible, arriving just in time to assist Mary Elizabeth in the birth of a baby girl.

Though the snow was still a foot deep, the next week Mary Elizabeth heard the first spring bird. She wanted to call the baby Avis, which means bird, but years earlier her friend Bertie Kintrea and she had promised that each of them would name their first daughter after the other. Though Bertie died young, Mary Elizabeth felt the promise was binding. She named her baby Roberta.

The baby's birth and the first spring bird seemed good omens that the tribulations of the past few years were over.

Chapter 10

I WHO LOVE POETRY
KNOW ONLY PROSE
Kirbyville Store and Old Mahnkey Farm:
March 1905 - June 1910

I who love poetry
Know only prose
Growing a bean vine
Instead of a rose.

I mend an old coat
I bake a corn pone
I pluck purple grapes
On a wall of gray stone.

But on the dark glades
Where the whippoorwills sing
I listen to poetry
Through soft nights of spring.

After the birth of their daughter Roberta, it truly seemed that life was smiling on the young Mahnkeys; Bertie was a healthy, happy baby. She and three-year-old Doug were the source of endless pleasure and constant companionship to their young, active mother. No longer was she lonely, living as she had for several years isolated in almost wilderness areas.

Pres's hard work and good trading abilities made possible still greater happiness; he traded the farm for a stock of goods in a little store in Kirbyville (Marvin Root Store). Mary Elizabeth was glad to be home again, to be nearer her family and friends. Living behind the store in the little town was much more to her liking than living off where she and Pres never saw anyone else for days.

Their move back to the Kirbyville area in March 1905 marked the beginning of several changes in their careers and personal lives. From this first store, until they sold the business in Mincy in 1943, they became progressively more involved with storekeeping and less with farming. Mary Elizabeth, always assisting Pres in farming, did not help in this first store in Kirbyville, for women did not work in country stores then. But later times changed. Beginning with their first stint with the Mincy store in 1914, when she became postmaster, she was part of the store business also. Through the years, though she eventually became actively involved in the business, Mary Elizabeth never lessened her role as homemaker and mother, combining these two careers, as well as continuing her writing interests.

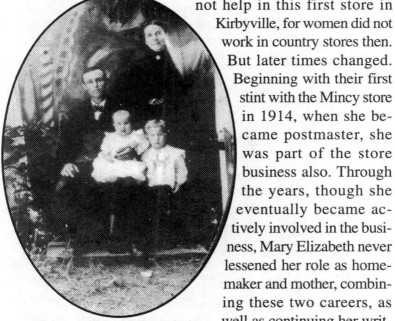

Pres and Mary Elizabeth
Mahnkey in Kirbyville, 1905.
Bertie was seven months old,
Douglas three years.

This period saw changes in the Prather and Mahnkey families. In April 1905 Ben Prather died after a brief illness of abscess of brain caused by an injury received while working for the railroad.

Mary Elizabeth had a premonition about Ben's death. She dreamed that his wife Janie was wearing a pretty hat with sparkling bangles that glittered when she moved her head. An older neighbor turned white when Mary Elizabeth told her of the dream. With a shudder the older woman said, "That's a sign the next time you see Janie, she will be in some sort of trouble."

The next time she saw Janie, she was a widow with two little girls.

In June 1910 the colonel died. Soon after his death Mary Elizabeth's mother and sisters, Deal and Mag, moved permanently to California. The remaining Prather brothers, Frank, Dick, and Joe, had already left the region.

After Pres's father's death, his mother closed the camp house. With the coming of the railroad to Branson in 1906, the heavy traffic along the Springfield-Harrison road began to wane. After operating a hotel and livery barn in Kirbyville for several years, Mattie Mahnkey moved to Tacoma, Washington, to join her son Bill. She never returned to the hills. Pres and Mary Elizabeth were the only members of either family to make Taney County their permanent home.

As the elder Prather and Mahnkey clans were dispersing, the Pres Mahnkey family grew. After they moved back to Kirbyville, two more sons were born, Reggie in 1907 and Bill in 1912.

Pres was not ready yet to give up on farming. After the brief storekeeping venture in Kirbyville, he and Mary Elizabeth moved to the old Mahnkey place when his mother vacated it. They farmed it from 1905 to 1910. Even this early

Taneyville, June 1908.
Douglas, Reggie, and Bertie with Mary Elizabeth

in their married life, most people had lost count of the moves
they made. They still moved by wagon.

The Mahnkey house was the finest house Mary Elizabeth and Pres had lived in so far, two stories with a one-story
room built off in an ell. Charles Mahnkey had built it years
before from pine lumber sawed on his place. Mary Elizabeth
enjoyed the beauty of the neatly trimmed and painted house
with its established landscaping. She loved living on this 200-
acre farm so near Kirbyville on the main road into Arkansas.

Reggie was born there on May 19, 1907. "You can see
we had begun to ascend the ladder," Mary Elizabeth said. "At
Reggie's birth we had a man doctor for the first time. Reggie
was a healthy baby, just like Bertie. He was a pretty baby, too,
with blond curly hair. Pres was always careful to keep the
ends cut off because folks would look at the curls and say,
'What a pretty little girl!' He wanted everybody to know it
was another boy."

But Reggie was a troublesome, crying baby. Mary Elizabeth hardly knew how to handle him because he was so different from her other two. As a baby Doug was sick but he never cried; he was patient. Bertie was never sick and she didn't cry. Reggie wasn't sick but he cried much of the time. His mother decided he was just ornery. Pres would rock him and sing to him, but still he cried on. Reggie learned to walk very early, hanging on to his mother's dress tail while still crying.

Mary Elizabeth would study her unhappy son, trying to understand him. Many years later on May 8, 1942 she wrote a poem that perhaps expressed her thoughts.

> Oh, child, why art thou hard to please?
> Why do I feel so ill at ease
> When my small talk and playful wile
> Doth win from thee no ready smile?
>
> Oh, child! What dignity is thine,
> As if thou lately left a shrine
> To come and stand and gaze at me—
> Perplexed by what thou canst not see.

She was content with her life and proud of her family in the fall of 1909 when she left Reggie with Pres, perched five-year-old Bertie and seven-year-old Doug on the big mare with her, and took them to their first day of school in Kirbyville.

Even with their limited resources, Mary Elizabeth made sure her children looked attractive. She washed their school clothes every afternoon. Most of the little boys, including Doug, wore overalls, which she thought looked dingy after they were washed a few times. She sent away for a pattern to make Doug some wash suits, pants and blouses. The boy did not share her enthusiasm. He was ashamed of them, wanting to wear overalls like the other boys.

Owning one of the first treadle Singer sewing machines in the community, she made shirts and night clothes for the boys and all of the clothes she and Bertie wore. Because of her eye for beauty and her wide reading, which included fashions, the older girls in the Kirbyville community came to her for advice on grooming and clothes. They would spend all afternoon in her living room fixing their hair or fitting their dresses. They even made some hats.

In Doug and Bertie's second year at school, Reggie was big enough to run out the gate to watch for the children coming home. Mary Elizabeth never tired of watching him. From his birth this restless, venturesome, and occasionally troublesome boy captured his mother's heart in a special way. Nothing he ever did dented that love, even though in later years his actions sometimes hurt her.

Busy as she was, Mary Elizabeth spent much time with the children and never tired of watching them play. While doing her household tasks, she could keep an eye on them in the front yard, safe behind the fence that protected them from the traffic on the road.

The mail carrier, who rode north to Kirbyville and back the same day with his padlocked leather mail pouches strapped behind his saddle, greeted them each day. Since their mother wrote and received many letters, they watched for him to stop briefly and hang their mail sack on the gate post.

Regular drummers, traveling for wholesale houses to supply the country stores, passed by in buggies or hacks pulled by good horses. Mary Elizabeth was pleased when they waved to the children or threw them a sample. The Arm and Hammer Soda drummer always tossed them a miniature box of soda just like the one sold in the store. Mother and children alike were thrilled with the enclosed card with a colored picture of a bird in its natural setting, for it illustrated the plants, rocks, and birds that they talked about on their many walks.

Traveling the road were business men, house-to-house salesmen, stockmen driving cattle, families moving, and hobos. No one was afraid of any of the travelers, even the hobos. Mary Elizabeth was kind to each hobo that stopped. She often built a fire to bake him some cornbread, and after he had gone, she would worry about where he would sleep. She always thought about her brother Joe who spent many years wandering over the country. Perhaps someone was offering him a hot cup of coffee as he trudged by.

One time a traveling circus passed by. The children called for their mother to join them when the first painted wagon appeared over the crest of the bald knob to the south. For the first time the children saw black men, lions, tigers, and an elephant that left huge tracks in the dusty road right in front of their house.

After several years of being alone in the house most of the day while Pres was out working, she had company and someone to share her love of books. As in her childhood when her brothers read aloud, she read to her children. And she kept up her own reading, for during this period her hunger for books was partially satisfied. The Missouri State Traveling Library left books in Kirbyville at the private home of Miss Masie Johnson. In her Kirbyville column of September 1908, Mary Elizabeth urged everyone to "take advantage of this splendid opportunity. Miss Masie is a very patient, efficient librarian and can assist anyone in choosing books."

Though the farming was generally good on the Mahnkey farm, in 1910 there was another bad drought. The crops failed, and without grass the stock suffered. But with the railroad nearby in Hollister, there was a market for railroad ties. Ready to do anything to improve their finances, Pres began making ties. Though he had never used a broad ax nor made ties before, he went to the woods to cut down the white oak trees, saw the butt ends, and with a broad ax square out each log into a tie by trimming it down to the exact measurements.

One winter day he hauled his first load of fifteen ties to Hollister. He got four dollars for the load. For months the only bread the family had eaten was cornbread. Since they raised their own corn, they could get their meal ground at the mill for part of the grain. That day he bought home a twenty-five pound sack of white flour and a can of white karo syrup. Best of all for the children, Pres, who rarely spent money for anything except necessities, brought each child a miniature glass suitcase filled with candy.

While they lived on the Mahnkey farm, Mary Elizabeth and the children often visited the Prather grandparents who lived then in Branson. Taking advantage of Pres's trips to Hollister to sell his railroad ties, they rode the six difficult miles to town with him on the wagon load of ties. When they got to Hollister, they had to cross the White River. Their choices were fording the river, taking the ferry, or riding the train across the railroad bridge.

Pres gave the children a rare treat. He deposited his family at the passenger station at Hollister to buy train tickets to cross the river to Branson. Mary Elizabeth enjoyed the children's excitement as they listened impatiently for the lonesome whistle, warning them the train was coming around the bend. Then with awe and trembling excitement, they watched the huge locomotive appear, looming, black, and puffing. They thrilled to the clatter of the cars, the steam exhaust, the vibrations of the rails, and all the noise, movement, and exhilaration of a huge engine pulling up just a few feet from them. Bertie always covered her ears and closed her eyes. She jumped when the blasts of steam escaped. Doug watched boldly.

"Boooooard!" the uniformed conductor called, standing by his step stool. Following the cluster of people boarding, the three children and their mother scrambled up the steps before the powerful engine gathered steam to puff across the bridge. The children were hardly seated before the conductor called, "Braaaaanson." They stepped off into the waiting arms of Grandfather Prather, "Hello there, kidlings," he would say. Depositing them in his buggy, he drove his spirited horse to his front gate where Grandma always greeted them with treats of cookies.

Their dog Jack usually followed the team and wagon wherever Pres drove, especially if the children were along. One time when Mary Elizabeth and the children were just settling in their seats on the train, Jack came bounding down the aisle chased by the conductor and porter. His tongue hanging out, his tail excitedly wagging in greeting, and shaking water from his cooling swim in Turkey Creek after his long hike, the dog jumped with joy at finding his family. The train was about to start. The conductor, after taking their tickets and realizing how short the ride would be, let Jack stay.

But there was no thrill or excitement for the many times Mary Elizabeth crossed the river during the first part of 1910. When Colonel Prather's health failed, she made frequent quick trips to his sickbed to be with her father and help her mother and sister Deal, who came back from California, to nurse her father. Though needed at home, she left the children with Pres and rode horseback back and forth in one day, fording the river on each trip.

Usually, fording the river was no problem; she was used to that. But starting home late one rainy day late in May, she found the White River muddy, with a crest of leaves and branches in the middle of the current that told her the water was rising. Feeling safe in a man's saddle, she entered the water, even though she wasn't sure how the young mare would handle herself in the river.

She knew immediately the water was higher than she thought for it ran across her lap. Knowing not to jerk or startle a horse in the water, she left the reins loose, calmly urging the mare. The filly wasn't frightened. Swimming easily and carefully in the strong current, she came to the other bank about thirty yards below the ford. "Even that didn't frighten her," Mary Elizabeth said. "She didn't try to lunge up the slippery bank. She turned sweetly and patiently back to the road. It was as though a gentle hand had hold of her bridle, guiding her all the way."

A few days later on June 4, 1910, at age seventy, Alonzo S. Prather died. He was buried in the Van Zandt Cemetery in Kirbyville with a Masonic funeral amid much recognition. "The whole majestic affair would have pleased his proud heart," Mary Elizabeth said, "but it didn't lessen our grief."

Chapter 11

LIVE ON HOLLYHOCK TEA
Railsback Farm and Kirbyville Store:
1910 - Fall 1914

When I grow old, I'll raise turnips
And try to like turnip stew,
But now that I'm young, I raise hollyhocks
And asters, and marigolds too.

Raising turnips is sadness
That is why I dread growing old,
Do you think I could live on hollyhock tea
Or shop with the marigold gold?

Perhaps my flowers will remember
And make intercession for me,
And old age will come along gayly
And help me make hollyhock tea.

In the summer of 1910, for $1,500 Pres's mother sold the
Mahnkey farm, 200 acres with good improvements. Once
again the younger Mahnkeys had to move. Some of their re-
locations were joyful and full of enthusiasm for a new challenge, or for promised better conditions. This move was a sad
one. Pres was leaving the home place his father had acquired

and improved with great effort. It was the symbol of his parents' success in this beautiful but hard land. Mary Elizabeth also hated to leave. She was happy there.

Even the weather on moving day seemed to sympathize with their moods. It poured all day. Undaunted, they unloaded and arranged all their things inside the house and barn before dark. As on other moves their dog Jack helped drive the sheep and cows.

Knowing they would have no time or means of getting supper, Mary Elizabeth had fixed their meals ahead of time. There was nothing left for Jack. Since the night was chilly and damp, she built a fire in the fireplace. While it was burning down, she stirred up some cornbread and baked it in an old iron skillet over the coals. When Pres came in, he asked her what she was doing.

"Cooking Jack's supper," she said. Since people in the hills paid no special attention to a dog, Pres thought that was the funniest thing he had ever heard. Mary Elizabeth said, "But Jack had worked as hard as anyone, and I couldn't bear the thought of him out on the porch without anything to eat."

After the Mahnkeys reconciled themselves to the necessity of moving, they admitted they had a good place. Known as the Railsback place, it was farther south on the road where the land was even better for sheep than the Mahnkey farm. Pres raised a good crop; the sheep did well.

Though not as fine as the Mahnkey house, the house was adequate. It was attractive when Mary Elizabeth cleaned it up and arranged her things. There were four rooms with a porch across the front. She was proud of the big cellar constructed of cedar poles. When she stepped into it on a damp day, she loved the sweet cedar smell. As she had at every place they lived, she improved the yard, removing the weeds and planting flowers. She made a round flower bed of marigolds and zinnias and sowed hollyhock seed by the side of the house along the back fence. "It always seemed to me," she wrote, "that when you started hollyhocks, you were starting something permanent and something to live with."

The greatest disadvantage of the place was that the children were too far away from Kirbyville to attend school. Reggie was still too small, but Doug and Bertie were anxious to learn and had learned fast and well the two terms at Kirbyville school. Mary Elizabeth taught them at home with what materials she had. All winter they worked diligently with their pencils and tablets while Reggie played nearby.

In addition to farming and raising sheep, Pres also operated a custom hay baler. He had begun doing this while living on the old Mahnkey farm.

During the hay season when Pres was gone most days and sometimes all week, Mary Elizabeth tended the sheep and did all the chores at home, including caring for the mean and dangerous jackass. The work was easier now; she had help. Douglas was big enough to do many light chores and to help take care of little Reggie. It was almost a full time job to watch the never-still boy who would tackle any obstacle and climb any tree like a squirrel.

Nine-year-old Doug also looked after his mother's safety. One time when the heavy wooden gate leading to the pasture fell on his mother, he was able to lift the gate enough that she could squirm out from under it unhurt.

Mary Elizabeth turned many chores into fun times. Every trip into the woods or fields after the milk cow or to see about the stock was an excursion into beauty. The children raced down the leafy trails and over the mossy glades. They climbed their special trees to look over the panorama of rolling wooded landscape to see Pilot Knob or to catch a glimpse of smoke from the train at Melba a few miles to the west.

They rolled down the green velvet slopes, landing in a soft pile of leaves. They threw rocks into the spring, always on the lookout for a rock with a hole in it to present to their mother. These rocks were lucky she said as she put them in a special box at home. The children learned to tread softly, not rustling the leaves or stepping on a twig, in order to watch a mother bird on her nest. Tired after their jaunt, they sat quietly by the spring, searching for lucky four-leaf clovers. They loved to see the bright smile on their mother's face when they found one to give her. They knew she would prize it, taking it home and pressing it carefully in her scrapbook.

Often while Pres was working at home, Mary Elizabeth and the children joined him in his work when they could help, or they would sit nearby to keep him company. The children amused themselves. Sometimes Pres made them each a hickory whistle. Then both parents pretended they were sorry when all three youngsters blasted away in happy disharmony.

Other times Pres was too preoccupied with his job to pay much attention to them, or to his wife. One day he was doctoring a calf by their spring when Mary Elizabeth and the children walked down. Finished with her work in the house, she brought the restless children for an outing. She sat down on a rock ledge and read aloud a story she had just written. As always Doug and Bertie showed their interest and appreciation. Pleased with the way it sounded, she glanced at Pres, hoping he would say something to encourage her. He made no comment, continuing with his work, oblivious to his wife's carefully hidden disappointment.

This Cedar Spring was a favorite spot with three pools of water in holes in the rocks. The beauty spot, hidden below the hill from the house, often enticed Mary Elizabeth and the children. During the dry summer when their shallow well barely furnished enough water for drinking, the young

Mahnkey family went to the spring on wash days.

Pres hauled the black wash kettle and rinse tubs in his wagon before going to the field to work. Mary Elizabeth and the children filled the containers with spring water and gathered wood for the fire to heat the wash water. By noon when Pres returned for dinner, the lines strung among the trees were full of clean clothes. While the clothes dried in the afternoon, everyone had fun. The children played in the spring, listened to their mother's stories, and took hikes in the woods. When Pres returned for them at sundown, the neat stacks of clean laundry were ready to be loaded into the wagon for the climb up the hill to their house.

In spite of the incessant work demands of the farm, Mary Elizabeth and Pres both found time for fun, especially during the winter when farm work was mainly nightly and morning chores. Pres made spinning tops for the children out of their mother's empty thread spools. They played for hours with the buttons from her dark blue, beaded button bag.

Pres and Mary Elizabeth gave parties. Pres's brother, Henry, would come by and ask, "Mamie, can we have a hop here tonight?" He'd help them clear the room so the young people could dance. Mary Elizabeth and Pres, both merry and drawing out others, were always the life of the party, whether held at their house or elsewhere.

Nobody else danced as well as they did. Mary Elizabeth ignored the tradition that married women were supposed to sit and watch the young folks dance. After sitting out the first few parties after her marriage, she joined in. Dancing was too much in her blood. Pres was always in demand as a caller, calling the set as he danced. She and Pres danced complicated steps, causing the other dancers to stop and watch them. Even in much later years, when they were truly old married folk, the young people would beg them to dance an old polka or schottische which none of them knew.

Though often taciturn, Pres knew how to liven up a group. Like his father, he was lively around gatherings, often being the first to joke or tell a story to get others laughing.

The greatest recipients of Pres and Mary Elizabeth's good humor were their children. Doug and Bertie would sit enthralled as one or the other of their parents told exciting tales. They were half way scared at their mother's "ha'nt" stories. On a stormy night with gestures and pantomime that made them shiver, she told them a story her brother Dick heard from an old sawmill man. She believed it was true.

"The old sawmill man said that one day when they were working very hard in the mill, someone yelled out to come and look at 'this critter' on the sawdust pile. The other workmen were quick to catch the note of something more than idle curiosity in the cry, and all quit whatever they were doing and rushed to see what it was. The thing on the sawdust pile resembled a pack rat, but was much larger, and it was whirling on the sawdust in some kind of mad play, just as if it were miles away from human sight.

"One of the workmen tossed a chunk of wood at the thing. Whether or not he hit it, they never knew, for it kept up that frenzied whirling with the sawdust rising in a miniature cyclone about it. Then the thing became still for a moment and one of the men started toward it. He went quite close to it, with the others standing frozen behind him, and the thing seemed to slide down the sawdust and out toward the hill. Slowly, smoothly it traveled, followed by all the workmen. When they hastened their steps, trying to catch it or get near enough to see what the thing really was, it moved faster and faster.

"When they got to the top of the mountain, the creature paused to resume the mad whirling. Then it disappeared right in front of their eyes."

Mary Elizabeth paused at this point in her story for the children to grasp the wonder of that miracle. Dramatically she continued.

"Just at that moment a terrific explosion sounded back down in the hollow at the sawmill. The boiler had burst. It had not burst because the men had left it untended. It would have happened anyway, the old sawmill man always said, for the work they were doing that day had them working in the loft above the boiler. If the men had not been enticed away by this eerie being, probably all of them would have been killed. It was never seen again and the men always believed it had been sent to save them."

Especially delightful to the children were the times their parents made music. Bertie and Reggie early showed their musical interest and talents, encouraged by babyhood memories of singing, whistling, and harmonica music. Pres was adept on his harmonica, or French harp. He kept it in a little box that the children never touched. Bertie was thrilled each time when, after supper, he got down the box, carefully unwrapped his instrument and blew a bit on it. He usually had trouble getting started. He'd blow a note or two, and turn to his wife, "Old Lady, whistle a little bit of that 'Wagonner.'"

Mary Elizabeth was an accomplished whistler. Her soft whistling around the house or out on the farm was always cheerful. When Pres asked her, she'd whistle the perfect note. He caught the tune as she whistled a few more notes, and then he played it through beautifully. He played many old fiddle tunes—"Soldier's Joy," "Redwing," "Fox and Hounds." In more serious moods he'd play slower pieces like "My Darling Nelly Gray." While the children kept time to the music, Mary Elizabeth sat quietly on one side sewing or darning as she listened proudly, complimenting his skill with smiles and approving glances his way.

Both parents knew many songs. They sang to the children, sometimes separately, sometimes together. Together they often sang "The Bowery" and "Barbara Allen."

Mary Elizabeth's repertoire also included many kinds of songs, Irish songs, sad songs, and songs where little children got lost. Following is an old song she heard near Kirbyville in her childhood:

> Sweet as the flowers in springtime,
> Sweet as the honey dew,
> Sweet as the roses in their bowers,
> I'm thinkin' tonight of you.
>
> Sweet as the rose in the garden,
> Sweet as the dew on the rose,
> I'd rather be somebody's darlin',
> Than a poor boy nobody knows.

The children grew and were happy living on the Railsback place, but renting this farm wasn't what Pres and Mary Elizabeth wanted. They wanted their own place again, or their own business. Pres's first venture in storekeeping in Kirbyville had suited him. His natural trading abilities and affability made him successful. When an opportunity to go into business again opened, he took it. The years of farming had enabled them to increase their livestock to the point he could make a trade.

One day when he returned home from Kirbyville, he hollered to Doug as he drove the team to the barn. "Go get your mother."

Mary Elizabeth knew something was up. The whole family joined Pres while he was unharnessing. With a satisfied grin he greeted her, "Well, Old lady," he said, "start packing. Joel Johnson and I bought the biggest business in Taney County today!" He bought half interest in the big general store and mill in Kirbyville at a cost of $1,100. That was a lot of money then.

The family was happy to move back to Kirbyville, to old friends, close neighbors, and school again for the children. Mary Elizabeth was pleased, though, as usual, she left with mixed feelings. To raise the money Pres had to sell all their stock. Once again she had to part with the animals that she had tended so carefully. "When I saw the new owner leading away Lucy, the mare that had carried the children to their first day of school, I just thought I couldn't stand it," she said.

But the sale concluded, they both looked forward eagerly, always hopeful, expecting big things from this new venture into business. From the time of this move, their involvement in farming was temporary or secondary to storekeeping.

This time in Kirbyville, in 1911, while in partnership with Johnson, Pres did not have much to do with the store itself. He operated the gasoline-powered mill, perfecting his technique of adjusting the burrs until he earned the reputation for making the finest cornmeal in the county. His meal when squeezed in the hand, made a little cake that fell apart easily, the test for good meal.

Mary Elizabeth always loved living in Kirbyville, though she admitted some houses they lived in were better than others. First they lived in a house behind the store; then they moved a mile south when Pres thought the children should be in the country. Then very soon he moved them to the Linzy place, one-fourth of a mile west of the store. Mary Elizabeth loved the Linzy place for they could keep a cow and have chickens. In the yard there was a pretty silver-leaf poplar tree. That home had special significance, for little Bill was born there on December 18, 1912. He was named William Richard, for Pres's brother Bill and her brother Dick.

After a few months, Pres bought the forty acre-place. Since they had lived in rented places since they sold the Stout farm, Mary Elizabeth's entry in her journal Monday, March 3, 1913, gives us a glimpse of her suppressed feelings and optimism. "Pres bought this place Saturday. I wonder if I ever scribbled off fair words before that meant so wonderfully much. To never, never have to 'pack up' and move. What a wearisome time I served at that. This is such a dear place.

"O the big splendid lilac bush even now putting out buds is worth $50, and the beautiful silver-leaf poplar is worth $100, and sold to Pres for $250. I told Pres if I had known this years ago I would have been a better woman, I know."

While Bill was an infant, Mary Elizabeth was too busy to baby him. In 1940, remembering back to those days, she wrote in her scrapbook, "But oh, how I loved him. While he nursed I would read—not much time for reading—and when he was barely toddling, he would come dragging a newspaper with such sweet baby talk. Some said this was remarkable for it showed reasoning."

Mary Elizabeth loved to tell little things Bill did as a toddler. When he was learning to talk he called milk, "new cow." She explained, "We had got a new cow, little Jewel, and I would give Bill a glass of the nice new cow's milk. He called all milk 'new cow' for a long time."

Pres did well in the business. Mary Elizabeth was glad he didn't have to work as hard as he did when farming. But she knew he was still not satisfied. Unhappy not being the boss, he sold out to his partner and went back briefly into the cattle business, renting pasture land on an adjoining farm and in the White River valley.

Mary Elizabeth had learned long before to accept her

place in their partnership and to do what she could to make the best of things and keep everyone happy. Her journal continued to record her daily life and her hopes. Though still frustrated by events not to her liking, she was not bitter or in despair.

May 2, 1913
Reggie "shed" two teeth yesterday and little Bill is trying hard to cut two.

July 14, 1913, Monday
I feel quite matronly and important today with 3 kiddies starting to school. Reggie wore his 4th of July sailor suit— bright blue striped—he looked so sweet and there was a very mournful primp to his little mouth when he kissed Bill and me goodbye.

Nov. 28, Friday
We have so much to be thankful for. Yet the cares and the solemn responsibilities of our growing family have caused Pres and I both to be grave and serious. I am so anxious that they shall be educated and learn to work and learn practical things.

Jan. 31, 1914
Big, big snow. Papa is having a time feeding—made the boys a sled, and how they and Berta [sic] enjoyed it. Billy ran from one window to the other to watch them. Finally he came up to papa dragging my old black scarf, begging sweetly without the power to utter a word that he might join them.

Sunday March 1, 1914
It was just a year ago now he bought the place. I could be so happy if he was only satisfied.

Wed. April 1
Yesterday we set out the orchard, and 6 rows of strawberries and 2 rows of Early Harvest blackberries and 25 fine big rhubarb roots. Pres set out five Montmoray King cherries. I hope we can do well, and they will grow and bear for us. But Pres is so blue it almost breaks my heart. I am discouraged with him. When he was in the store and making money he was so cross and so mean about everything I wanted done or any poor little thing I wanted to buy that life was so unpleasant. Guess he will always be that way.

But better times were coming. On Wednesday, July 15, 1914, Mary Elizabeth wrote, "'Tis settled. Pres had traded this place, the cattle, and team for the Mincy store. [South of Kirbyville about seven miles] We get the dwelling-house, 30 acres of land, and store-building. He is down there today invoicing. Darling Boy, for you I am so glad and I will be good."

Chapter 12

I LOVE THE LITTLE COUNTRY TOWNS
Mincy Store: Fall 1914 - 1916; 1917 - 1918

I love the little country towns
So quiet and serene,
With houses nestling small and white
In shaded lawns of green.

We do not speed, we drift along
On muted, drowsy wings;
We loiter by the wild-rose banks;
We pause at stone-walled springs.

Blue mountain haze, like Galilee,
Is waiting just out there;
We feel its cleansing, healing charm
As answer to a prayer.

Pres soon realized, as did Mary Elizabeth, that his best
chance for success was storekeeping. Though he operated the
Mincy store himself, he was in partnership with the Moore
brothers. The family settled into their new home and quickly
became a part of the community. Mary Elizabeth's involvement in the partnership increased. For the first time she helped
in the business. Though Pres was officially postmaster, Mary
Elizabeth ran the post office, waited on customers, kept the

books, and otherwise helped operate the store.

Although it caused some adjustments at home, Mary Elizabeth enjoyed her new role. Doug and Bertie were old enough to help. The business that Pres managed was the center of the neighborhood. In addition to the nearby school-church, it was also the social center. Mary Elizabeth loved it.

A typical late fall day in 1914 would find Mary Elizabeth finishing her work in the little post office cage in the back of Mincy general store when the last customer walked out. Twelve-year-old Douglas likewise relaxed from the rush of patrons at mail time. Being busy meant customers and mail patrons. Mary Elizabeth placed the last of the letters still not called for into the alphabetized cubby hole which corresponded to the letter of the last name.

The mail carrier from Melva, a flag station on the railroad seven miles west, delivered the Mincy mail on horseback. Mary Elizabeth had carried out the big key ring, which hung beside the door of the post office, to unlock the mail pouch from the saddle. With the store full of people, she called Doug into the store to help while she sorted and distributed the mail in the latticed office. Though the work was slacking down since most of the cotton was ginned, Pres, with Bill Williams, his only hired helper now, was busy in the cotton gin behind the store, another facet of the Mincy business. Until his mother sent for him when the mail came, all morning Doug had been helping in the cotton gin.

Business was greater this season because of the good cotton harvest. Farmers had money to settle their accounts and stock up on staples. Though Bertie and Reggie attended the Mincy school just a short distance east of the store, Doug was needed at home until the cotton harvest was over.

Little towheaded Bill toddled around in the store, hanging on to his mother's skirt. Mary Elizabeth picked up the child and started across the dusty road to their big house to fix dinner, telling Doug to mind the store until Pres came.

She quickly stirred up some cornbread, cut off slices of meat from a cured ham to fry, peeled some potatoes, and snapped the beans she had picked from her garden before breakfast. Opening a can of home-canned peaches and setting out the rest of the cake left from yesterday, she soon had a meal ready. When Bertie and Reggie ran in from school a half an hour later, all was ready but setting the table. Bertie removed the starched white cloth covering the things on the table, set out seven plates, knives, and forks. There would be six family members and the hired hand. The spoons were already in a spoon holder on the table protected from flies by the cloth, as were the salt and pepper shakers, sugar bowl, jelly, and pickles.

Bill and Bertie on the porch at Mincy about 1916. "You can see the beautiful snowball bush and the rain barrell," Mary Elizabeth wrote under this picture in her scrapbook. "I sit there in Ben's [her dead brother] little rocking chair so often in the twilight."

The children chatted happily about their morning at school. Reggie romped with little Bill through the house, Bill squealing in delight. Pres and Bill Williams tromped in, washed up, and continued their animated talk about the good cotton year. For the next half hour the kitchen was as busy as the store was earlier. Bertie and Reggie ran back to school after wolfing down their meal, anxious to join in the noon playtime.

Though Pres ate more slowly, he did not take time to smoke his pipe. He needed to relieve Doug. He told Mary Elizabeth that she wouldn't need to come to the store until late afternoon. He was almost caught up with the cotton ginning. Doug could go back to school next week.

After the meal was the lazy time of the mild fall afternoon. Down the road the noise of the school children at play had ceased, meaning noon recess was over. The baby was asleep. It was quiet at the store, and even the gasoline engine Pres used at the gin and mill was quiet for the first time in several days.

Relaxing in the wooden rocking chair that had belonged to her dead brother Ben, Mary Elizabeth rocked contentedly for a few minutes after reading her letters. There was one from her mother in California and one from her brother Dick. For a few moments she let herself think about them, and about the others of her family. She wondered where Joe was wandering now. Only occasionally did she get letters from him, sometimes with gifts of jewelry and other exotic things. Where he might have got them worried her.

She reached for the book she had brought home from the store. She had prepared a counter at the store to display the books she ordered through the mail from the Missouri State Traveling Library to lend to her customers. She set the book back. She'd read it later. Finding her pencil and paper, she jotted down some items she picked up in the store for her weekly column.

In all the years nothing prevented her from sending in her news, not moving, birth of children, sickness, deaths, heartaches. Doing her column was a weekly satisfaction as necessary to her well being as sleep. Almost as regular were her entries in her private journals. These writings served as a record of events, a release for her emotions and for her creative spirit. She had begun writing verses when the rhymes inside her needed to come out. She wrote them on scraps of paper from the children's tablets, on the backs of old envelopes, or in her journal. She found it easier to write the verses in Kirbyville where everything was familiar, but she wrote anyplace.

This day she didn't write down anything right away. She was enjoying these few minutes of inactivity away from the store, where she had worked almost continually for many days. She looked out the windows toward the woods. Sumac and poison ivy were still red. Dogwood was scarlet; goldenrod brightened the fence row. Banks of oaks forming the edge of the woods were burnished russets and tarnished oranges. New grass from the recent rains glowed in fresh contrast against the varicolored timber. Another year was almost over.

The letters from her family put her into a nostalgic mood. She remembered the colorful autumns when she was a child walking the woods with her mother, how they almost tiptoed through the crimson and burnt orange wonderland unable to believe the display. She thought of the autumn horseback rides her crowd of young people used to take in the evening, and she thought of that October ride that caused her first baby to come too soon.

She was beginning to think like her mother who spoke to her so often about long ago times. Lately Mary Elizabeth's thoughts and journal entries were becoming retrospective. She wondered if it was a sign of maturity. She and Pres rarely looked back, their thoughts on the future. But she knew she was becoming reflective, sometimes when she was content, as she was today, and sometimes when she was sad.

The startling thought came to her that she was half way through her life. She was thirty-seven years old; in January Pres would be forty! They were no longer young, evidenced in Mary Elizabeth by some obvious physical changes. Since the births of the little boys she had put on some weight. Her hair, just as her father's, grayed prematurely. It was almost all white now. Since she was thirty-one, she had worn false teeth. None of these conditions bothered her. Early graying was hereditary in her family; most women lost their teeth early in life. The saying "a tooth for every baby" was accepted as the price women must pay. They did not know to take extra calcium, and Mary Elizabeth's not liking milk may have caused her to lose her teeth even faster.

These symbols of youth's passing were superficial as she thought and acted young. She was in the prime of life, nursing her baby, working long hours without tiring, greeting each day with enthusiasm. And Pres? Only a few gray hairs. Trim and muscled, quick and lithe as a boy. Just the other day a group of boys in their teens challenged him to a foot race. Mary Elizabeth chuckled as she remembered the expression on the boys' faces when Pres quickly outstripped all of them, turning around and grinning at them over his shoulder.

Mary Elizabeth was pleased with their home and business at Mincy. There was a good school almost at their doorstep. Doug, growing up to be a great help to his father, loved the beautiful broad valley from the first glimpse he caught of it while driving the stock to their new home. The little boys played happily in the shady lawn, and Bertie had lots of friends.

So did Pres and Mary Elizabeth. In all their moves (except back to Kirbyville which was always home), they had never before felt so welcomed and accepted by any community. Though there were fewer than thirty residents in Mincy proper, the area around it was quite populated, making their crossroads store a natural trading center. Their few months' residence already showed that they would do well. Pres was pleased. He owned half interest in the store, mill, cotton gin, blacksmith shop, and their home, with enough acreage that he could still dabble in stock and farming. Maybe he would be satisfied to stay. Hopefully Mary Elizabeth would continue to like it.

As often happened when she hated to leave one place, she soon grew to love the next. Mincy was easy to love. She believed she could stay forever. Here was a new sense of achievement for her with her growing involvement in the business. Life was fine. She leaned over her paper and began writing her news item.

"The gnarled old cedars hazardously clinging to the bluffs are gay with necklaces of ruby and garnet, for the entwining ivy turns color first of all. Soon the staid and decorous hickory trees will be casting golden confetti, and we know that summer is gone."

Though the family could never account for it, when everything seemed to go so well, the Mahnkeys did not stay long at Mincy this first time. In less than two years, in December 1915, Pres sold out his interest. While he remained in Mincy to feed out his hogs and finish collections at the store, Mary Elizabeth and the children lived in a shack on Gardner Mountain, just west of Mincy. The three months of camping out there were very difficult, more because of the uncertainty of their future than the physical conditions. When Pres and his partners traded for a hardware store and house in Hollister, he told Mary Elizabeth that he did not care if she spent a hundred dollars for furnishing the new house. He felt magnanimous; he figured they were $1,287 better off from having moved to Mincy.

Mary Elizabeth did not like living in Hollister. She felt out of place in the society of the town, though she was happy for the good school for the children. She had no place to keep chickens, have a cow, or make a garden.

In May 1916 when Pres had an opportunity to buy out his former partner in the Kirbyville store and mill, Mary Elizabeth was the first to say, "Let's move." However, a few months stay back in Kirbyville showed her that her home town was not as it used to be. She began to long for the "quiet and everlasting peace and beauty of the hills" of Mincy, where her boys would not be idle in the streets of Kirbyville. In March 1917, Pres sold out to Stottle, another merchant in Kirbyville (even signing an agreement not to start another mercantile business in Kirbyville) and bought back the Mincy business.

Mary Elizabeth wrote in her journal February 21, 1917, "I read not long ago that God sometimes granted our prayer just to show us how little it really added to our happiness. And now I know why all this trading went on. And we have made the grand circle and got back to Mincy and in so much better shape than when we were there before, for then Moores owned a half interest in everything." Pres sold out to Stottle for $3,636. He gave the Moores $2,400 for house, 30 acres, store and goods, gristmill, and cotton gin.

Their years at the Mincy and Kirbyville stores were in the height of the prosperity and importance of the country store in the rural Ozarks. This was just before roads were improved and the automobile became widespread. Throughout the region, about every five or six miles, there was a store at a crossroads or at other natural locations easily accessible to the public. The store was the hub of the community, and when the school and church were close, every community activity centered at the store. Mincy was a typical country store and trade center.

When they returned to Mincy in 1917, Mary Elizabeth was appointed postmaster there, as well as in the other stores they operated until they retired. When she stepped across the road from her home, she often looked proudly at their business enterprise.

The store building was a one-story, unpainted, rough-sawed wooden structure with a wide porch across the front. Rising above the porch roof was a square false front. The center door was flanked by two big windows. Over the front and on the side by the road were pasted signs advertising Velvet smoking tobacco, Missouri Mule and Climax chewing tobacco, Rooster snuff, and various patent medicines.

Inside a potpourri of smells greeted her. Perhaps the tanned leather smell was foremost. New smells of denim overalls, shoes, and dress goods mingled with the fragrance of brown sugar, spices, vinegar, tobacco, and wood smoke, ashes, tobacco juice, and dust from the many muddy feet tramping over the bare wide boards of the floor. The scents of wet fur and spoiled eggs were blended with metallic odors of nails, horseshoes, and garden tools.

Mary Elizabeth was busy in the hustle of waiting on customers. Farmers needed nails, plow points, horseshoes, parts for their machinery, kerosene, medicine for livestock, leather strips for repairing harness, and gun powder. That and hundreds of other farming supplies, tools, and parts were on display. The men often congregated in the side room that was off limits to women, though she knew that sometimes the men had a jug of whiskey hidden in the jumble of goods there, and they took advantage of the little hole in the outside wall to relieve themselves.

Men brought in furs in season to trade for groceries or other supplies, but much of the weekly produce the families brought in to trade came from women's efforts. Mary Elizabeth counted out baskets of eggs and stored them in wooden egg cases in the side room. She bought fresh churned butter on pick-up days and roots the women brought to trade. She and Pres had to be careful when buying both fur and herbs to know the quality, and to look carefully to avoid being taken in by some crafty people. They had to scrutinize the roots, especially, to spot the worthless May apple root sometimes brought in with ginseng or golden seal.

The men traded and visited, either in the side room or, in cold weather, sitting around the cast iron stove on nail kegs or split-bottom chairs. Some chewed tobacco and spit into the flat box of ashes in front of the stove. Occasionally they would miss and hit the hot stove. The spittle would sizzle until it burned up. In summer, the men loafed on benches on the porch. While the men were thus occupied, the women did their trading and visiting in the main store.

Mary Elizabeth or Pres would weigh their roots or butter, count out the eggs, or figure up the worth of the fur. The women would then select their groceries. Very few foods were packaged or canned. There were canned sardines, salmon, cove oysters, and peaches, but most items were dipped out of big containers and sold by the pound. Brown and white sugar and white flour came in barrels, as did soda and soda crackers.

The women were interested in the piece goods and other sewing supplies, as they made most of their family's clothing. Across the store from the groceries were the dry goods, shoes, and hats. Carefully figuring how much credit they received from the produce they brought, women selected what they could afford. If there was any money left, the children were sure of a stick of hard candy. Even if there was no money left, Pres usually handed each child a stick of candy.

As automobiles became more numerous, a tall gas pump ornamented the southern end of the porch. Gasoline at ten cents a gallon became another item to sell. After receiving her bluing, coffee, and sugar in return for her eggs, one old lady would say to Mary Elizabeth, almost in embarrassment, "Just figure out the balance of the eggs in gas. Reckon we'll take a trip somewhere in the old car tomorrow." Pres would push the lever back and forth to pump the gasoline into the round glass container before putting fifty cents or a dollar's worth of gasoline into the gas tank.

Often the customers for gasoline were not local people. After Powersite Dam at Forsyth was completed (May 1913), forming Lake Taneycomo and attracting tourists, some of them found their way into Mincy Valley. One of the local customers who spent time loafing at the store was Jerry Youngblood. Mary Elizabeth wrote that when he heard the honk of an impatient motor car by the gas pump, he would turn his cud of Star tobacco over to the three teeth on the other side of his mouth and crow derisively, "Step out, Mahnkey. One o' your touristes is a-bleatin' f'r ye!" The old-timers pronounced the word toor-is´-tes.

Many times the farmers would not have the money or produce to trade. Until they raised their calves or pigs, or until the crop was harvested, they needed credit, especially during droughts or economic depressions. The Mahnkeys extended credit to many. Giving credit was risky; they had to know how much to extend. They needed to know how much money the patrons might be able to produce, watching to see that they did not extend their credit beyond their ability to pay. Giving credit meant the Mahnkeys would be short of money in restocking the store and paying their wholesalers.

Their freighter was Isaac Strahan, their neighbor just south, who was also the Baptist preacher on Sunday in the Mincy schoolhouse-turned-church. Once a week early in the morning, he took in his wagon the load of eggs, butter packed in wooden kegs, and a crate or two of chickens to the railroad at Hollister. Late that night he would rumble back with the replenished stock of goods Pres had ordered.

Pres and Mary Elizabeth were scrupulously honest. Never did they renege on any obligation. One time in 1911 Pres kept his word even though it meant hardship for his family. He had signed a surety on a note for a man who then skipped the country. To pay off this man's note, Pres had to sell four of his own calves. Business dealings such as this earned the Mahnkeys a reputation for honesty and fair dealing.

Not everyone in the hills, however, was so conscientious about honesty. As storekeeper, Pres often resorted to various means to get his money. He was always willing to take something in trade to square the account. Sometimes men worked for him to pay up. Other times he went to the homes to collect.

One collection trip caused Pres unwittingly to be a hero. He heard that a debtor, who lived across the river, was going to leave the country. Since Pres didn't know these people very well, he took along Bill Young, a big fellow who used to be a constable. He also had a boat to cross the river.

As they were walking from the river to the debtor's house, they came to an old log cabin where the children told them their mother was in labor and their father had gone for the granny woman. With Bill Young's uncertain help, Pres delivered the baby. There wasn't even soap in the house, so Pres sent Bill to find some eggs. Pres used the white of eggs beaten into a lather for soap. When the father and granny woman arrived, mother and baby were fine.

When a customer settled up his account, Pres usually told the woman to pick out a piece of goods to make a dress. He wouldn't give the man a pocket knife, because giving a knife was bad luck, but he would sell him one for a penny.

The store was the hub of the Mahnkeys' businesses. To the south was the blacksmith shop from which at all hours came the ring of the hammer on horseshoes, plow points, and other tools. Though Pres could operate a forge and shoe horses, he didn't run the smithy.

There was a big cattle corral and scales. Cattle buyers driving herds from the south stopped at Mincy, bedding the cattle and spending the night. Many times the big scales were busy all day weighing cattle.

These cattle men took advantage of another facet of the store. The rear corner of the row of counters on the south was covered with white oilcloth to serve as a lunch counter. Mary Elizabeth had lettered some cardboard signs, "Pork and Beans, Fixed up 25¢," "Salmon Fixed up, 50¢." "Fixed up" meant the can's contents, dumped into a bowl, would be served with crackers and pepper sauce. Pepper sauce was hot peppers in vinegar. A water bucket with one common dipper sufficed as the drink to wash down the meal. There were no soft drinks or canned drinks of any kind.

On the other end of that back counter, beyond the tanned and aromatic side of leather, tools for cutting halters, bridles, and harness straps, was a big round longhorn cheese on a re-volving circular table. The cattle buyers, or others, would in-dicate how big a chunk of cheese they wanted. A big knife was hinged at the center of the cheese. Marks on the outer edge of the table indicated how far the cheese should be turned to cut a slice weighing the desired amount. Many people made meals of crackers and cheese, finishing off with peppermint or horehound candy, or for the men, chewing or smoking tobacco.

Behind the store about fifty yards was the barn-like building that was the gristmill. Farmers brought in their white corn, usually already carefully shelled and picked over. For his toll, or fee, they gave the miller one-sixth of the corn to get their corn ground. The miller at Mincy before Pres used a toll box which physically measured out his portion—five boxes to the farmer, one box to the miller.

When Pres began operating the mill, he by-passed the toll box by weighing the total amount of grain, and calculating the amount of his toll.

Marion Huff had his corn ground this way a couple of times. The third time he drove right by Mincy the ten miles down to Lowry, Arkansas, to the mill there. "Don't you like the way I grind your corn, Marion?" Pres asked him.

"Yeah, Mahnkey, you do a good job grindin' the corn, but I don't like the idy of you not usin' that toll box. I never did have no confidence in a man that pushed the pencil."

After that, for Uncle Marion Huff, Pres used the toll box.

The other Mahnkey enterprise at Mincy was the cotton gin. Compared to southern states the cotton industry in Taney County was quite small, but from 1880 to the late 1920s, the crop was a substantial economic benefit to the county. In 1890 it amounted to $100,000, a considerable sum for that time in an Ozark county where one was fortunate to grow enough cotton for half a bale an acre. In the rich river and creek bottoms and even on cleared ridge lands, farmers grew cotton as a cash crop.

Mary Elizabeth and Pres both grew up hearing the familiar whistle of the cotton gin, powered by huge steam engines. The whistle sounded before daylight during the season, which ran from October when the frost opened the cotton bolls, until

all the cotton was ginned. Mary Elizabeth had happy childhood memories of romping over the big burlap wrapped bales.

Having a gin of their own thrilled her. The exciting, cum-
bersome steam engine had given way to a gasoline engine, but
the 500 pound bales that Pres rolled out from his press were
identical to those she had known in her childhood.

When the cotton season began, Pres worked from early
morning until into the night trying to keep up with the arriving cotton. Pres and Doug, with three or four hired hands,
worked almost nonstop. The entire store operation fell on
Mary Elizabeth. Without any other help she took care of the
store, the post office, the farm chores, the baby, the young
children, her housework and cooking, including feeding the
hired hands. Bertie and even young Reggie helped. Far from
complaining, Mary Elizabeth loved it. Pres was working as
hard as she and they were getting ahead. They were more
equal partners.

Some nights she would finish before the men. After the
last animal was fed, the children put to bed, the dishes
washed, and floors swept, she occasionally could sit by the
kerosene lamp to read, sew, or write, waiting for Pres and
Doug to come in. It did not happen often, but in 1914, the
good cotton crop caused them to work late several nights. To
give light, Pres wired flashlights at three or four places in the
gin and one right where they were working. He couldn't use
kerosene or gas lanterns because cotton was very combustible.
The air was filled with the cotton dust; any fire or smoking
would have caused a fire.

Mary Elizabeth did not worry about a fire because she
knew how careful and strict Pres was about fire precautions.
She did worry about the ever present dust, especially in the
little room with the press where they baled the cotton. Sometimes one of the men would get a dust chill and miss a day

of work. The only protection they used was to tie dampened handkerchiefs over their faces.

The fall of 1914, Pres hand-ginned a hundred bales of cotton. The war in Europe caused the price of cotton to rise to $100 a bale. Farmers and gin owners profited.

As a writer Mary Elizabeth savored and recorded every detail. Her journals and columns were filled with descriptions and anecdotes gleaned from her hours in the store. Sometimes she put them into short verses.

> "Inefficient? Shucks,"
> And Granny shook her head
> "In my day we wuzn't so polite—
> Plum lazy is what we said."

Annoyed by outsiders' disdain for the Ozark people, she never missed an opportunity to show the wisdom of the hill people. Tourists who camped at a nearby spring often came to the store. She wrote, "The head of a family expressed himself as amazed and disgusted at the general ignorance of the ones he had met. 'I never saw in one place so many ignorant people,' he said. The little boy from the nearby farm house who had been sitting quiet and thoughtful, listening, said, 'And seems like a-most of 'em camp at Gran'pa's spring.'"

At Mincy the busy times were interspersed with slack times. Work was offset with play. School, church, sports, parties, and books all entered their lives.

Education was always high on Mary Elizabeth's list of priorities. As she had missed much school in her childhood, so too did her children miss because of moving so much or working, but whenever possible she saw to it that they attended.

Little Bill started school at Mincy in July 1918. At home

all the children had jobs, even five-year-old Bill. His job was to keep the little brown leghorn chickens out of the garden. The teacher at school was trying to impress on the children to keep their minds clean and not let unwholesome or damaging thoughts in. She asked, "Now, for example, what gets into the garden to ruin it?" She was thinking about weeds.

Bill jumped up excited that he knew the answer. "Chickens!" he said proudly.

Abashed when everyone laughed and he realized he gave the wrong answer, he began to be more conscious of weeds. One day while he was riding behind his mother horseback to a place he was not familiar with, they passed a grape vineyard. "Look at all those weeds!" he exclaimed.

"No, Bill," his mother said, "Those are grapes."

Bill studied the vines for a minute, screwing up his face in thought. "Well, you call them gwapes and I'll call them weeds."

On Sunday the white schoolhouse became the Sunday School and church. Since Mary Elizabeth taught the children's class, the Mahnkey children always attended, though many men and boys in the community did not. Isaac Strahan conducted the church services.

Sunday afternoons often found the young men playing ball. Pres encouraged it. He fixed up a basketball court near the store. Later at Oasis he helped the boys make a baseball diamond in his creek field, even buying balls, gloves, and bats so they could play. Sometimes he would play with them.

The second time the Mahnkeys moved to Mincy, in the early spring of 1917, war with Germany was imminent. Mary Elizabeth kept up with all the news, and she worried greatly. When war was declared in April, Pres was appointed registrar for the draft. Many of the hill boys who came to register could not read nor write. With understanding and tact, Mary

Elizabeth helped them fill out their questionnaires. The men were willing and patriotic about their duty, but one fox hunting lad probably expressed the feelings of most. As he signed his name he said, "Well, I know I've got to go, but if I could have my druthers, I'd druther stay at Mincy."

Mary Elizabeth recorded how she could not let all these boys leave home without some send off. She suggested to Reverend Isaac Strahan in July 1917, "I think the boys should have some honor shown them."

He nodded his head and said, "That's a good idy."

"I think we should get up a prayer meeting," she said.

He nodded his head again and said, "That's a good idy!"

She saw right away that he wasn't going to do anything, so since prayer meetings were hardly her line, she held a dance. Later the neighbors laughed good-naturedly about her party. "That's like Mamie," they said, "suggesting a prayer meeting and then giving a dance!"

Mary Elizabeth and her children cleaned out the old mill. There was a lot of space inside the sturdy building. They flew flags in the trees, giving everything a festive appearance.

On Isaac Strahan's weekly trip to the railroad for Pres, he brought back candy, popcorn, and other party supplies. Another special trip in the wagon to Hollister brought back ice. Packed in sawdust and wrapped securely with burlap and tarps, enough ice came through unmelted for them to make ice cream.

Each family brought a basket dinner. The tables were covered with dishes of fried chicken, beets pickled with hard-boiled eggs, cottage cheese balls, pies, and homemade light bread.

Mary Elizabeth asked the men to move Bertie's parlor organ to the mill. People brought guitars, banjos, and fiddles. Everyone stayed until night. Pres called the square dances and he and Mary Elizabeth danced with the young folks.

Mary Elizabeth was always glad she held the party to give the boys a beautiful memory to take with them. Two of the boys never came back. Two others were gassed in the war and lived only two years.

Mary Elizabeth always enjoyed the tradition of old-time picnics for the Fourth of July. From her childhood she had gone to many of them at various places in the county, Walnut Shade, Kirbyville, and more. She remembered how fervently the speakers talked, including her own father whose patriotism was well known.

She remembered one celebration at Taneyville about 1890. It had a parade and all kinds of contests, including a horse race with a ten-dollar prize and bicycle races with lesser prizes. In addition to dancing, musical novelties, and gramophones, at night there was a balloon ascension with

OLD TIME PICNIC

On the Old Picnic Grounds
Mincy will Celebrate
July 4 and 5
Patriotic Speeches and Songs

Dancing Floor and Refreshment Stands
BASKET DINNER

Horse Races ⎫
Foot Races ⎭   For Prizes

Basket Ball Games

Poster of the picnic the Mahnkeys planned in 1918 at Mincy.

161

fireworks display, followed by a sham battle. Two thousand twenty-ball roman candles lighting the sky over the fifty men and boys re-enacting a Civil War battle lent a realism no one ever forgot.

The sad summer of 1918, in the midst of the great war, seemed an appropriate time to hold such a patriotic picnic at Mincy, though perhaps not quite on such a grand scale. Accordingly, Mary Elizabeth had her editor at the *Taney County Republican* print up some notices which she posted to advertise the event for July 4 and 5. She and the children mowed and cleaned up the grounds between the store and mill. Once again they scrubbed the old mill, set up tables, built refreshment stands, and organized everything. There were basketball games, foot races, and horse races with prizes for all furnished by Mincy store. There was dancing and group singing. Old Civil War veterans wore their faded uniforms, politicians took advantage of the crowd to campaign, and well-liked orators spoke from the speaker's box. Fireworks lighted the sky the night of the Fourth. For two days the community celebrated the nation's independence and its continued love of freedom. The war in Europe, where many of the community's young men were fighting, was foremost in everyone's mind.

On November 11, 1918, Mary Elizabeth was waiting on Pearly Williams in the store. Just as she finished counting out Pearly's eggs, the women heard shooting and loud detonations coming from the north.

"What's that?" Pearly asked frightened.

At first Mary Elizabeth was startled, but having read her daily paper, she knew the time for the end of the war was near. She put her arm around Pearly and said, "Why, the war is over!"

Just then the telephone on the back wall rang two longs and a short, the store's number. Mary Elizabeth was right.

Germany had surrendered. Forgetting the rest of the trading, the two women sat on the front porch and cried. "Many people were crying all over the land for the boys that would never come home," Mary Elizabeth said. "We were just crying with them, although we were deep in the hills in front of a little country store."

Chapter 13

A JEWEL KNOWN AS COURAGE
Away from Taney County - Texas County and Tacoma, Washington: November 18, 1918 - January 28, 1920

I went back to try to find
A treasure I had lost
Back down a lonely rocky road
All black with early frost.
A jewel known as courage
Set in with pearls of trust,
By going back I found it
Untouched with mold or rust.

The war brought more prosperity to the hills, with higher prices for farm produce such as cotton, cattle, and eggs, but in the rural areas there were still no opportunities for high paying jobs such as were available in the big cities. Some people left Missouri for the attractive war jobs. All of the Mahnkey and Prather relatives in the West wrote back glowing accounts of the money they were making and spending. New cars! New homes!

Though the business at Mincy was good for an isolated country store, and the whole family loved the place, it seemed to Pres that compared to others they had nothing. One can only guess Mary Elizabeth's reaction when he again moved his family. All she wrote in her journal was, "He began to get anxious—the old symptom of itchy feet. He swapped the store to a Mr. Hyde for a farm over in Texas County, and I hoped that would be all the moving he would care to do."

Just a few days after the Armistice of World War I, the Mahnkeys moved to a new life. Once again Pres was excited and looking forward to this new future, although they were moving where they knew no one. Mary Elizabeth seemed equally optimistic. The farm was eight miles north of Houston, about seventy-five miles northeast. Seemingly without regret they gave up the steady, though small, income from the post office and the security of the store trade. They took Doug out of his first semester of high school at the School of the Ozarks, a private school near Hollister where hill boys and girls could live and work their way through school. They headed to their new farm—the largest yet, 242 acres.

Physically, this move was the easiest one they ever made. Pres traded everything, business, house, furniture, stock, and machinery, for the farm, house, furniture, stock, and machinery at the new farm. The swap even included the canned goods in the cellar and the pictures on the walls. It must have been difficult for Mary Elizabeth to leave brother Ben's favorite rocking chair, Bertie's organ, and all the jars of preserves and pickles she and Bertie canned during the summer, but the surprise of all the nice things they would find in their new home compensated for what they left. One thing they knew about was the piano in the new house!

They moved only their personal belongings and clothes, which Pres and Doug hauled in a covered wagon pulled by a team of mules he bought for the trip. Mary Elizabeth, Bertie, and the little boys went by train as far as Cabool. Pres's beloved Aunt Cil Breakenridge and Uncle Andy Pogue (brother and sister) accompanied them.

Pres and Doug followed three weeks later. It took them five days to make the trek. They were aware of the epidemic of influenza which had been raging for several months, but they had not realized the extent of its toll, even though Doug had contracted it at the School of the Ozarks, and the school closed for awhile. On the journey they saw many new graves in the country cemeteries they passed. In some cemeteries there were as many as twenty new graves.

At first sight of the place in Texas County, Mary Elizabeth was pleased. There was a white painted house with three rooms downstairs and two upstairs. There was a good barn, three good horses, several cows and a herd of sheep. Pres was back into farming.

The neighbors were very friendly, welcoming the Mahnkeys. They called in the afternoons to sit beside the fireplace visiting in the old-fashioned way people used to do when Mary Elizabeth was a child.

One day a young man rode up with a parcel in his hands. "Would you like some beef? We butchered the other day," he called out. Pres started to get out some money. "Oh no!" the young man protested as he dismounted. "Mother is just sending it to you."

Though at first the farm seemed a good trade, it was not long until they discovered its many drawbacks. Perhaps they had made a mistake? One problem was the distance from the school. For several years they had lived right by a school. Here there were two schools, both a long walk away. The shortest way to the nearest school was through piney woods. Mary Elizabeth took the three younger children their first day to Piney Ridge School, tying strips of colored cloth on the bushes as they walked for the children to find their way home. When the short term ended that winter, Bertie and Doug went to Arthur's Creek School, three miles in another direction. Doug did not attend the Piney Ridge School because Pres needed him at home to help get the farm in shape.

Pres soon realized the extent of the farm's bad points. The land was thin, rocky, piney. There was no hay land, or much pasture. The fences were down and the buildings in bad repair. Pres and Doug spent the first few weeks getting things in order. Pres had to spend his small capital on hay for the stock and seed for next spring's crops. He worried about getting through the winter with no income.

From the very beginning Bertie and Doug did not share their parents' faith in the new farm. They hated it. Bertie complained openly. Her mother told her she should be thankful they had the grit and nerve to get up and move. Douglas said nothing, but helped in any way he could.

Even little Bill sensed the despair. Late on a January afternoon he and his mother walked to the end of a dreary lane to Aunt Cil's house. Mary Elizabeth wrote Bill's reaction in her journal January 18, 1919, "I don't like it at all around here and never will. But I'll sure grin and bear it. Yet the wintry woods have a strange lonely beauty—the pines make it so. Last night the big moon came up out of the dark woods and Bill said, 'Looks like he'd be afraid way over in there.'"

Mary Elizabeth had to make a quick trip in January back to Mincy to see about some reports at the post office. "It seems now almost a miracle how I went down into the danger zone and out untouched. The flu is all around now—all the folks at Mincy sick. But such wonderful weather. I saw buttercups in bloom in the road from Melva to Mincy and the children have seen butterflies. An old saying that flowers blooming out of season is that they decorate the dead, and it seems true this winter."

Then the weather turned cold, colder than in Taney

County, and their only heat was the fireplace. Every Saturday to get enough wood for the next week, Pres, Doug, and Reggie worked all day sawing firewood and hauling it to the house.

The Mahnkeys did not go hungry that winter, but had a limited diet, getting by on the Hydes' canned fruit and stored food. There were some turnips, wild huckleberries, and some dried cowpeas. Every day all winter they ate cowpeas. The children complained, used to having a store and everything they wanted to eat.

Their scant cash was doled out carefully for the few groceries and supplies they had to have. Everyone gave up luxuries. Since Pres knew they could not afford it, he gave up the flat tobacco he liked to chew. Mary Elizabeth came back from the store with a few groceries she set on the table. When no one was watching, Pres dug down in the basket to see if she brought him a piece of flat tobacco. She always did.

Mary Elizabeth continued to enjoy one of her luxuries; Pres was certainly entitled to his. She continued to get the daily paper and enjoy the many letters she wrote and received. The mail hack passed by the house. Every winter day she would sit by the window to watch for the mail. Each day except Sunday she got the Springfield paper.

When Pres realized what a bad investment he had made, he became more discouraged and despondent than he had ever been. He never went to town. He even considered going to the woods and taking his life. When spring came, he had none of the optimism spring on the farm used to bring. "I can't make a living on this place," he said. Mary Elizabeth knew the signs. She knew there would be another move and braced herself for it. He had a farm sale, selling off his stock and many other things, even the piano Bertie prized. Getting his Aunt Cil and Uncle Andy to live on the farm, in March 1919, he moved his family to Tacoma, Washington, to join his mother and brothers, Bill and George, who were working in the shipyards.

With money from the sale, the family got the train tickets and clothes they needed for the trip. Doug, soon to be seventeen, got his first man's suit. Mary Elizabeth bought a pretty gray silk to make into a dress. When she got home and spread it out, six-year-old Bill admired it.

Aunt Cil teased him. "That's what your mother will wear when she leaves you. She'll be going out in society in Tacoma, and in the city women don't take little boys with them."

Bill looked at his mother with a hurt expression. After they got to Tacoma, Mary Elizabeth made the dress. Whenever she took it out, she saw Bill looking at her with that wounded expression. She never wore the dress.

The move to Washington state was another disappointment. In her journal many years later Mary Elizabeth referred to it as "our wild goose chase to the coast." Though Doug and Pres both got jobs immediately in the Todd shipyards at $4.64 a day, the war boom was over. They worked only until that late summer of 1919 when a strike closed the yards. They arrived too late to get the advantages of the high paying jobs and quick advancement that wartime economy offered. However, they were able to save some money, so that when they returned to Missouri, and with the sale of the Texas County farm, Pres was able to return to storekeeping, buying another store and stock of goods in Taney County at Melva.

While in Washington everyone contributed to the family finances, even little Bill. Reggie got a newspaper route after school. Bill accompanied him. Mary Elizabeth was happy the boys had this to do. The country boys got very restless penned up in a city yard.

After the school term ended, Mary Elizabeth had Pres's brother Bill move her, Bertie, and the little boys to a berry farm a few miles west of Tacoma near Puyallup. They were happier there in a little cabin the owner furnished. The quiet of the country after the city racket was balm for Mary Elizabeth. The children loved it. The boys played until dark and Bill slept through the night. The next morning she stewed the bright red raspberries they picked with some sugar and poured the sauce over two pieces of light bread on Bill's plate. He ate every bit. For weeks in the city he had not been eating or playing or sleeping well.

Bertie was fifteen and big for her age, but since they did not lie about her age, she was not old enough to get a job in the city. Here in the berry field she was happy working with her mother and little brothers.

Reggie loved the farm. The owner used a good horse for hauling the berries to the house. He soon let Reggie, always followed by Bill, hitch up the horse and do other important jobs. The boys were proud.

Boy-like, Reggie enjoyed cutting up. The field boss told the workers that the next child that threw berries would be sent out of the field. Mary Elizabeth, knowing Reggie had been throwing berries, warned him not to ruin things for them."And do you know, she said, "it wasn't ten minutes until I saw Reggie reach down in his box and take up a handful of berries and make a sort of snowball out of them. He threw it at Bill and hit him right on the forehead and the red juice spattered all over his silky white hair and his overalls. I just reached up over my head and broke a branch off a tree. Then I went back to that young man and nearly wore his pants off of him. I hated to do it in public, but I sure made a believer out of him.

"When I went back to work, my hands were shaking so

I could hardly pick berries, and the tears were rolling down my cheeks. I was so ashamed at having to do a thing like that in front of everybody. Then an old lady in the next row spoke up and said, 'Honey, I know it's hard, but you did exactly right.' That's how I became friends with Mrs. Selsby!"

Pres and Doug came to Puyallup on weekends at first, then buying an old car to drive to work, they moved out with the rest of the family. They helped pick in the evenings and weekends. They also liked it. Pres was an expert picker, as quick at that as he was with any activity. When the shipyards closed, he and Doug worked full time for the farmer, digging up apple trees to prepare the land for the more profitable berries.

Mary Elizabeth and the children picked raspberries, next hops, and then blackberries. When those seasons were over, Mary Elizabeth and Bertie worked in an apple cannery where many men who lost their jobs were also working, doing tasks like cleaning or other menial jobs. Mary Elizabeth was glad that Pres was spared that, because men in the hills did not work at such jobs. His job, trimming the berry vines, was more like man's work.

Mary Elizabeth took advantage of the stay in Tacoma to educate the children. She put Bertie and Reggie in school. The family needed Doug's wages, but she insisted that he take night courses in a business college, impressing upon him the importance of the education and the family's sacrifice by paying for his tuition with the five dollar gold piece Bertie had won in a county spelling contest back in Taney County.

When famous people like the singer John McCormack, tenor with the Metropolitan Opera Company, or Woodrow Wilson, were in town, she made sure that at least Doug saw them. Uncle Bill Mahnkey took them to museums and on drives through the city and country, even visiting Bob

Prather's, widow Gertrude, and Mary Elizabeth's sister Mag and her husband.

Mary Elizabeth was dubious from the first about the trip west. She thought all along that it was not right; she could not understand why others failed to realize that the work would not last forever. Perhaps Pres's mother wanted Pres to be there at any cost. Mattie Mahnkey said to Mary Elizabeth with a great sense of achievement, "Well, now I've got my last child out of Missouri."

Quick to sense the snub, Mary Elizabeth said of her mother-in-law, "She seemed to like to lord it over me because she was a city woman by that time, and I was still the woman from the hills. But the family was still country! When John McCormack came to sing at the auditorium, I tried to get them interested so I could go, but they wouldn't think of it. They had never even heard of Mr. McCormack!"

Pres also knew they couldn't stay in the West. He began plans to return to Missouri. He sent Doug back to Aunt Cil on the Texas County farm. At Thanksgiving Mary Elizabeth and the three other children went home, followed shortly by Pres. Once again Mary Elizabeth returned to the hills. Their decision to return was deliberate. They could have stayed, for they were making money.

The train trip home was long and tiring. "During all the time we had been in the West," Mary Elizabeth said, "we had loved to watch Mount Rainier. Every time we looked at it, in the morning or during the day, it was different and more beautiful. We left Puyallup in the evening and next morning when the children awakened, they looked for Mount Rainier as they always did first thing in the morning. For a long time little Bill looked at it fading away behind them, and then he said, 'Oh, look, Mama! We're on the wrong side of the mountain.'

"I had such a strange feeling. It seemed sort of portentous. Indeed it was the wrong side of the mountain for Bill.

"Then, at last, after we had changed trains at Kansas City and stayed at a hotel in Cabool and then taken a mail truck ride to Houston, Doug met us with a team and wagon. He had our little dog with him. At the farm Aunt Cil had a good hot dinner for us. We had come back to the hills and all was well!"

When Pres returned to the farm, he did not share Mary Elizabeth's joy. Though glad to be back in Missouri, he did not think the land looked any better than it had before he left it. But now he had over $1,000 they had saved. He made a trip to Taney County to see what he could get for them there.

Though Mary Elizabeth knew a move was coming, she continued her work as though she expected to live there always. They celebrated Bill's seventh birthday in December with a special dinner and cake as they always did on birthdays.

Pres came home, encouraged, hopeful again. He had bought the store at Melva, a little settlement south of Hollister on the Missouri Pacific Railroad deep in the hills where Caney Creek joined Turkey Creek. They were back in the mercantile business. They moved there on January 28, 1920.

Chapter 14

FOOTPRINTS IN THE SILVER ROADSIDE SAND
Melva: March 11, 1920

Because we walked the woodland trails
So happy, hand in hand,
Because I saw his footprints
In the silver roadside sand
I will not have a motor car
For I know that I would see
That gallant, laughing little lad
Who used to walk with me--
And now that I could buy a car
Still walking I will go
Because for him I could not buy
The boots he wanted so.

Even though the day was dreary and the ground muddy with melted snow, the evening of March 10, 1920, little Bill Mahnkey kept a lookout for Doug coming back on the handcar with his section gang. Mary Elizabeth also watched for Doug, though not as obviously as Bill. Thinking of the close companionship of her two sons made her smile.

Bill was at his father's store in Melva where he could look down the road that went by the store, down the glade where it turned by the flag station depot to cross the two sets of tracks and drop down the fill to a small bottom before fording Turkey Creek.

Bill had watched for Doug almost every night during the five weeks since moving into the house about a hundred feet up the hill from the store at Melva. This evening when he saw the handcar come up and Doug alight with his crew boss and his friend Arthur Davis, Mary Elizabeth nodded her approval as he scrambled into his coat and ran down the road happily, followed by his little dog, Trixie. Doug, dirty, wet, and weary from the hard, physical work of handling the railroad ties and repairing the tracks, brightened as he saw Bill racing eagerly toward him.

"Doug!" Bill said excitedly as he reached him. "Doug, we got a new kind of candy in the store today. I brought you a piece." He looked up at Doug, the blond hair of his Dutch boy haircut sticking out from his cap. In his hand he clutched a piece of moist candy. Doug ate it eagerly. Dirt and all, it tasted good to the hungry young man. Hand in hand the brothers walked up the hill past the store to the house.

Bill talked about his day at school and how he, Reggie, and Hubert Box threw rocks across Turkey Creek which was swollen by the recent rains and the rapid thawing of the big snowfall.

After escorting Doug into the house, the cheerful fellow ran to the kitchen where his mother and Bertie were putting the final touches to supper. Without being asked, Bill put out the plates and silver.

"Mama," he begged for the tenth time, "can't I have those boots Papa got in last week? The real leather ones like Doug and Papa have?"

His mother smiled, answering as she had before, "No, Bill. We can't afford them. You've got your rubber boots." It pained Mary Elizabeth that she couldn't buy them for him.

Bill didn't pout. He had known the answer before he asked. He just looked down at his boots, screwing up his face in disappointment.

The family was animated at supper. They all liked Melva. Though the house wasn't as big as their house at Mincy, it was adequate. The little boys liked their school, which was only 400 yards south across a hollow. Bill was learning fast after a late start. He had received only smatterings of schooling before, at Mincy and in Texas County. They moved so much that he hadn't yet completed the first reader.

The boys quickly became friends with other children, especially the boys in the two Box families, thirteen-year-old Hubert and five-year-old George, whom everyone called Budgie.

Doug was happy for his job on the railroad. His earnings would pay his expenses next summer in Springfield in the summer college term where he could continue his school work that was interrupted when he left the School of the Ozarks. After that he wanted to teach.

Now that Doug was gone all day, Pres and Mary Elizabeth depended on Bertie's help in the store. Running a country store was something they knew well. They resumed their sharing of the work. Pres was enthusiastic and optimistic.

Melva was a thriving community which developed because of the railroad. Whereas Mincy's trade was a crossroads trade dominated by farmers, Melva was a railroad town. After the discovery and development of some veins of lead, zinc, and copper in the hills east of Melva in the late 1800s, other prospectors and miners were attracted to the area. The hoped-for riches did not materialize, but there was mining activity for several years.

Melva became a flag stop on the railroad and a work

center for two or three crews of workers. Miners and section hands lived in modest houses in or near Melva. Some section hands lived in temporary cars on the long siding next to the work train and cook car.

Melva was a center for fruit growing—apples, peaches, strawberries, and tomatoes. When the Mahnkeys moved to the town, there were several sheds below the tracks by the creek for storing fruit before shipping. The nearby hills also furnished lumber, ties, and cedar and oak posts, all shipped from Melva depot.

That night as the Mahnkeys ate their meal, they had every reason for optimism. Business was brisk during February, and with March here and spring coming, it should pick up even more. Every indication pointed toward the town attracting still more people to build on the empty lots the founders laid out in 1906. Pres, besides owning the store and dwelling, owned several choice lots.

After every move during the past few years, Mary Elizabeth hoped it would be permanent. Now Melva offered the best promise of that. Pres would not likely get restless with such a thriving trade and the added convenience and attraction of the railroad. He could order and ship directly without freighters.

Melva even had a hotel and restaurant run by Mrs. Buell. The town was not without culture. A Presbyterian missionary, Miss Lucy Woods, taught Sunday School in the schoolhouse, and, of great interest to Mary Elizabeth, kept a small library.

Thursday morning, March 11, was miserable though the temperature was mild. There were heavy rains during the night. In the morning hours it intermittently rained and hailed, with occasional brief periods of sunshine. As usual most of the men of the town had left for work. Doug's section gang went south toward the Arkansas line to repair the tracks. An-

178

other crew went farther south on the work train to work on bridges and trestles.

As Billy Box left for work that morning, little Budgie did an unusual thing. He followed his father, insisting he wanted to go with him on the work crew. Billy had to scold his son to make him go home. The boy cried. Billy joined his brother Ranzy on the work train just as it pulled out.

Doug's crew worked all morning in the bad weather. One of the men on his crew, Alva Howard, seemed to be depressed. He told Doug that working in that red clay made him think of a grave.

Back in Melva the day began as usual for the women and children, as well as for the few men left in town such as Pres and old Marion Oliver. The Mahnkey boys ran to school, but their teacher did not come because she couldn't get across the flooded creek. The boys came back home.

Pres opened the store as usual. He warned Reggie and Bill to play near the store because it looked stormy. Since the rainy weather kept most customers at home, Mary Elizabeth and Bertie worked at home.

Mary Elizabeth was unaccountably uneasy, not being able to settle down to any job. She ironed a few pieces. She found a torn knee in Bill's blue overalls and sat down to mend it. When she looked down at it, she somehow couldn't put a needle to the garment. She had the piece to make the patch, but all at once there was something breaking her heart. The feeling was similar to the one she had years before while sewing on her first baby's dress. Bill's overalls looked pitiful with the torn out knees; she folded them up and laid them away. She also did a strange thing she later could not account for. She took Bill's underwear from the wash and put it in the top of the trunk her brother Ben gave her when she was twelve.

That morning the mothers of the two Box families went

about their usual activities. After finishing her morning work, Anna Box, Billy's wife and mother of Budgie, five, and two girls, eleven and eight, decided to visit her sister-in-law. Florence Box, wife of Ranzy Box. Florence lived in a small square house with her four small children right on the creek bank across the tracks from the boxcar station.

Bertie went to the store as she always did near noon, Bertie came to relieve Pres so he could go home to dinner. Pres's anxiety had increased all morning as he watched the buildup of clouds in the southwest up Caney Creek hollow. Always afraid of storms, he feared today's weather was leading up to a bad one. Mary Elizabeth tried to cheer him up by tricks she knew to get him out of his despondency. Nothing worked.

In the store Mrs. Susie Melbourne and her little boy came in. She wanted to make a long distance call. But in order to reach the central operator in Hollister, someone had to turn the switch which was on Florence and Ranzy Box's house. Because of the danger of lightning coming into the house, Florence had disconnected the switch. Bertie sent Reggie and Bill down there to close the switch. After completing their errand, the two boys, their dog Trixie, and Hubert Box went up the creek to play, attracted by the raging waters.

The boys were familiar with the danger of creeks in the Ozarks flooding quickly after heavy rainfall. Though muddy water swirled down Turkey Creek from the south, what fascinated the boys was the roar of brown frothing water and big limbs that emptied into the creek from the southwest out of the hollow in the hills known as Caney Creek.

The boys were awed by the flood. None of them dared get too close to the water. They knew its danger. Besides, they were all afraid of water; they couldn't swim. The noise of the water was so loud they did not hear the roar in the clouds;

their fascination with the creeks prevented them from noticing the ominous buildup of clouds, or even that it was becoming dark.

The Box women did not miss those signs for they had
to light a lamp, nor did Mrs. Buell at the hotel. Mrs. Buell ran
to her neighbor, the missionary Miss Woods. The two women
huddled against the huge stone fireplace and chimney in the
Woods house.

While Mary Elizabeth was getting dinner, Pres watched
the sky with growing alarm. Right at noontime when he was
looking out the door, he exclaimed, "My God! A waterspout
is coming right down old Caney." Mary Elizabeth ran to see.
She wasn't afraid; she just marvelled.

She later described what she saw, "The whole hollow
seemed to be filled with black smoke that seemed to have
been leveled off by some mysterious power! On top of it little
white clouds seemed to be dancing."

"That's a cyclone," Pres shouted. "I've got to get the
children."

He ran the short distance down the hill to the store.
"Close the store!" he shouted to Bertie. "There's a big storm
a-comin'!" He began herding her and the Melbournes out.
"Where're the boys?" he asked frantically.

They ran against the wind to their house. They couldn't
keep from looking back to the hollow where a black cloud
was rolling on the ground toward them. Mary Elizabeth was
outside the house also watching the cloud.

"Where are the boys?" she cried. Once again no one answered. The wind was so strong they were having trouble
standing up.

"Quick," Pres yelled above the wind, "get into the base-
ment!" They all ran into a small storage space under the
house. There they waited, praying that the boys were all right.

It sounded to Mary Elizabeth as if a train of railway cars went right over the house. Mrs. Melbourne clutched her little boy. Bertie reached for her mother's hand. Pres paced back and forth in the crowded space. He watched anxiously as the corner of the house lifted inches off the foundation, wavered, and then settled back. The group saw the wind destroy the store. Lumber, roofing, and furnishings spun around like leaves in a whirlwind. No one said a word.

At the creek Bill was the first one of the boys to notice the storm. He looked up to the hill across the creek. "Oh, Reggie, look!" he exclaimed in wonder. Over the hill big up-rooted trees were flying and twisting up in the sky. Hubert spun about quickly and raced across the little bottom field to his house. Reggie and Bill ran after him. Anna and Florence were both looking out the window. Just as Hubert bounded in the door, Florence saw Bill and Reggie already past the house running up the road to the depot as fast as they could.

"Reggie, Bill!" she screamed over the deafening roar. "Come here!"

Bill turned back. Reggie pulled at him and yelled, "Let's go over here to the freight house!" Bill pulled away and ran into the Box house. Reggie followed him. Though only twelve years old, Reggie realized it was dangerous here. The house was too light and flimsy. When he got inside and saw the other eight children and the two women, both of whom were pregnant, he shouted, "Folks, let's go to the depot!"

It was too late. The terrible roar was over them. Anna held one of her children and reached out for the hand of one of her nieces. The wind, rain, noise, and tremendous air pressure hit all at once. Anna remembered, "Everything went black just like night—just like black smoke. It was as if something had burst."

Footprints in the Silver Roadside Sand

It looked to Reggie as if the cook stove jumped across the room. The house turned on its side and was torn apart in the creek. The next thing he knew, he and all the other children were in the cold, swift water. Turned over and over he fought, gasping, and flailing his arms to keep his head up. Something, perhaps a board, struck his forehead. Blood flowed from the gash. He was carried downstream. He was pushed struggling against some willows which grew on the bank, but were now completely surrounded by the flooding waters. He grabbed a branch. The force of the strong current against him bent the branch, but it held. Getting a better hold closer to the trunk, he was able to stop his headlong motion and keep his nose just above the water level. He couldn't touch bottom or get any foothold. Blood streamed down his face, but he could neither feel it nor distinguish it from the water splashing against him.

Gasping and spitting water, he dared not use his hands to wipe the water and blood from his eyes. Blinking rapidly in the dim light, he saw Bill being swept by, his cap gone, his blond hair plastered to his terrified face.

"Bill!" Reggie screamed, reaching out one hand as far as he could to try to grab him. But Bill was too far away to reach. Reggie narrowly escaped being swept after him; he tightened his precarious hold on the tree with both hands. Bill was carried farther down the stream. Reggie saw him go under. Then no more. Reggie stared at the spot for some time. Getting a stronger hold on the branch, he pulled himself up and struggled out of the water across the creek from Melva.

Anna and Florence Box were also thrown into the swollen creek amid planks and debris, but they somehow managed to hold on to the floating remains of the house and were not washed down the creek. When Anna regained consciousness, she was on a pile of rubble. Holding onto parts of the demolished house and bracing herself as well as she could, she grabbed Florence. The two women clung to each other struggling and screaming for help. Anna prayed, "Lord, help me to know what's become of my children!"

Bill and the seven Box children were carried down the stream.

In minutes the tornado passed. Pres, Mary Elizabeth, and Bertie ventured out into the strange, unnatural darkness. With trepidation they crept out into the rain and wind, thankful none of them was hurt, but afraid for what they would find. Great black clouds still rolled and twisted overhead though the roar was disappearing over the hills toward the northeast. The comparative stillness from the ear-splitting cacophony was almost as frightening as the noise. Part of their house roof was gone, but there seemed to be no other damage to the house. When they hurried around the house, they saw an incredible scene. Nothing was the same. The store was flattened. The hotel was gone. Only the stone foundation, chimney, and a north wall stood on the Woods house. Theirs was the only house still standing in the whole town.

Frantic with fear for the boys, they hurried down the slope. Pres and Bertie ran all the way down the hill and across the tracks toward the Box house where Bertie thought the boys would be.

Mary Elizabeth, coming more slowly, still in a daze, passed some women huddled in a group, Mrs. Buell, Miss Woods, and Maggie Oliver. Mrs. Buell and Lucy Woods were all black, even their faces. The soot from the big chimney which saved their lives covered them so that they were hardly recognizable.

Aunt Sarah Oliver was lying in front of her ruined home with a broken thigh. The women told Mary Elizabeth that since all telephone lines were out, Sarah's husband Marion had gone down the tracks to Hollister for help.

"Where are the children?" Mary Elizabeth cried. There were no little boys anywhere. She knew hers would be with the others.

"I'm afraid they are in the creek," Maggie said bluntly.

Gripped in the terror of what she would find, Mary Elizabeth ran as swiftly as she could down the hill, across the tracks and on down to the creek. As she ran she noticed the depot was still standing, as was the schoolhouse on the next hill. Building stones and pieces of glass were everywhere; boards, roofing, and fence rails were piled around as if carelessly spilled by a giant hand. Trees were uprooted and thrown down in every direction. In places piles of boards with protruding nails barred her way.

She saw Pres and Bertie reach the creek, where the Box women were struggling in the water amid the wreckage of the house.

"Where are Bill and Reggie?" Bertie shouted.

"They have gone to Heaven to be with all my children," Florence cried.

"Papa! Bertie!" Reggie screamed when he saw them. He was running along the opposite bank of the creek crying hysterically.

"Where's Bill?" Bertie shouted over the roar of the water. Reggie cried harder and pointed downstream.

Almost as hysterical as Reggie, Bertie started running down the creek screaming, "Bill! Bill!"

Mary Elizabeth's first reaction was relief when she saw Reggie. But she instantly understood the situation at the sight of Bertie racing down the creek screaming for Bill.

She reached the creek just as Anna and Florence were struggling out of the water. Pres picked up a pole to try to balance himself to wade into the deepest part of the creek, but gave it up. Keeping to shallow water, he helped the women reach the land. In her mounting concern for Bill, it did not occur to Mary Elizabeth until later that Pres might have been swept away by the water or struck by pieces of the house that littered the swollen and treacherous creek. Pres couldn't swim.

The Box women scarcely looked human. Each was big with child. The wet clothes were molded to their bodies, their dresses almost torn off of them, their stockings off, and hair streaming. Florence was badly hurt. She had broken ribs, a broken jaw, an eye badly injured, and several bleeding gashes on her head. Mary Elizabeth forgot her terrible fear for a moment in sympathy for them. "Let's take them up to the house," she told Mrs. Buell and Miss Woods, who took them to the Mahnkey house to care for them until other help arrived.

Just then big Ben Layton galloped up the creek road on his huge mule.

Ben was the first help to arrive from outside the storm's path. He lived about two miles down and across the creek toward Hollister. At his house he had seen the storm coming and took his wife and two children just below his house to an overhang on Turkey Creek where they would be safe. Many years later in 1977, he described his experience to Doug. "It was just as still as it could be. I could hear the air cracking and a-popping. I knew it was a cyclone. I never had seen one, but I knew it was—just as black as could be, and it was big in the air and come down small at the ground."

The tornado didn't reach his family, but he was fearful for those in its path. He grabbed a slicker, jumped on his big mule, not even taking time to saddle him, and rode up the west side of the creek toward Melva to find a place he could cross. He met Marion Oliver who was running along the tracks. Oliver's face was bloody and he was bareheaded.

"Melvy's blown away," Oliver panted, "and Sary's layin' outside in the rain."

About that time it rained for a few minutes as hard as Ben had ever seen it rain; then it quit. Without looking for a better crossing, Ben headed his mule into the creek. The mule waded the deep churning creek water that was rising perceptibly even as he crossed. Ben ran the mule as hard as he could go to Melva. His first help was rescuing Reggie.

Ben said, "I went down to the crick and I stood with Pres and Mrs. Mahnkey, and she was wringing her hands. And Reggie was on the other side. We could see blood coming down his face. Somebody rode a horse out in there, and the water hit him, and he just come back. And I told Pres, I said, 'Pres, I can go git that boy. This mule will wade that. He's a good mule.'

"Pres said, 'Take him to the Rittenhouses. Don't bring him back across the creek.'"

Pres could see that most of the house across the creek was standing. He thought Reggie would be safer there than he would be attempting to cross the creek. The Rittenhouses would comfort the boy and care for him.

Ben continued his account. "I got on that old mule and he just kept one foot down here and there. I got up on my knees on there, and it was just his head and hip bones sticking out. Water come up to my knees." Ben and the mule forded the creek again as he did several other times that day and the next looking for children's bodies. Ben was a powerful swimmer, afraid of nothing. "Nervy" is the word people used to describe him.

When Ben reached down from his horse and grabbed Reggie, the terrified boy, wet, cold, and shaking, clung to the big man. Ben took him to the Rittenhouse home as Pres instructed. There was no one there. During the storm John and Maude Rittenhouse had taken refuge in the old original log part of their house which withstood the wind. Though they were not hurt, the roof of the lumber part was lifted loose, and clothes which were hanging on the wall were sucked out under the eaves.

As soon as the storm passed, and John and Maude realized they were safe, they hurried up Caney Creek about one fourth of a mile to the Alva Howard place to see about Alva's wife, daughters, and little son. John thought he heard the children yelling.

When Ben put Reggie down, Reggie didn't want to stay alone in the empty house. Worried about the Howards and knowing Reggie was safe, Ben was anxious to get to them. He pointed to the Rittenhouse dwelling and said kindly, "Reggie, go ahead in there."

"There ain't nobody at home," Reggie protested.

"Go in anyhow. Go on in and set down." Ben's heart went out to the boy especially when he saw clearly the big cut across his head, but there were now other lives to save. "I'll be back directly," he said kindly. "Just wait here."

The tornado had lifted the Howard house into the air with Cora Howard and the children inside. While in the air, the floor gave way, letting everyone and everything fall out. Cora fell on her head holding her three-year-old son in her arms. She was killed, but the boy was not injured. Three girls were injured. After Ben helped the Rittenhouse couple take the injured back to the log house, where they found Reggie waiting, he came back to the creek to search for the other victims.

When the water had subsided somewhat, and other people arrived, Reggie was finally helped back across the creek. Bertie took care of him, bandaging his head, cleaning him up, and putting him to bed, though he didn't stay there long.

Mary Elizabeth could do nothing. In her heart she knew Bill was lost. Outside help soon arrived. Ben Layton and others were searching the creek. Someone gave her an imitation sealskin coat. She waved off all other offers of assistance. Wandering around in a daze, she picked up the post office money box, stamps, and a few pieces of mail. Then she and Pres sat on a stone ledge by the creek.

Told of the tornado by Gertrude Peppers, who ran up the tracks to get them, Doug's crew raced at top speed to Melva. Not knowing what had happened, but having heard Reggie was safe, Doug cried, "I'll find Bill."

Mary Elizabeth was numb as she watched Doug race down the creek bank. He waded into the water where Claude Stacy was pulling up boards and roofing. When Claude moved a big timber, the mangled body of a child surfaced in the muddy water. Bracing himself in the current, he gathered up the body and turned to hand it to Doug. Doug couldn't touch it or stay there longer. He was afraid the next body they would find would be Bill's. He turned away and went home.

By this time there was much good help. The work train was back. A train going by stopped, and Marion Oliver returned from Hollister with a relief train.

After carrying the Howards to the Rittenhouse home, Ben Layton joined the others in searching for the children in the creek. He waded neck deep into holes of raging brown water. He remembered, "I went on down that crick there, I guess half a mile, down to a shoal, and there was two babies, a-hanging and floating on top, and the clothes was wrapped around a willow. If it hadn't been for that, they'd a-floated off. They looked to me like twins. [Probably the two five-year-old Box cousins.] But I rode that mule out in there. I used to be stout as a mule myself. I weighed two hundred forty pounds. I waded out there and got them babies." Farther down the creek he had to dive down into the treacherous water to retrieve the body of an older child.

Volunteers put the injured Box women and the Howard girls on the relief train along with the dead; the train left for Branson.

Little Bill was not found until about five o'clock that afternoon, Hubert Box not until the next afternoon. Both boys had been carried farther down the creek than the other children. Ben was on the scene in both instances. He pulled four of the eight drowned children out of the water.

Bill was trapped in the water under a big elm tree that had uprooted and fallen into the creek. It took two other men besides Ben with a wedge and crosscut saw to cut through the trunk. When the log broke in two, the current rolled the tree over. Bill's body came to the surface.

Ben ended sadly, "And he had them boots on. I can remember just as well as if it was yesterday, them little rubber boots."

Chapter 15

WHERE SAD WHITE ROSES GROW
Recovery: Melva and Mincy Valley
Night, March 11, 1920 - January 1922

> Strangers have bought the Van Zandt place
> And I wonder if they know
> Of a little plot upon the hill
> Where sad white roses grow.
> Will they see that way, that solemn way
> That leads up to the hill
> Where the gate is closed in sorrow
> And everything is still?
> The old Captain lies here sleeping
> In the fields he loved so well
> Where melodious tones still echo
> From his old farm dinner bell.
> We have two darlings lying
> Within this sacred sod
> Oh, remember, please, dear strangers
> This acre belongs to God.

First sighted at Oasis about eight miles away, the tornado that hit Melba continued in its northeasterly direction where it caused two other deaths and much property damage. Tearing up trees, barns, and more houses, it crossed the White River east of Forsyth and apparently dissipated just south and east of Taneyville. Its path was 400 yards wide and over twenty miles long.

At Turkey Creek in Melva where the storm did the greatest damage, Ben Layton and others continued searching the creek and helping the injured. There was nothing more the Mahnkeys could do at the creek. Long before Bill's body was found, the family knew he must be dead. They returned home to comfort Reggie, see about the damage to their house, and salvage what they could from the store and post office.

When Ben Layton carried Bill's limp body home in his powerful arms, though Bill was large for a seven-year-old, he seemed pitifully small compared to Ben's six feet. Ben's soft brown eyes were full of compassion for the family as he brought them their child.

Pres asked Mary Elizabeth, "Should we send him to Branson with the other children?"

"No, bring him home."

When Bill was carried home, his little dog, Trixie, lying hurt on the porch didn't raise her head as the men entered. Inside there was Bill's glass of milk still waiting beside his plate.

Some men prepared the body, cleaned him up, and dressed him. They had to ask Mary Elizabeth if he had any underwear. She remembered she had put it away in the trunk that morning. The men dressed him in his Sunday suit and laid him out on a board supported on the backs of two chairs. They covered him with a sheet. The only mark on Bill's body was a small blue bruise on his forehead.

The men had combed Bill's hair back from his forehead. Since Mary Elizabeth cut his hair in the Dutch boy style, hanging straight down with bangs over his forehead, Bill didn't look right to Doug. He combed his hair the usual way so that the bangs covered the blue mark. Bertie slipped in and put on his finger her ring that he had always admired.

It was the custom in the hills for neighbors to sit up with the dead. But that night with so many in town dead, homeless, and injured, there was no one to come. Little Bill's body lay in the cold room all alone. The Mahnkeys all went to bed, though they didn't sleep. Doug's friend Arthur Davis spent the night.

The morning of March 12 was cold, dark, and dreary. When Mary Elizabeth opened the door there was Drake, a big red hound, looking up at her. This hound belonged to the former owners of the house. When Mary Elizabeth and the children first came to Melva in January on the train, this hound had taken up with Reggie and Bill, following them around and playing with them. His owners took him with them when they drove their team on their move to Oklahoma. Mary Elizabeth thought he must have come back to comfort them.

That morning there were many curious sightseers and some well-wishers who wanted to visit with Pres and Mary Elizabeth; the Mahnkeys did not want to see anybody. In spite of their deep sorrow, both went out looking for letters and government property from the post office. The night before, Pres had walked around with a lantern picking up what he could find. Right up to time to go to Bill's funeral, Mary Elizabeth was out salvaging. It was something she could do to keep occupied.

She said, "We picked up what we could find of the post office stuff and put it into a box. We slid it under the bed, in the old hill fashion of putting things under the bed, and after all, we had no roof on the house. Then when the post office inspector came, I brought out the box and showed him what we had. 'What else have you got?' he asked. I told him, 'That is all.' He grabbed hold of a little old suitcase that was there and said, 'What's in this?' 'Open it and see,' I told him. He opened it up and it was filled with little old pitiful odds and ends just like any family would have. Not a bit of sympathy out of him, even though the tracks of the little children that had been killed were still around the store."

Red Cross representatives from Hollister and Branson gathered a fund for the storm victims. They wanted Pres to take some for his loss and for funeral expenses for Bill. Pres and Mary Elizabeth's independence and love for the child made them refuse. "No, we'll bear these expenses ourselves," they said.

But they did accept the offer of a neighbor. With his wagon and team he took Pres and Mary Elizabeth and the little wrapped up body across the hills to Kirbyville for the funeral and burial.

Just at sunset they laid Bill's body at the foot of Colonel Prather's grave in the Van Zandt cemetery near Kirbyville. The line in the services which stayed with Mary Elizabeth was, "Is it well with the father? Is it well with the son?"

In addition to the sudden appearance of the red hound, another strange coincidence occurred that day. Old Captain James Van Zandt, who had married Mary Elizabeth and Pres twenty-one years before, was also buried in the same cemetery. Though the storm did not kill the captain, it destroyed his house. Everyone thought the shock caused his death.

Mary Elizabeth stood by her little son's grave. Since it was March there were no flowers. Even a single blossom would have comforted her, for like his mother Bill loved flowers. She remembered the many walks she used to take with Bill through the woods and fields gathering and appreciating the flowers. Mary Elizabeth said, "Perhaps I wouldn't have thought so much about that, but Captain Van Zandt was a famous Mason with city friends. He was buried under a mountain of flowers. And not a flower for little Bill. I think Captain Van Zandt would have wanted Bill to share those flowers."

But beauty and love were expressed in other ways. She continued, "Bill had more than flowers. After the men had been at Captain Van Zandt's funeral, they all came over and stood around little Bill's grave and wept with me. Even men and boys!"

Douglas and Bertie stayed home from the funeral to be with Reggie. Reggie was wild. He couldn't stay in bed. With a big bandage tied around his head he ran all over town where the buildings were torn up. All his life after that storm, Reggie was afraid of a black cloud or a storm. At any indication of a storm, he ran to a cellar.

The next day was the funeral for the Box children in Branson. Florence Box's baby, born dead the night of the storm, was placed in the casket with his eighteen-month-old brother. Doug represented the family at the funeral. One wide grave held four little caskets of one family and another grave beside it held three more.

At home in Melva that day Mary Elizabeth's depression was severe. She tried to iron, but couldn't; Bill had helped her wash those same clothes. While mending a few things, she picked up Bill's overalls with the torn knees, trying to mend them.

"The storms of life are o'er for you, my darling, and the rest of us are still battling them," she wrote years later in her journal. "O life! How we are shaken and shattered—but love remains."

The candle within her soul almost went out. At no other point in her life was it harder for her to hold on to her own metaphor of life as a worn fabric. This time it was too thin to patch. She couldn't find the brighter side.

The days following the storm were bitter ones. But Mary Elizabeth was not one to wail and beat her head. "It distressed me terrible when people came in to express sympathy—the women a-bawling and clinging to me," she said. "My grief seemed too deep for that."

Even in her agony she had sympathy for the school teacher, Jean Layton, who received the blame for the children's deaths. Each morning the teacher rode to the school on horseback. On the morning of the storm the flooded creek prevented her from coming. When the storm cleared, the schoolhouse stood untouched. A school board member said to the teacher, "If you'd done your duty, the children would be safe!"

Jean Layton was sobbing as she came to see Mary Elizabeth. Gathering the teacher in her arms, and not understanding why people were so cruel, Mary Elizabeth told her, "You shouldn't feel it's your fault. It was just meant to be."

Though she exonerated the school teacher of fault, Mary Elizabeth wondered if she herself were being punished. She said, "I remembered when I had been so hurt about the coarse black sateen that they used for lining the casket of our first little baby girl. I had held that resentment for years! It always seemed that anyone would have put in white for a tiny baby. Somehow, when I thought of Bill lying there in his little white casket, so pretty and childish, I just wondered was I being punished for having wanted a white casket for the little girl?"

Alert to any premonitions, she made another connection with a dream she had during their trip West. In the dream one of the children was on fire. In desperation as she was trying to put out the flames, she began heaping dirt over the child. When she completely covered the child, the fire was out.

The next time she visited Bill's grave was on horseback after the heavy rains that followed the storm. The raw mound was of yellow, sticky clay. Hunting around she found a little bucket. "Then I climbed the fence into a new plowed field, where the earth was all rich and black and brought back some of that good earth for the grave," she said. "I don't know how many trips I made, getting that nice dirt. Then when I was putting on the last bucketful and making the grave all nice and smooth so grass and flowers would grow on it, my dream suddenly came to mind. I was patting the earth on that little mound exactly as I had patted it in that terrible dream."

The loss of the child was devastating to the Mahnkeys in itself, but the storm also caused other losses. It wiped out their business and livelihood and damaged their home severely. They had no insurance. The storm ruined the thriving town they had invested in and on which they set their hopes for the future.

The town was not rebuilt. Everyone moved away, the railroad station closed; the country roads leading into it became private trails that were eventually fenced off. In a few years there was nothing left to show there was once a town except a few house foundations, stone chimneys, and walls. Today the only way to reach the site of Melva is to hike down the railroad tracks.

Pres and Mary Elizabeth sold their house. They were forty-five and forty-three years old. In April, with only $200, a team of mules, a gray mare, one cow, and their household goods, they trudged across the hills to Mincy Valley, renting the place on Gardner Mountain to live the next year. A new house had been built since they lived there in 1915.

In June the tornado claimed its last victim. Years later Mary Elizabeth wrote about it in her journal, "Along that road now lost to sight is Trixie's grave, Bill's dog. Berta and I found her and buried her and heaped a pile of rocks on her grave. She was with the boys in the storm and was hurt."

The storm at Melva left a darkness on the family for the rest of their time. They rarely talked about it; there was just somber, wistful grief that showed through during all the years. Perhaps this tragedy was more difficult because the family did not talk about it. Even Mary Elizabeth's journal failed her. Her journals, in addition to being records of her life and opportunities for reminiscences, were also outlets for her emotions. But this time she could not write. Her journal stopped abruptly with her last entry just before the storm. The only record in that book was this comment in Bertie's handwriting: "A cyclone came March 11, 1920 and took Little Bill away from us and also took the store. We are now living over at Mincy."

Mary Elizabeth did not begin another journal until June 1931. It was fifteen years later in 1935 that she finally recorded in her journal her only written account of the day. She wrote it, not as a release for her, but as a factual telling of the events as if she wanted to fill in the blank in her life's history. Scattered in the later journals are short pangs of remembrances to show her deep love and loss.

Not until the late 1930s and early 1940s, did she begin to express her grief, loss, and guilt in her poetry. Though she rarely mentioned Bill by name, those who know her story can glimpse her feelings, such as in this one written at Mincy in the 1940s:

> He was so simple, God
> Little he knew
> Of how life would try him
> Of what he might do.
>
> How did we fail him, God
> And let him slip by
> Into dark waters
> To struggle, to die.

But life had to go on. That spring, on the Gardner Mountain place west of Mincy, Pres and Mary Elizabeth put out a crop. Doug and Reggie cut cedar posts to get enough money for Doug to attend the summer term at Southwest Missouri State Teacher's College (now Southwest Missouri State University). Mary Elizabeth and Bertie put out a garden. As the summer wore on, to avoid saddening the family, Mary Elizabeth tried not to grieve too much, but she didn't succeed.

One day when she was depressed Bertie said, "It could have been worse."

"How could it have been worse?"

"You might have been left alone," Bertie answered.

Mary Elizabeth remembered then how she had stood on the rock ledge while Pres went in the creek after the Box women. The wind was so strong it pushed her back. She realized the storm could have taken Pres and her other children. "I began canning corn, beans, tomatoes—anything from the garden. When cabbage was right, we made kraut." Painfully she was learning to cope by doing something constructive. Though not written until 1939, the following poem explains her solution.

To a Melancholy Lady

Raise some guineas
Raise some gourds
Make a little gesture towards
A richer life in service passed
To leave some imprint at the last
If not great deeds
Or golden words
Then raise some guineas
Raise some gourds.

Her candle began to glow again.

In late August 1920 Doug began teaching at Bee Creek, a school almost on the Arkansas border. To continue her schooling Bertie lived in Forsyth with Ben Prather's widow, Janie, who ran a boarding house. Reggie attended school at Mincy, but during every storm, he ran home and clung to the door.

Mary Elizabeth resumed her Sunday School class at the Mincy school building. "It took a lot of nerve to go to Sunday School past our old home, but I went," she said. "I always looked at the house as we passed and missed Bill every minute."

The next spring, 1921, they rented the Bill Moore farm, just a mile from Mincy. The family enjoyed having Bertie home the following summer and next school year when she began teaching the Mincy school. With both Bertie and Doug now living at home and teaching nearby schools, it was a busy household. Their young friends came every Sunday to visit, often staying all night. The family life gradually resumed its normal pace.

Toward the end of the school term a set of revivalists from "one of these very vigorous, loud-talking religions," as Mary Elizabeth called them, began a series of protracted meetings in Bertie's schoolhouse. Though Mary Elizabeth didn't like this kind of meeting, she went one night since it was at Bertie's school. She said, "I didn't like the preaching, for it was so loud—not like I've always felt that religion should be. Then at the close, a bunch of loud-praying women began to holler about my need of being saved. They got hold of my dress and clung to me so I couldn't get away. I was almost fainting with the turmoil. It seemed like I was being sucked down into some horrible darkness. I reached back and caught hold of Otis Yarnell, and hung to him like a drowning person. Finally he got me loose from the clutches of those women who were so bent on saving my soul."

Mary Elizabeth's behavior in the meeting caused talk. She was even hearing bits of it when a good friend of the family stopped the talk. One day he came across a group of people who were discussing it. He interrupted, "No one in that gang is qualified to show Mrs. Mahnkey the way to heaven!"

Mary Elizabeth's religion was precious and personal. She was religious, but not overtly so. Saying public prayers and attending church or publicly demonstrating her salvation did not constitute religion to her. She usually tried to do what society expected of her, playing her role to the best of her abilities. But when community pressures conflicted with her convictions, she rebelled. Religion was a way of life, a deep personal faith and commitment she lived every minute. Though baptized in the Christian Church in Kirbyville in her youth, she had no real church preference. Her main interest was the children's Sunday School class. Because of their proselytical manner, she was skeptical of preachers, usually keeping her distance.

Pres was even more wary of preachers; he rarely attended church. Mary Elizabeth fully understood.

When the parson comes a-calling
My husband slips away
He's timid like with preachers
And don't know what to say.

But if our parson really knew
Some of the many ways
He helps the poor and needy
He'd listen in amaze.

He'd forgive his Sunday fishin'
His cussin' now and then,
If he really knew the story
I know he'd say A-MEN.

Soon after little Bill's death, Pres went to church without anyone suggesting it or prodding him. Deeply hurt, he reached out for solace. He sat near the middle of the room with his family. The preacher believing this was an opportunity to save a lost soul, seized the opportunity to direct his sermon at Pres. He preached that people would be punished one way or another for their evil deeds, such as not attending church. He said that sometimes a death in the family, even that of an innocent child, would be sent to remind people of their sinful ways in order to get them to confess their sins and join the church to be saved.

Everyone there knew that the preacher was speaking directly to Pres. Suddenly Pres heaved a sigh mixed with a great sob. He rose and walked out, never entering a church again except for a funeral much later.

The two years following the storm finally passed, healing as time does. Pres did well with his hogs the summer of 1921. With what money he had and with the help of Doug and Bertie's school teaching money, he and Mary Elizabeth borrowed the remainder to buy a new business. He bought the store, gristmill, cotton gin, blacksmith shop, barn, and good creek bottom farm at Oasis, a little community on Long Creek west of Melva about six miles, in the extreme southwestern corner of Taney County. In the inflationary time of 1922, it cost $7,000. They moved in January.

Chapter 16

DOWN TO THE OLD OASIS MILL
Oasis I—the Business:
January 1922-June 1935

When Andy Youngblood comes to the mill
In that old truck of his'n
The neighbor kids all pile in too,
And then they go a-whizzin'
Down to the old Oasis mill
On Long Creek's sandy shore,
Where they swim and hunt for pawpaws,
And then they swim some more.
I wish I was a little kid
Out on that pleasant hill,
To ride with Andy in his truck
When he goes to the mill.

"This little valley is almost an island," Mary Elizabeth wrote in her journal September 23, 1934. Oasis was a beautiful, out-of-the-way place, a sparkling green valley surrounded by high blue hills and edged on the north by the cream and gray limestone bluffs which channeled the waters of spring-fed Long Creek.

In 1922 when the Mahnkey family drove in from the east through the dry ridges and cedar hills and down the steep dirt road which opened onto the valley, they thought it truly was an oasis.

Mary Elizabeth caught her breath, for even though it was winter, she had never seen anything quite so perfect. Man's industry and needs in this valley harmonized with nature. The fields, still somewhat green, as if protected from the harsh elements by the protecting wooded hills, framed the little community and the mill pond which extended about a quarter of a mile upstream from the dam. The tall, red, wooden mill house and cotton gin hugged the creek bank. The white, two-story combination store and dwelling stood directly across the road.

A row of catalpa trees lined the lane from the store to the large red barn. Willows and other trees formed a narrow border on either side of Long Creek as it made a big bend around the valley to the mill where it turned north to disappear into forested bluffs. A few other buildings, a low, hand-hewn shingled blacksmith shop and two or three other houses, clustered around the store where the road from the east converged with one road that forded the creek to follow it north and another that led south to Blue Eye and on into Arkansas.

Using the rich bottom fields for crops and the power of the stream for energy to run the mill machinery, former settlers here had done nothing to deface this valley. The partnership of man and nature gave the natural wildness a homey beauty and peace nature alone could not give. How appropriate was the name Oasis! Not only for its touch of human endeavor in a wild region, but as a haven for Mary Elizabeth and Pres after so much uncertainty, heartache, and financial difficulty. Mary Elizabeth's desire to find a place to settle was fulfilled at last. They remained at Oasis until 1935, fourteen years, longer than either of them had ever in their lives lived continuously in one place.

No period of years is without its difficulties and unpleasantness. These years were no exception, but the problems were the results of the times, their stage of life, their grown-up family, and their own personalities. Looking back on these years, Mary Elizabeth called them "hard years"—hard in adjusting to their tragic loss, in letting their grown children go, but mostly hard in trying to get out of debt and recoup their financial losses, since part of this time was in the Great Depression.

These years were also peaceful and productive with time for reading, writing letters, and visiting. All three children married, with the grandchildren bringing much joy. The Mahnkeys became part of the community, making many friends. Mary Elizabeth's growing acquaintanceship with writers, folklorists, and other professional men and women over the nation blossomed. During her stay in Oasis, she began her "In the Hills" column in the Springfield *News and Leader*, she entered contests, and she sent poems and stories to other publications, even occasionally getting a small check. She received local recognition with the publication of her book of poetry, *Ozark Lyrics*. She was emerging as a talented writer and observer of Ozark traditions.

The business operation at Oasis was similar in scope to their operation at Mincy. Once again they had a crossroads country store and post office in an area remote from any town. Even in the midst of the Depression in 1932, the post office itself brought in forty dollars a month. "Who is making that much on a farm?" Mary Elizabeth bragged in her journal. The gristmill was bigger than the one at Mincy because it had machinery for milling wheat flour, though Pres ground only corn. Pres revived the cotton gin, which had not been used for a few years. There was a blacksmith shop operated by Pres's brother Bill, who returned for a few years from the West after the shipyards closed. Bill also devised a sawmill for making shingles, using power from the mill's turbine.

In addition to these businesses, Pres added an aspect not present in the Mincy enterprise. Recognizing the appeal of Oasis, its beauty and good fishing, he built three cabins along the mill pond shore. He and Doug dismantled an old, long-vacant house on his property to get the lumber. He rented these cabins to fishermen and tourists who were beginning to visit the Taney County Ozarks.

The store and dwelling faced north overlooking the creek. There was a one-lane steel bridge across the creek, with no fill leading to it on the southern valley side. The other end abutted right against the bluff allowing only pedestrians to cross.

The useless bridge at Oasis was often the subject of conversation for newcomers. Wondering why there was a high bridge with no access on either end, a salesman at the store asked, "Why do you have a bridge like that? To make fools ask questions?"

"Yes," Mary Elizabeth answered, "and it works every time."

To give access to the bridge from the north, in 1925 there was finally financing for workers to blast out a path for a road around the bluff. Pres donated the dirt and helped build the fill on his side. With a passable bridge, the country roads north and south became Highway 86.

Across the front of the store building was a wide porch which wrapped around a few feet on either side. A sign on the false front above the porch roof read:

C.P. MAHNKEY
GENERAL STORE
OASIS, MO

The general store at Oasis about 1930. The Mahnkeys lived in
the rooms above the store.

The family living quarters were upstairs. The store was
built on a slope so that one could enter the house portion from
the back on ground level. There was also a ladder with stair
steps, which could be pulled up out of the way with a rope,
leading from the house to the rear of the one big room of the
store. A curtain hung across the upstairs entrance to the ladder, giving the living quarters some privacy. She laughed in
describing the step ladder "that I have 'clum' so often I should
be reduced." When minding the store alone during slack
times, Mary Elizabeth often worked upstairs, keeping a lookout for any customers through the door and through the three
front upstairs windows of the building.

The store hours were long—actually no regular hours at
all. Perhaps someone would come to mail a letter at six
o'clock in the morning. In the evening, if a customer wanted
to loaf and talk, one of the family stayed with him.

Occasionally, even after the family retired for the night,

people needed to do business in the store. Men stopped by for many reasons; the Mahnkeys helped them any way they could. On March 7, 1934, Mary Elizabeth wrote in her journal about a farmer who needed to store overnight some oats he bought to sow the next day. "Pres had gone to bed. I had on my bedroom slippers and my teeth out reading my *Saturday Evening Post* and had to go down and let him in. His wife and all nine children were with him. She told me the boys would have to get out and hunt up the cows, for the baby was out of milk— a bottle baby is a curious product in this country. It was so late and the little boys tired and sleepy, so I came up here and got a bucket—half filled it with night milk. I imagined their relief."

Since the store, with the post office and a telephone, was the hub of the community, the Mahnkeys were in a position to know what was happening to the neighbors, often helping them. One day a woman became ill while in the store. Mary Elizabeth cleared off a counter, laid her up there, covered her with a quilt, and tended to her until she felt better.

Another time Mary Elizabeth helped a neighbor woman in labor.

> One night a poor distracted fellow came and got my husband out of bed to go to the telephone for a doctor, as one was needed and Granny Gibson was across the river at another stork party. The doctor was gone, so we decided that I had better go down, for no one else was there, only another neighbor woman. I ran lightly along the road, not afraid in the deep soft summer darkness, for Rexie, the little dog was with me. Yet horribly frightened too, for this was a crisis, and I did not know what to do. But the sick lady told us what to do. "Take an' git some little peach tree limbs, water sprouts, if'n you can find 'em, take off the outside bark, an' scrape the inside bark down, and make hit into tea." This we did and she drank the bitter brew

uncomplainingly. Then I sat down by her bed and talked of many, many things. I even repeated old poems, and directly she fell asleep and slept sweetly till daylight and the arrival of gallant old Granny Gibson. My husband said he always knew that I was a fluent talker, but this was the first time any one had ever out talked the old stork in his determination. Yet sometimes I shudder to think what might have been if the peach tree twigs had been scraped the wrong way.

Though Mary Elizabeth never read the cards that came through her post office, for she was too busy and respected people's privacy, one day it was fortunate for her patron that she did notice the short message. There was a card from a woman who had moved away to her daughter who still lived there. Mary Elizabeth could not help reading the big, black-lettered words:

COME AT ONCE!

She knew something was seriously wrong. Since the woman's daughter and son-in-law often didn't come in for their mail for several days, she phoned them. In no time they charged past in their wagon. When they returned several days later, they stopped at the store. Mary Elizabeth asked what was the trouble.

"Oh! Mama was in jail!" said the daughter.

She explained that her mother had rented part of her farm to an old man, who began stealing her apples and giving them to his hogs. When she told him to stop, he sassed her. Angry, with what Mary Elizabeth called "that good old Arkansas spirit," she hit him in the head with a rock. He had her put in jail.

Sometimes in the store Mary Elizabeth was troubled over things she saw or heard that she couldn't figure out. She didn't ask any questions, heeding the advice of an old friend, "Jes' play shet mouth, a game that's always hard to beat."

Mary Elizabeth was always good to the traveling salesmen, or drummers. She noticed they always managed to get to Oasis late in the afternoon. Naturally, they had to stay all night. Since the word got out that she was a good cook, they timed their calls to arrive at supper time. She baked cornbread, went to the chicken house to catch a chicken, and sent it to the store for Pres to kill because she couldn't bear to kill one. Then she had to wash sheets and clean up the spare room.

A special treat for the drummers was when she fried them home-cured ham. She said, "I suppose they got chicken most of the places they stopped, for other meat was out of the question in the summer. A chicken kept itself on the hoof, so to speak, until it was needed."

The highway coming through in 1925 made quite a difference to their business, at first bringing in more customers. But gradually as more people got cars, they drove elsewhere to trade. However, one good thing resulting from the highway was that the drummers began to travel in cars instead of horses and rigs. Since there was no reason to stay at Oasis, Mary Elizabeth prepared fewer chicken dinners.

Operating the country store had its unpleasant side. Mary Elizabeth worried that Pres's temper might get him hurt. One time a younger man was quarreling with Pres about his account. The young man said, "Oh, I'll git you out here some day with them glasses off, and I'll give you a goin' over!"

Pres jerked off his glasses, ran around the counter and confronted the young man. "Go out right now, young feller, if you want to go."

The man backed off.

Never sure of herself in arithmetic, and having to handle

money in the store, Mary Elizabeth counted out the change carefully. One time a young man wanted her to cash a check of sixty dollars. Recognizing the name of the cattleman who wrote it, she cashed it. She was a bit bothered, though, when she counted out the money to see the fellow give a sly grin over his shoulder to Tuck Collier who was sitting on a sack of beans by the stove.

Tuck spoke up, "Mrs. Mahnkey, you've given that young feller ten dollars too much!"

The shrewd old man knew by that grin that she had made a mistake in the boy's favor. Mary Elizabeth had given him a twenty instead of a ten.

Another time she was making change for an old man. He counted it over and then said, "It's short five dollars."

Knowing his tricks, Mary Elizabeth had taken care to give him the right amount. She answered, "If it's short, you've either put five dollars in your pocket, or you're standing on it."

A little boy waiting in the store for his turn whooped and laughed, "Look, Mrs. Mahnkey, it's under his foot!"

But Mary Elizabeth said most people were honest. One young woman rode to the store on an iron gray mule carrying big water buckets of eggs. How she got them up on the mule Mary Elizabeth did not know, for she could hardly lift them herself. She said, "Then down in the eggs I found a brand new clean envelope. I went carrying it back to her with a little pleasantry about writing a letter after she got to the office. She had the most stricken look on her face, 'Oh, Mrs. Mahnkey,' she said, 'I am so ashamed, but some way or other I got that envelope mixed in with my things the last time I was here. I'm just returning it.'"

Cashing checks for people they did not know was always a risk. A fellow came in one day about sundown and bought a few items. Mary Elizabeth thought he was a nice young fellow, as he looked very clean cut and friendly when he handed her a check. But since she had never seen him before, she wouldn't cash his check. The young man waited until Pres finished milking and came into the store. Mary Elizabeth left to strain and care for the milk. When she came back in, Pres was selling shoes to the young man, who paid for them with the same check he offered her. It bounced.

"He hit Pres just right when he asked for shoes," Mary Elizabeth said. "Pres loved to sell shoes. I couldn't ever sell them. Seems that I always said the wrong thing or gave them shoes that pinched or rubbed."

Country storekeepers did not try shoes on customers; usually customers knew their sizes. Clerks would hand out the shoes for people to try on themselves. The Mahnkeys handed them a piece of paper to stand on to prevent soiling the shoes.

Sometimes hill people would bring in a bundle of sticks of different lengths. They would joke about there "being one more this year" or "the bresh gettin' pretty scarce out on the hillside where I have to cut these measures every fall." Each stick was cut the length of a child's foot; even adults bought shoes by the stick if they forgot their shoe number. Once, while Pres was away at a sale, a customer bought eight pairs of shoes—for his six children to begin the school term, for himself, and for his wife. When Mary Elizabeth saw Pres coming over the hill, she ran out on the porch and bragged, "I sold eight pairs of shoes!"

Mary Elizabeth was rarely afraid. Only two times in the store was she really frightened. One day when she saw three cars stop down the road, she thought she was in for something. A swarthy woman, dressed in a ragged blouse and a full skirt, came into the store. A gypsy! She purchased odd amounts of food—three cents worth of sugar, a nickel's worth of beans, four cents worth of oatmeal. When she mentioned her baby was sick and asked for some outing flannel for a dress, Mary Elizabeth gave her an extra measure. She felt sorry for any baby having such a mother.

The gypsy said, "You have been kind to me. I saw that extra measure of the flannel. Now I want to bless your money so it will increase."

"I have no money."

"Oh, you must have money in a place like this." The gypsy started behind the counter toward the post office corner.

Mary Elizabeth blocked her way, saying bravely, "You can't come back here. This is government property."

The gypsy ran out to the waiting cars. Quickly Mary Elizabeth locked the front and side doors and raced upstairs to get Pres's pistol. She could see the gypsy men gathered around the barn. Afraid the woman would tell them she was alone and that they might rob her, she prepared herself to shoot anyone who stepped on the porch. Fortunately, they all got into their cars and left. As she watched the cars easily ascend the long mountain road out of the valley, she decided they had powerful automobiles, for most local cars puffed and wheezed before they reached the top.

Once when she was alone in her upstairs lookout, she spotted a car coming, much bigger and finer than any in the country at that time. The motor was so quiet she would have missed it if she hadn't been looking right at it. The driver, a large, handsome well-dressed man with his hat pulled down over his eyes, stopped down the road a short distance, left the motor running, and ran into the store.

"I need some groceries and I'm in a great hurry," he panted. "You don't mind if I help you pack them up?"

Mary Elizabeth got a big cardboard box as he began grabbing items off the shelves, saying, "Tomatoes! Salmon! Pork and Beans! Crackers! Corn!"

When they had the box full, he took out a billfold and thumbed through the bills. She tried not to stare at the hundred and five hundred dollar bills. Sorting through the bundle, he pulled out a fifty dollar bill.

Mary Elizabeth looked at it, "I don't believe I can change that!" She lied. She didn't want to unlock the post office money while alone with him.

"I must have some change." He looked down at her frightened expression and added in a kind, reassuring voice, "Mother, I wouldn't harm a hair of your head."

She walked to the post office. Her hand did not tremble on the hard combination as she unlocked the money. She knew the man had harmed others, but she also knew he would not harm her. She counted out the change. No one in the country saw the fellow again. Believing that he was heading for a hide-out in the hills, Mary Elizabeth was glad he bought good substantial groceries.

One aspect of the Oasis valley that made it so picturesque was the tall, red gristmill across from the white store. The mill was built of massive hand-hewn timbers. Mary Elizabeth admired the beautiful rugged wooden beams, just like the timbers at the Mincy mill, but she never considered giving a dance in Oasis mill. That was all over. The three-story mill was built in 1876 when the name was Cedar Valley. Later a dam was built at a narrow place in the creek, across solid rock. Impounded water released into the mill race turned the overshot wheel. The old wheel had been replaced by a turbine before the Mahnkeys' time.

Pres never ground wheat. The availability of store-bought, hard wheat flour lessened the demand for home-grown soft wheat flour. However, the demand for cornmeal remained great. Pres used water power to turn the turbines until a big flood in 1927 washed out the dam. Then he installed a gasoline engine.

Willing to do almost anything to get back on his feet financially, Pres repaired the old cotton gin. Though the heyday of cotton in the hill valleys was over, he realized that possibilities were still there for extra income for farmers and for him. Acquiring good seed, he encouraged interested farmers to plant cotton. At harvest time, hiring two men and with Reggie to help him, he worked night and day at the gin. During the Depression time, it brought in needed income to the area.

Mary Elizabeth enjoyed the cotton harvest. She said, "It was such a pretty sight. The farmers would drive in with great big wagons full of that fluffy white cotton. Somehow I was always nervous when Pres was running the gin. It was old and I was afraid something would fall off or be thrown out and kill him. But he made a little money on it, and that was what we needed." Cotton ginning at this time in Oasis was profitable for only a couple of years. The farmers quit raising cotton and turned to tobacco, which was a better money crop and did not require quite as much labor to grow.

Though the Mahnkeys never planted any cotton, they had to harvest one crop. A blacksmith near them ran up a large store bill, saying he would pay it when he sold his cotton. Before picking time he left for Oklahoma, telling Pres he could have his cotton crop for the picking.

Even after their work of picking the cotton, its sale didn't pay the bill. Mary Elizabeth said, "Pres wrote the man a sassy letter saying that if he was as good a Christian as he pretended to be, he would send him the rest of the money. We never heard from him."

Chapter 17

COMMON THINGS HAVE BEAUTY, CHARM, AND GRACE
Oasis II—The Community and Family: January 1922 - June 1935

I stick smart weed and beggar lice
In with my bouquet
And then I smile
When my friends say,
"How beautiful, how delicate
What can these blossoms be?"
"O yes," I say, "O yes,
But it takes one just like me
To show you all
That common things
Have beauty, charm, and grace,
But not until you see them
Stuck in a crystal vase."

"For getting a good slant on people of all kinds, in all kinds of moods, in all degrees of goodness and cussedness, you can't beat country storekeeping. You see all and know all," said Mary Elizabeth.

More than just an observer and humanist, she recorded. Her best writing dealt with the commonplace things and people around her. She lived the life and she captured that life for readers to see its beauty, its worth. During the Oasis years she became known for her folkish tales, even sometimes using the pen name, "The Backwoods Contributor."

Her writing output during this period increased greatly for she had more time to devote to it. In 1928 she learned to use a typewriter. In 1931 she got a battery-operated radio. Keeping abreast of the world news as well as that of her little community, she sent prose and poetry to periodicals or newspapers that might be interested. Her success in being published, however, was limited mainly to contributors' columns, such as "The Forum" of *The Country Home* magazine and "The Wastebasket" of the Springfield dailies. The first of her monthly "In the Hills" columns, which appeared in "The Wastebasket," was in 1930. Many of the stories and events recounted in this biography came from her writings during this period.

Mary Elizabeth recognized the bad and the good in people, even in the old-timers, native older people whom she generally admired. But she wrote, "They were very human. They fell out and 'fit' over boundary lines and over strayed cattle and hogs, and often I've seen one group of children hustling down the trail before the others because they had been forbidden to speak to So-and-So's children under penalty of getting all the clothes 'whupt off'en 'em'."

She followed an older woman's advice, "The onliest way to get along with that gang is to give 'em a good lettin' alone."

She admired most old-timers for their dedication, industry, and honesty. Some of them had very little education or opportunities.

One of the older hill men whom Mary Elizabeth admired was Johnny Jackson, who lived in Blue Eye country (according to Mary Elizabeth, the community got its name because of the very blue eyes of the first postmaster). Uncle Johnny and his wife worked hard. They made a tomato crop one year, setting out the plants in ground so hilly and rocky Mary Elizabeth wondered how the old couple could even stand up on it. Cheerfully, Uncle Johnny brought eggs to Oasis to sell. He rode in on his gray mare with his worn sweater collar full of snow. In the egg basket when Mary Elizabeth counted out the eggs, she found snow and bits of cedar. Then she knew that on the way over the mare had shied and bumped into the cedars with him.

Though he had a reputation of being a fine fiddle player, no one could remember hearing him play. Mary Elizabeth explained, "He had joined up with that religious band that tried to pull me in, and they considered fiddle-playing a sin." One Saturday he came into the store to sit and talk all afternoon, dressed as many old-timers did in their good shoes and a clean Sunday shirt and new overalls. Uncle Johnny picked up a fiddle someone had left there. For a few moments he sat holding it. He ran his hand over the polished woodwork; he began twisting the keys and twanging the strings with gentle but expert fingers.

"Play us a bit," Mary Elizabeth urged. The others in the store watched him in anticipation. The temptation was too much; he began playing soft and low, then louder. Uncle Johnny played all afternoon. Pres and Mary Elizabeth agreed it was the finest fiddling they ever heard. The store was filled with old tunes he had loved years before, like "The Girl I Left Behind Me," "Forked Deer," "Hell Among the Yearlings," and "Billy in the Low Ground."

The Mahnkeys heard that next day in church meeting he prayed for forgiveness. He said he was tempted to play the fiddle down at Mahnkeys', and if God would forgive him, he would never do it again.

"I suppose he never did," Mary Elizabeth said, "For no one ever heard of him touching a fiddle again."

One night when the old fellow came to the store to get coffee, he was so tired he could hardly walk. He said he and his wife hauled in hay all afternoon. Pres cussed and asked what all his big stout kinfolks were doing. "Oh, they had to ride to town to get commodities," said Uncle Johnny, "and all they got after ridin' all that way in the heat was a little old butter and some black strap molasses."

It wasn't just the older people that Mary Elizabeth understood. Her sympathy for and understanding of young people was apparent in her writing. In a time when an unmarried girl was ruined for life if she had a baby, and when no one talked about it in public, Mary Elizabeth wrote:

> A young mountain lad, all unconsciously played the part of Arthur Dimmsdale in *The Scarlet Letter* in one of the little dramas that are occasionally enacted in our hills, with no audience, with no comment, yet with tears and agony. A little neighbor lass had loved him far too well, and not at all wisely, but fiercest family coercion could not bring her to utter a name as father of her little love child. She devoted herself to her baby, and when it died, she was a piteous, heartbroken little figure. The day of the burying, when kind neighbors assembled to assist to prove their sympathy and loyalty, a lanky lad stood silently watching, his dark face sullen and morose, the mask worn by the true mountaineer to hide all emotion. As the girl mother, wildly weeping, took her place in the rough vehicle, he detached himself from the group of men and boys, and with swift effortless stride, reached her side and seated himself by her, thus publicly announcing his guilt, his paternity. The next day they were married.

Another such case Mary Elizabeth caught in this verse which she published in her column.

Two Dresses

I had three dresses
But now I've got two,
For the plain little white one
Trimmed in bright blue
I cut into garments,
So tiny and small,
For my poor little baby
A-comin' this fall.

The boy that I worshipped
Told me black lies
An' run off an' left me
With tears in my eyes.
O, poor little baby
With no name at all.
Maybe God will forgive me
And help me this fall.

Mary Elizabeth retold many stories. "One of my father's many good stories was about a Quakerish old lady, who sat serene and unmoved at one of the fall camp meetings when there was singing and shouting and weeping. At last one of the sisters approached her, threw her arms around her and shrieked, 'O, Sister Johnson, don't you love Jesus?' Sister Johnson unfolded her little white kerchief, folded it primly again, and said, 'Well, I reckon I ain't got anything against him.'"

Some of the most appealing of Mary Elizabeth's gleanings during the Oasis years are short sayings or anecdotes. The following were written during the early 1930s.

Augusta Atchinson is the bright intelligent daughter of a widow, and she always worked hard, picking berries, working in the cannery, doing farm work, etc., and we used to say "poor little Gusta. The other day she married a big handsome youngster named Guy Poor, so she is now "little Gusta Poor."

The poverty of the poor is their destruction. Thus we read in Proverbs. Thus we actually observe in real life, for Floyd, the thin-legged, black-eyed oldest son in the poorest family of the neighborhood had come suddenly and unexpectedly into a fortune, some nickels and dimes from a kindly tourist. He was gloriously blowing it at our little store for pop, candy, gum, and gently I said, "Floyd, child, why not buy yourself a nice little shirt?"

"Huh," very derisively, very haughtily, "I've gotta shirt."

After an unusually hard winter, a neighbor drove down to the mill and store, and his horses were piteously thin. One of the ubiquitous humorists said, "Well, well, you've done somethin' the buzzards couldn't a-done. You've picked them hosses' bones and never busted their hides.

Huldah Huckstep was a wonderful woman. Nearing eighty her crisp comments were worth attention. A certain friend would not praise her little daughter for her small tasks well done nor for her sweet and lovely conduct, because she feared it would make her vain. "And yet," said Huldah Huckstep, "you pat your dog on the head when he pleases you."

There is no other place in the nation where the depression has wrought such slight havoc as here in the very southern Ozarks. The real Ozarker merely tightened his belt and marched on at his task. It is as Uncle Frank Jackson remarked. In front of our little crossroads store, he had mounted his filly to go home, the saddle festooned with stovepipe joints and a long well bucket. He was stoutly maintaining his seat on the lunging animal, and said grimly, "Oh, she won't buck long."

Renting out the cabins and meeting the tourists and other newcomers in the store gave Mary Elizabeth many opportunities to know this new breed of people in the hills. She liked and respected many of the tourists and newcomers, appreciating their contribution to the development of the area; others she bemoaned. Like the native hill people, there were good and bad.

Her fame as an Ozark reporter and writer reached the editor of a St. Louis paper. He asked her for "short snappy paragraphs of the reaction of the natives to the tourists." She abhorred stereotyped thinking about either tourists or Ozarkers.

Said I to myself, "How silly!" What could be the 're-action'? What is a tourist, only a person like you or me, out in a different place, probably interested in seeing everything new and different? We used to meet many delightful people at Oasis. They would pause for a closer look at Long Creek and the bluffs. As I crossed the road coming from the barn one afternoon, a big beautiful car stopped, and a couple seemed anxious to talk to me. Idly I pulled up a little weed by the roadside, crushed it in my fingers, and told them this was wild sage. How eagerly interested they were! So I showed them growing also close by the pennyroyal, and blue vervain. Maybe if I had written this in a certain style, and said I was barefooted and had just tossed away a chew of tobacco, the 're-action' might have pleased the editor. My re-action was that of any ordinary native endeavoring to please the passing guest, folks who were charming and intelligent. The ones who were not interested in new places and people sped by to the nearest cold drink spot. They did not see the skip-jacks in the clear water, nor the kingfisher, nor the old mill.

One newcomer, whom she admired, settled in, took his share of responsibilities in the community, such as serving on the school board, and sent his son to Mary Elizabeth's Sunday School class. She wrote:

> And I am persuaded that the hills will always claim their own, and everlastingly be renewed and strengthened by such as these good people. We are proud of our growing fame as a resort country, and then, we are proud when old fields are reclaimed, and new grasses started and little boys from such families go to the little village Sunday School.

Often she found something to laugh about concerning the tourists.

> We had three little cabins along the creek bank that we could rent to tourists. Since we were in such an out-of-the-way spot, we rented them to the same tourists year after year, for not many people could find them. One young couple came from Tulsa each summer. They were Roy and Mildred. Roy loved to fish, but Mildred would fuss every minute they were there. She didn't like to fish! She didn't like the country! She didn't like anything, not even fresh air, I reckon. She would trail along after Roy, just moaning and groaning. We used to laugh about it, and yet we were sorry for him. Then one summer he didn't come. The next summer, there he was again, and Reggie ran down to help him get settled in the cabin he always took. Then Reggie came back and said, "Roy has his wife

with him, but it isn't Mildred!" Sure enough, he had gotten a divorce from Mildred and married a long-legged young thing that would stride ahead of him on the way to the river and out fish him and all the young fellows in the neighborhood.

Usually the hill people came out ahead of the tourists when confronted one to one. From the store porch Mary Elizabeth witnessed old Andy Smith coming from the north to cross the bridge to the mill with a sack of grain lying across the mule's back. There was an unwritten law that the first one on the one-lane bridge across Long Creek had the right of way; others must wait their turn. The driver of a large touring car loaded with tourists followed him onto the bridge and blasted his horn again and again, trying to hurry Uncle Andy and his plodding old gray mule. Uncle Andy knew he had priority.

There's a twickety-twock on the bridge;
Uncle Andy is coming to mill
On his old gray mule, so steady and true,
From over yan side of the hill.

The old gray mule lays back his ears
At the sound of a motor horn,
And a rich powerful car whines down to a creep
Trailing the mule and the corn.

Serene, undismayed, Uncle Andy rides on,
Secure in his right of way.
"Let'em toot, let'em cuss,
I'm fust on the bridge
An' I'm goin' to mill today."

Storekeeping, milling, ginning, writing her column, and tending to household and farm chores continued at Oasis as at the other places the Mahnkeys lived. However, because of the length of time they stayed there and the ages of their children, the stay at Oasis was made sad for Mary Elizabeth and Pres when their children left home. They both admitted they were now past their prime. Though vigorous and active in their fifties, they knew the time of old age was approaching. Pres pushed himself to the limit to get a stake, often becoming despondent and ill when things got worse. Though feeling just as depressed, Mary Elizabeth kept her cheery demeanor for the world to see, confiding her thoughts to her journals.

During these years Pres lost his mother (1927) and his brother John Henry (1934); Mary Elizabeth's oldest brother Frank died (1922) and her youngest sister Mag (1930). Only Dick, Joe, Deal, and her aging mother remained of the Prather family, and they were in California.

When the Mahnkeys moved to Oasis in January 1922, Doug and Bertie were in the midst of teaching their school terms. When school let out, they both rejoined the family, obtaining schools nearby for the next term so they could live at home. Doug taught Cedar Valley (down the creek) for two terms; Bertie taught Brush Creek (up the creek) for three terms. Both rode horseback to their schools.

Doug ran for and won the office of county clerk of Taney County in 1926 and moved to Forsyth where he made his life-long home. He served four terms, until 1934, when, like his grandfather, he was elected to the House of Representatives in the Missouri State Legislature. On June 13, 1928, he married Merle Walker from Bradleyville. Mary Elizabeth felt as if she already knew Merle because years before she had attended the Bradleyville Normal with Merle's parents W.A.

(Doc) Walker and Josie Harris.

During this time Doug was also studying for the law. It was still possible to practice law without a law degree from college by passing the very difficult bar examination. At every opportunity Doug studied and took preparatory courses. Twice he did not succeed in the examination. Hurting for him when he failed, while others with some influence passed, Mary Elizabeth remembered times when her hopes were not fulfilled. She wrote in her journal April 27, 1934, "I had hoped my children would have been spared the bitterness that was in my cup."

Bertie seemed happy as a young grown woman at home. She enjoyed her teaching. Mary Elizabeth hoped that she, like Doug, would be able to attend some college. Bertie had many boyfriends, "but few tarried, probably because Pres was so strict with her," Mary Elizabeth said.

The coming of the highway in 1925 caused them to lose their girl. Mary Elizabeth explained, "It seems a sort of give and take for Pres had worked so hard to get a road across that bridge. Finally there was the road gang ready to do it.

"Many of them were nice young fellows and some had young wives with them. With Bertie and Reggie at our place, the store was soon headquarters for all of them. Someone had left an old organ at the store and Bertie could play it. Reggie would play his banjo, and then a young, tall, dark, handsome young fellow, named Roy Jones, would play the fiddle. He was really a young man of striking appearance and so musical! Everyone said these three could make the best music they had ever heard anywhere. Often the store was open until midnight, with playing and singing making echoes. I was always worn out, for I had so much to do and the gangs of people bothered me."

In July 1925 Bertie eloped with Roy. "I just thought I

couldn't live," Mary Elizabeth said. "Pres was stunned, too. You could imagine that he would have raved and sworn, but he didn't. He just sat down and dropped his head. He didn't have anyone in mind that he wanted Bertie to marry. He just didn't want her to marry anybody. He wanted her to have a business career, for she had such a good mind for business. Roy had nothing but his fiddle." Roy also had a wild reputation.

Pres stated that they could not come back; Mary Elizabeth did not argue. She knew time would help. About a month later, early one morning, Essie Youngblood's husband came to the store and said, "Essie's going to have company today. She said for you to come up and stay all day." From his grin Mary Elizabeth knew something was afoot. She quickly finished her work, put some things in her basket and walked rapidly down the road to Essie's house. When she turned the bend, Bertie came flying down the road to meet her.

"The newlyweds stayed up on the creek with Roy's grandpa's folks, and Roy helped make the hay crop," Mary Elizabeth said. "Then finally, I couldn't stand it any longer. I had a talk with Pres, and then I wrote a note to Bertie, telling her to come down. She came down a-horseback and everything was fine. When they had been married thirteen months, their boy, Leon, was born on June 16, 1926. It was the old story you hear so often. Pres was foolish over the boy, and Leon always worshipped his grandfather."

However, it took much longer for Pres to get completely over his hurt at her elopement. It was not until seven years later that he entered Bertie and Roy's home.

The Joneses went to Pontiac, Michigan, to work in the automobile industry, returning to Missouri briefly in 1929 to live in one of the cabins on the mill pond. Winnie Bee was born there April 17, 1929. Her name was Winifred, shortened to Winnie. It was Pres who tacked on the name, Bee, which has stuck all her life. Every time Mary Elizabeth looked out, she saw little Leon tagging after his grandfather, driving up the hogs, going fishing, or going after the cows. In March 1930 the Joneses returned from Michigan for good. Roy worked out when he could, farmed, and drove the mail route from Kirbyville to Mincy.

Reggie was the last to leave home. When the family moved to Oasis, Reggie was fourteen. He attended Doug's school, worked with his father in the store, mill and gin, and with the farm work in their valley fields. A hunter and fisherman, he loved action; he loved the out-of-doors. Following Doug and Bertie's lead of school teaching did not suit him at all.

His proficiency on the banjo took him to dances all over the "wild and lawless country that was not far from us, and it made us so uneasy," Mary Elizabeth said. "One day he came to me and said, 'Mother, I want you to sign my papers so I can join the Army.' I protested that he was too young, but he said, 'If you don't, Mother, I'm a goner!' I didn't hesitate any longer."

In October 1926, he joined the Army. Mary Elizabeth agonized over his leaving, but consoled herself that there were no local jobs. The hills couldn't hold him. He was an active, restless young man seeking adventure.

The Army suited Reggie. Mary Elizabeth didn't worry about him the first few years, though she missed him dreadfully. She wrote February 20, 1934 in her journal, "C.P. [she nearly always used Pres's initials when referring to him in her journals] is gone again this morning. So sad and lonely. Used to be when I was left like this, Reggie was here to help me and we joked and played all day, and laughed about eating up C.P.'s candy and pork and beans."

In 1928, Reggie married Bertha Klein from Bismarck, North Dakota, where he was stationed. Remembering back on it, Mary Elizabeth wrote in her journal June 1, 1947, "Reggie's marriage was quite a shock. He was not intended for family cares."

Reggie soon discovered that his thirty-one dollars a month army pay was not enough to support a wife and apartment. Though Mary Elizabeth lived for his letters, she began to dread what they would contain because Reggie gambled and drank excessively at times. On April 27, 1934, she wrote in her journal. "Very disturbing letter from Reggie Monday. I don't know what to do—really Lord—I do not. 'These children Thou gavest me.'" Reggie didn't get the hoped for promotion to corporal. "But his troubles were greater than that! I dare not write it down." All his parents could do was send money from time to time.

In the drought year of 1934 on the day of the first rain since early spring, she thought about Reggie. "August 17— Poor Reggie. He would never listen to us. And Papa and I have been rather remarkable persons for the opportunities given us. I'll say—he is out in this delightful drizzle now— planted six rows of beans." She and Pres could always spring back. Even after the devastating drought, Pres was planting in the first rain, hopeful of a fall garden. But she feared for Reggie's ability to cope.

When Reggie left for the Army, Mary Elizabeth had to fight loneliness. For twenty-four years she had had children with her. Coming from a large family and accustomed to the activities of her own three grown children, during the years 1925-26 when all three left home, she and Pres both suffered. Though they saw people constantly at the store, and many of these people were dear to them, they weren't family. Mary Elizabeth missed Doug's good advice and loyalty, Bertie's constant companionship, and Reggie's youthful exuberance.

When Bertie and Roy lived nearby in Oasis, their children began to fill that space. Doug's children when they arrived were no less precious. Pat was born in 1930 and Mary Jo in 1933. The birth of a new grandson had to be announced to the world. She wrote in her Oasis column:

> Little Charles Patrick Mahnkey was an honored Oasis visitor Sunday, but he was disappointingly silent regarding the beauties of the Long Creek Valley. However, as he was only three weeks old, we pardoned him. We were glad to see Doug and Merle again, so proud, yet humble, in the beautiful new role of parents.

One of Mary Elizabeth's original sketches from her scrapbook showing Doug with his new son, Pat, during the campaign year, 1930.

This is my solace as I grow old—
Little boy hands to pat and to hold,
Little boy listening, smiling, bright-eyed,
Little boy nestling close by my side,
Little boy eager to hear granny tell
The old, old stories we both love so well.
The years may have taken much pleasure and joy

> But I find them once more,
> With this dear little boy.

It wasn't long until the actions and sayings of Pat and his little sister got reported.

> I learned early to be careful in telling mossy old jokes before Mary Jo. I was talking about our first real drought, in 1901, when there was no dew, no showers, when the barrels fell apart, and the dry, crusty earth cracked open. "It was so dry, the old sow wouldn't hold slop until she had been soaked overnight." Mary Jo fixed a judicial and enquiring eye upon me as she said, "But what was there to soak the old sow in?"

Chapter 18

ROSES & GARDENS ARE KINDRED THINGS
Oasis III—Friends and Growing Reputation:
January 1922 - June 1935

He was a high-hat, pompous and stately.
(In anguish I twisted my apron strings.
Wealth and dignity are fearsome things.)
Wondering what I should try to say
To this potentate who had come my way.
(Twisting and folding my apron strings
Wealth and dignity are fearsome things.)
Then he stooped to caress my flowering moss
He smiled at my rose on its cedar cross.
And I dropped my twisted apron strings
For roses and gardens are kindred things.

Though she had many acquaintances, Mary Elizabeth did not become close to many people. But when she found a kindred spirit, she treasured that friendship the rest of her life.

Much of the companionship and joy Mary Elizabeth enjoyed during the Oasis years was through her increasingly wider circle of friends. Those in Oasis she saw frequently, those from Hollister and Branson and out of the county, occasionally.

From the beginning she and Mettie Davis liked each other. Mettie lived across the creek and up a woods trail about a mile. Both women loved to read and to discuss books they read. Mary Elizabeth wrote little jingles for Mettie about her children. Mettie treasured these poems, as well as all of Mary Elizabeth's writings. She saved them in scrapbooks.

Pres and Mary Elizabeth were not always on the giving end of acts of kindnesses. They received their share. Mary Elizabeth said, "I think Henry Davis [Mettie's husband] was the best man that ever lived. Pres took the measles one time. The idea of him taking the measles, and us there alone with a store, farm, and post office! Henry came down every day to help me. He carried in wood, made fires, and built egg cases [for the store]. Mettie was always sending down their little girl, May, with something for me, wild onions or maybe sheep sorrel to make a pie."

Both women loved flowers, inside and out. During the winter Mary Elizabeth's house plants usually died; it was impossible with their one wood heating stove to keep the plants from freezing. Every spring Mary Elizabeth would ask Mettie to get her some cuttings from Mrs. Tuttle, another friend who lived near Mettie. Mrs. Tuttle always managed to keep her plants alive in her stone house.

Margaret Tuttle and her husband, C.S. Tuttle, lived downstream at the end of a trail that followed the creek under a high bluff and then climbed a high hill overlooking the valley. Mary Elizabeth loved to walk or ride horseback there, especially in the spring.

The Road to Tuttles

As I went up to Tuttles
I did not go alone
For dear old friends were with me
By every log and stone.

> Johnny-Jump-Up hailed me,
> And Buttercup so shy,
> And from a ferny ledge
> Sweet Blue Bell winked her eye.
> Bob White then saluted
> With call so clear and sweet,
> While his little wife went whirring
> From the pathway at my feet.
> And there was Long Creek singing
> In the valley just below;
> While the Redbuds and Dogwoods,
> Waved their banners to and fro.
> As I went up to Tuttles
> I did not go alone,
> For dear old friends were with me
> By every log and stone.

When Mary Elizabeth reached the house, Mrs. Tuttle laughingly accused her of not coming to visit *her*, but "to stand on the front porch and gaze and gaze."

However, it was more than nature's beauty which brought her to Mrs. Tuttle's home time and again. In the companionship with this older lady, she found a rare and cultured beauty which filled an aesthetic need. Mary Elizabeth admired her ability to live elegantly in very straitened means. She described her home.

> The kitchen was the living room, also the dining room. And here was the cream separator, a small model on a clean scoured oaken bench. Then there were fat sacks of beans, and cowpeas, ready at hand, when she could find time to hull them. There were baskets of eggs, often a basket with cheerful little chicks. Big blue and white crocks, even sitting along the wall on the floor. Yet it was orderly, everything seemed rightfully in place. The window panes

were diamond bright, the tissue thin old white curtains as white as snow. And house plants bloomed in all the windows and hung from hooks and sat on top of the cabinets and in every place where there was room for one. Her long dining table was always set, with a spotless cloth, and then, another cloth white as snow spread over all. I used to marvel at the napkins, made from bleached flour sacks, exquisitely hemstitched, many with crocheted butterfly corners.

One afternoon I asked a newcomer lady to go with me. Of course we were invited to eat. This day it was fried chicken and fresh light bread, buttered thickly. I asked the newcomer lady to notice the napkins. On the way home she said something that gave me quite a jolt. "Wasn't that silly to put all that work on flour sacks?"

Another dear friend was Cinda Kenner. During the later years at Oasis when Cinda and her husband Allen moved in, they were with the Mahnkeys often. Since neither Pres nor Mary Elizabeth ever learned to drive, Allen Kenner drove Pres many places.

Other friends who lived in Hollister or Branson visited often, coming for her to take her with them to special events or for overnight. Mrs. Frank Dawes had read her columns in the Springfield paper and sought her out when she moved from Nebraska into the nearby hills.

Mary Elizabeth's circle of friends and acquaintances comprised a far greater area than Taney County. Other people visited her. Vance Randolph stopped by often. The Mahnkeys admired the noted folklorist and gave him material for his collections. During a visit on May 21, 1934, he told Pres that Mary Elizabeth was a wonderful writer, and the Depression was the only thing keeping her from making money.

May Kennedy McCord, folklorist and radio personality

from Springfield radio station KWTO, became one of her
greatest friends during the later years at Oasis. Mrs. McCord
wrote in *Missouri Magazine* of her first meeting with Mary
Elizabeth at Oasis:

> We were received with dignity, and the quiet, sweet-faced
> woman seemed a bit overcome that we should make a pil-
> grimage to her shrine—indeed her strange, grey eyes
> struggled to hold back the tears. But she knew we were
> kindred spirits though we had never met her.
>
> Mary Elizabeth Mahnkey has never been far t'other
> side of the mountain—she longs for the beautiful things
> of the world—for the companionship and sweet under-
> standing of those who speak her language. These she does
> not have over much. She is lonely—but never would it
> pass her lips. She is not the complaining kind—a true
> daughter of the pioneers!
>
> We came away silent and admiring, withal a bit sub-
> dued, but with no words to describe this woman with the
> light in her face from the candle within her soul. Mary
> Elizabeth Mahnkey, an Ozarkian, whose poetry ranks with
> the great.

Missouri artist Thomas Hart Benton visited her. Writer
Rose Wilder Lane was a long-time friend. One time when she
visited Mary Elizabeth she brought along her mother, Laura
Ingalls Wilder from Mansfield, Missouri. This was before
Mrs. Wilder wrote her series of "Little House" books.

Mary Elizabeth was a friend of the writer, artist, sculp-
tor, and creator of the Kewpie dolls, Rose O'Neill. One time
Doug's family took Mary Elizabeth to visit Rose at her home,
Bonniebrook, in northern Taney County. Miss O'Neill was
lounging on her porch in her long red robe, surrounded by
three or four admirers. As soon as she saw Mary Elizabeth,

she jumped up, ran out into the yard, and hugged "my dear, dear Mamie," putting her cheek to Mary Elizabeth's in her customary affectionate greeting for good friends.

Another visitor was John B. Neihardt, a well-known epic poet who lived in Branson at the time. As any aspiring writer, Mary Elizabeth wanted to show him her writings, but did not. She wrote in her journal October 29, 1934, "I did not seize the opportunity to deluge him with stale manuscripts and my silly poems, for O, I know how it is to be gobbled up by selfish people."

Her friendship with Fanny Dawes and Neihardt helped bring about the first publication of her poems in book form. Through Fanny Dawes, Mary Elizabeth became involved in the Taneyhills Study Club of Branson and Hollister. Mrs. Dawes came for Mary Elizabeth to take her to several meetings.

One of the projects of the Study Club was to start a library in Branson, a project of great interest to Mary Elizabeth. To raise money, the ladies asked her if they could publish a book of her poems. Pleased and honored that these educated women thought so highly of her poetry, she readily assented. Fanny Dawes took a box of Mary Elizabeth's poems that she had written through the years; a committee read them and decided which ones to include in the book. She let them have the money from sales of the book to begin the library.

Mary Elizabeth admired Fanny Dawes's business ability. Mrs. Dawes had the books printed at the Sunshine Press in Springfield, making enough advance sales to pay for the first 500 copies. Then in July, 1934, when the book came out, Mrs. Dawes took Mary Elizabeth to a luncheon the Study Club held in her honor. "It was a proud day for me. At last I had some recognition among my home folks," she said.

Though Fanny Dawes was the instigator of the little

book of poems, the introduction by John B. Neihardt assured the book of an audience of serious poetry lovers. Mary Elizabeth admired Neihardt's poetry and was honored by his interest in her poetry, but she was bothered by his introduction.

She explained, "In his introduction he seemed to be apologizing for my work. I didn't think the poems were literature, of course, but it seems bad to start out apologizing for something—like a woman apologizing for a cake when she knows it is the best she could make."

The next edition of the poems was published by the print shop of the School of the Ozarks, because she had always admired the school. There were plans to publish a third edition. "Fanny still insisted that we have that same introduction; I said we'd just forget it," Mary Elizabeth said. "I'd rather not have the book than have to see that introduction again. So the book stopped right there."

This is the preface by Neihardt that she objected to.

> My interest in these lyrics is less concerned with the great art of Literature than with what I believe to be far more important in the last analysis—the personality of the human being who wrote them. The sympathetic reader cannot fail to note how often, here and there throughout the collection, something like a warm, soft light breaks through, lives briefly in phrase or line, and then is lost awhile in undistinguished words as commonplace as common living mostly is. As the friends of Mrs. Mahnkey know, the light thus briefly but often revealed is that of a rare human spirit, and the warmth grows out of the womanly heart of one who is truly a good neighbor to her fellows and to everything that lives.

Without understanding Mary Elizabeth's sensitivity and her growing self-perception as a literary artist, most people do not understand her objections. Like Fanny Dawes, they see Neihardt's introduction as a compliment. As a critic he recognized that the strength of her poetry was her ability to capture the beauty and warmth in commonplace living. He recognized the glow of her candle.

After Mary Elizabeth's death, other editions of *Ozark Lyrics* were published by the School of the Ozarks (1972 and 1980). Doug and Bertie selected the poems for these editions. Needless to say, there was a different introduction. In 1985, The Little Photo Gallery at Forsyth printed still another edition.

The original publication of the book of fifty-five poems was a bittersweet experience. Though appreciative of the Study Club's sponsorship, she grew to be unhappy about it. Because the book was a money-making project for the club, discussion in the club meetings, in Mary Elizabeth's opinion, became mercenary, thus spoiling for her the beauty and emotion portrayed in the poems.

In contrast to the introduction's hint that the poems were not really art, there were some complimentary comments from reviewers which pleased her.

Noted folklorist Vance Randolph wrote, "They are the only verses in which I have ever heard the authentic music of the Ozark hills."

Marion B. Pickens, Editor of *Missouri Magazine*, wrote that "the rich simplicities of nature run like a golden thread and withal a quiet contentment, a wholesome creed of living, that reaches out from the printed pages and soothes."

Editor of the *Taney County Republican* W.E. Freeland wrote in his editorial, "The charm of Mrs. Mahnkey's poems is their unstudied expression. She writes what is in her heart and does not worry about the yardstick of rhetoricians. After all, unrestricted expression makes human values."

Even this last complimentary review indicated that the

poems lacked form. Her reaction to the repetitive comments about her irregular verse form is evident in the following poem:

> Illiterate, he? and yet he sees
> Wild gnomes, and harps in leafless trees
> And pale gold stars bend low to tell
> The secret of this strange, bright spell.
> Yet some disdained his lyric song
> For meter, verb and tense were wrong.

Because of the criticisms she sometimes made light of her "pomes," and referred to herself as an "Imposter."

> "Do you write of moods?"
> "No, I write of *woods*
> Or *dogs* or an old *stone wall.*
> By this you know,
> Ere you further go,
> That I am no poet at all."

But rather than belittling her ability, perhaps she is asking us to look more closely at what she is saying. "I write of woods" may have meant the beauty of an Ozark fall as in "October."

> There's a murmur in the woods of mystery.
> There's a ripple on the water as of tears.
> And all this blaze of royal, glorious colors
> Cannot allay our vague and nameless fears.
> For it is a funeral train of solemn splendor;
> Sweet summer soon will rest upon that bier,
> And summer's friends are terrified and fainting.
> The end for them is drawing very near.

This verse is not only an appreciation of the beauty of woods and scenery, but could be a metaphor for the end of life.

She says, "I write of dogs." In "Prisoner," she tells about her dog's night hunting forays. She ends the poem by comparing herself to the dog, a comment on women's place in her society.

> This may be envy that I feel
> That I must stay at home
> Tied to convention's high stone wall—
> Never free to roam.

And "old stone walls?" In the verse above, the stone wall is a metaphor for society's restrictions. In the following poem, Mary Elizabeth uses a literal stone wall to show that a man labeled a failure is really a "Benefactor." Common people like him make life richer for everyone.

> They said old Steve Bailey
> Was not much good
> But he cleared all brush
> From the white oak wood.
>
> He walled with stone
> The dripping spring
> Where birds alight
> To bathe and sing.
>
> He planted grape vines
> And a walnut tree
> Then left this beauty
> For you and me.

These qualities in her poetry were those that her readers understood, as did many of the women of the Taney Hills Study Club. Though she was a paid member of the club only

Roses and Gardens are Kindred Things

one year, she attended meetings frequently when friends came for her. Because of her help with the donation of the book of poetry and other assistance, such as writing news items for the club, she was made an honorary member. "How rich I am in friends," she wrote October 12, 1934, after a wonderful time spent in Branson and Hollister visiting with friends and attending a meeting of the Study Club.

An excerpt from Mary Elizabeth's journal, August 17, 1934, after attending a meeting of the Taneyhills Study Club.

I joined 'em for culture
And what did I see
Forty-one stylish stouts
A-drinking their tea.
Shakespeare was lovely
And Browning was cute
I resigned from the club
An uncultured brute!

These ladies and others who knew her then, and many today who learn about her, cannot understand why she avoided the intellectual life of Taney County that was begging for her, and one that she needed in her seemingly drab life devoid of artistic and intellectual stimulation. Instead of participating, she maintained a self-imposed isolation from the women in the higher echelon of the county's society. The women wanted her and needed her, often seeking her out. From all over the area important and cultured men and women visited her. Humble and appreciative, she enjoyed their visits on her own ground, but she was often uncomfortable in strange company. She never really belonged.

Shy ("In anguish I twisted my apron strings") and sensitive to every slight, whether intentional or not, she avoided places where she might feel uncomfortable or be hurt. This sensitivity was one of the reasons she did not want to go to New York City to receive her award and why the trip exhausted her so. Outside her own people, she felt she had to guard constantly against any ridicule.

Her admirers have speculated how far she might have gone in the literary or intellectual world had she not been "trapped in the Ozarks," or to put it more accurately, trapped herself in the Ozarks. But had she left, as did her talented brothers and sisters whom very few remember, today no one would be interested in her. Her strength and her abilities came from the Ozarks, the land and its people. A remarkable woman, in a remarkable time, in a remarkable place. These ingredients all combined to develop Mary Elizabeth Mahnkey. The Ozarks produced her. She reproduced the Ozarks for the world to know as honestly and with as much understanding as anyone else has ever done.

Friends of Mary Elizabeth, and even her children, were not aware of her feelings of inferiority or the vein of sadness that underlaid her life and thoughts. Both she and Pres kept their troubles to themselves. Some times were harder than others. Even the seemingly happy and productive years at Oasis were shadowed by the debt they owed on the property. Not until they sold it, were they once again free of debt—a condition always weighing on them. Today with everyone using credit, it is difficult to understand how oppressive their debt load was to them. It meant bondage, uncertain futures, perhaps even the poor farm. No sacrifice was too great to prevent losing their pride and independence.

They worked hard to keep the dam and mill pond as a functional unit of the Oasis enterprise, for the power at the mill, for fishing, and for the aesthetic values to tourists. In spite of their efforts, the flood of 1927 washed out their little dam. The U.S. Army Corps of Engineers already had plans for building Table Rock Dam on the White River above Branson. Some land was being purchased along Long Creek, which would be totally inundated when the lake filled. These worries and the futility of it all must have been on Mary Elizabeth's mind on July 20, 1927, when she planted a late garden. This was the first summer they were alone after Reggie left. She wrote in her personal notes:

> I went down into the garden real late last evening, and there where Pres had cleaned out the strawberries, and the earth between the rows was all soft and loose, there I planted a row of beans. Today it is cool and cloudy with now and then a drop of rain, so the beans may have a chance to sprout and grow. I wonder how things will be when they bear? And who will cook and eat them?
>
> Sometimes I feel such a deadly weariness, and an intense dislike, almost hatred, for this place. Yet there will come a time, when I will look back with tears and longing, for the gentle peace and grace of these last few years Pres and I are spending here together. How patiently and faithfully he works, nothing too small or mean for him to try to see if something can't be made from it. He bought a little crippled sow at a sale last spring, and this little thing has raised five pigs that are the talk of the country. He can sell them for fifty dollars soon. The grass seed he has sown, against my protest, and worse than the protest, blighting ridicule, has made a wonderful meadow. Our barn is bursting with hay and he sold $185 worth to John Burnett.

The year of 1934 was a hard year. In the midst of the Depression, those with credit at the store had difficulty paying their accounts. Trade fell off. Then to compound the problems, the country was plagued with the greatest drought since 1901. Except for early greens, there were no gardens, no corn, no hay, no pasture for the stock. Bertie and Roy were barely making ends meet. They sold some veal calves in August for less than a dollar apiece.

Both Mary Elizabeth and Pres caught colds more often. Though their health was still good, they began to experience more problems.

Mary Elizabeth could pull herself out of the blues quicker than Pres. She could not understand why Pres could not see the brighter side. February 22, 1935, when in a good mood after a cheery letter from Bertie, and after bringing from the store some prepared foods for supper, she wrote in her journal, "We could be doing worse, Old Pal, what say? If he were not always so sad and glum and always so assured of calamity!"

She was the romantic, the idealist. She could transcend cares by love and feel paid by beauty. Pres was a realist, the worrier. He knew there was no real silver and gold in the beauty that his wife treasured. He was not sustained by her metaphor of turning life's fabric to show the brighter side. He saw only the patches where they tried to make do and the worn spots that would cause future trouble.

Weary from work which often brought disappointing rewards, with his feet firmly planted on the hard, rocky ground of reality, he unwittingly hurt Mary Elizabeth time and again. On July 20, 1934, she had a wonderful day with some friends in town, capping the day's pleasures by buying some gifts. She brought home some dress material for Bertie (39¢) and a bracelet to match (10¢). For Winnie Bee she bought a ten cent ring. She wrote in her journal that night, "As usual Pres took all the joy out of it by saying, 'Better have got her something to eat.' I told Pres that there had been times when a flowery strip of brand new dress goods coming in as an unexpected gift would have lifted me out of the depths into heaven almost."

In October of that year she received a totally unexpected royalty check of ten dollars from *Ozark Lyrics*. She wrote, "I said at once I was going to get Papa a new overcoat. Of course he dashed all the sparkle—and broke my glass of hopefulness and joy. He said he 'needed other things worse than an overcoat.' It is a heavenly gift. I'll send it to Reggie and Bertha. Tears, tears, tears."

Letters from the children, unexpected visits of grandchildren or friends, a walk up the creek, or an all day excursion with friends away from home would relight her spirit. Always she was glad to get back to her comfortable home and beautiful valley and to her "cranky Mahnkey," who usually had dinner ready. For in the peace of her home she always anticipated the quiet, free time when she could write.

> I have a wee bit garden
> A clothesline and a cat
> A butterfly all yellow gold
> A cow all smooth and fat.
>
> I have a dear kind husband
> He milks the cow, he hoes,
> But he does not see the butterfly
> A-swinging, or the rose.

The last year at Oasis was one of uncertainty about selling, for they both knew they had to leave. Talk of the dam at Table Rock was already decreasing the value of their property.

Though Bill Eychaner made them repeated offers for the place, none were sufficient to assure them a suitable place to live after they paid their debts. But when the offer reached $5,000, they sold.

Though preliminary investigation and permits to construct the dam at Table Rock site on the White River were underway as early as 1912 and 1921, and actual license to build it was granted in 1932, the dam was not fully completed and dedicated until 1959. After the water reached the power pool level, all that remained of the creek valley was its name on Long Creek Bridge which now crosses the lake on Highway 86.

In the center of the lake north of the bridge, are two small islands. A few trees, sticking up like a footstone, mark the top of the hill bordering the field south of the Oasis store; north of the trees, a small island, like the headstone of a grave, is the top of the bluff that the old steel bridge butted into.

One hundred feet under the water line lie the steel beams of this one-lane bridge that Pres once hoped would bring prosperity to Oasis.

Chapter 19

O LITTLE HOUSE
Interlude in Forsyth:
July 29, 1935 - August 29, 1936

O little house, why do you sigh
When gay spring winds come dancing by?

And then, sometimes, I see you weep,
For bright drops down your gray roof creep.

You weep because we go away
And you will be alone some day?

Though they were sad to leave their friends, Pres and Mary Elizabeth were satisfied with the sale of the Oasis store. Rural stores everywhere were declining. Mary Elizabeth said, "The highway and the motor car were the death of small community stores. We sold Oasis. It was a hard trade to make, for Eychaners, who were buying the farm, store, and camp, also wanted our cows. I thought so much of our cows. We finally sold all of them but Buttercup. They bought our cream separator, our ice box, and everything. We bought the little house on a hill top in Forsyth that Doug and Merle lived in and made so comfortable. It is clean and sweet and beautiful. Seven rose bushes blooming—mocking birds singing. We moved there June 11, 1935, taking Buttercup with us."

Pres Mahnkey on the porch of the little house east of Forsyth about 1935.

Their stay in the little house was a temporary one, until Pres found another business. Before deciding on the little house, they had considered buying back the store at Mincy. Mary Elizabeth had written in her journal June 6, "Papa went to Mincy and looked the old place over. I wanted it O so badly—but Hublar asked $2,500 and would not give possession until January 1."

Glad to be out of debt and to be in a position to give financial assistance to both Bertie and Reggie, Mary Elizabeth put aside her disappointment in not moving to Mincy and quickly settled in the little house at Forsyth on July 29, 1935.

She had very little time to think about their future business plans, however, for she soon received nationwide recognition for her writing. She was chosen best rural correspondent, receiving the Crowell Publishing Company's first annual award and the resulting trip to New York City. The award, coupled with the publication two years earlier of *Ozark*

Lyrics, gave her statewide stature in the literary world. Following this recognition her poetry was later accepted in anthologies, such as *Voices from the Field*, Lord, 1937, and *Living Authors of the Ozarks and their Literature*, McCullough, 1941.

It was to the little house that she returned from her New York trip to Doug's and Bertie's welcome-home dinner. Excited, exhausted, and so glad to be at home and away from the spotlight that she almost cried, she tried to resume her usual life style. But the experiences were so overwhelming and the mental and physical stress so great that several months passed before she was herself again. "Perhaps I expected too much when I thought we could settle down to our old peaceful existence after such an upheaval in our lives as my trip to New York," she said.

During the ten days of the trip she had been the center of attention, sought after, interviewed, escorted to many places, fed unfamiliar food, and housed in strange surroundings. Back at home, after climbing wearily out of the taxi and walking into her house, her stamina deserted her. She was back in her own country, in her own little house with her family; the ordeal was over. But the most upsetting thing was that her home seemed different—as if the trip had changed her niche in life. She was frightened that she felt out of rhythm there as well as in New York.

Her face drawn white with fatigue, she rested in her favorite rocker as her spellbound family plied her with questions. She could not eat though Doug's wife, Merle, had cooked a country dinner of new potatoes, fried chicken, green beans, fresh corn, and tomatoes, with coffee the way she liked it, black and strong. Only Pres noticed that she took nothing but a little coffee.

The grandchildren wouldn't let her rest. They plied her

with questions. "Nanny, we didn't hear you on the radio. Grampa turned on all the knobs but we just heard static and funny noises. Did you talk?"

"Yes, darling, I talked."

"Were you scared?"

"No, they had everything written out, so I just read it. You couldn't scare an ole hillbilly like me with a mike. I've had lots of practice talking over the old crank phone at Oasis."

The children asked all the important questions about her trip. Was the whistle of the train too loud? Did the train make a lot of noise when it started? Could she keep from falling over when the train went fast? Did she eat any ice cream on the train?

She answered all their questions. "You children are as full of questions as those reporters. They asked me about everything here at home."

"Did they ask you about us?"

"Yes, and I told all about you. They were especially interested in Papa."

"What'd you tell them," everyone wanted to know, looking at Pres to see his reaction.

"I said, 'My husband's name is Charles Preston Mahnkey. Mahnkey rhymes with cranky. He's the harmonica champion of the Ozarks. Yes, he wanted me to come to New York. No, he's not much interested in my work, but I notice he always reads my column. That's the first part of the paper he reads!'"

Pres beamed.

The boys were fascinated by the ship-in-a-bottle from Mayor LaGuardia. Everyone admired the silver platter and vegetable dish that were given as part of her prize, though Mary Elizabeth complained, "I'd have rather had a cup or some good knives and forks I could use. Why in the world would they give such elegant things to a country woman?" She gave the platter to Mary Jo and the vegetable dish to Winnie Bee. "One day you girls will have the home and furnishings to go with these."

So excited was everyone that only Pres noticed how ill she was. He encouraged her to lie on the couch.

All afternoon visitors came until Pres and Doug had to ask them to come back later. Now that she was home, Mary Elizabeth relaxed the tight hold she had on herself for the past ten days. "I was actually ill," she wrote in her journal, "and almost had nervous prostration for months."

During the rest of that summer she rested often. Pres prepared some of the meals for them, as his garden, hogs, and milk cow didn't keep him busy in this in-between time after they sold Oasis and until they found another business. Though the future was uncertain, their time there was peaceful with time to renew and sort out priorities. "C.P. and I are all alone and happy in an elderly quiet way," she wrote.

For the first time in years they had no business to care for. The small farm they lived on hardly counted. It didn't take long for Pres to become restless. Though times were still hard in the summer of 1935, the economy was improving slowly. Trader that he was, no one was surprised to hear that he traded for another store.

Helpful was the money from Mary Elizabeth's prize of fifty dollars and the sixty extra dollars over her actual expenses from the Crowell Publishing Company. Even more wonderful was the twenty-five dollars a month for one year from *The Country Home* for a column Russell Lord commissioned her to write entitled "Ozark Correspondent." She also got an occasional check of five dollars for some special writing assignments to papers, such as the St. Louis *Post Dis-*

patch, or a two-dollar check from someone reading one of her poems on the radio, like Mirandy of Persimmon Hollow— Mrs. Fred Baersfeld, National Farm and Home Hour personality from Chicago. Almost a year after her trip she figured up in her journal that she made "$524.64 income from writing since June 1935. Pretty good for an old bird like me."

Considering that in many years she and Pres did not make much more than a thousand dollars on their store, mill, and post office combined, they greatly appreciated this income.

Although two years passed before she recorded her trip in her journal, Mary Elizabeth appreciated it more and more as the months went by. She never mentioned it to anyone or wrote about it in her column or journal without some adjective preceding the word. Usually it was "amazing trip." In retrospect she marveled at her experiences. "Queer the adventures I have, or that are having me, now at the close?"

Sometimes the results of the trip were almost more than she could handle. She worried about her health, about not being able to snap back to her usual energy level. The trip drained her more than she thought possible. She wrote in her journal, "I feel pretty bad again tonight. Nerves—I who have always been so brave and so unshaken."

Perhaps part of the reason for the slow recovery was how she was treated after getting home. Being a celebrity did not suit her. She was stared at, feted, sought after by casual acquaintances and reporters both local and out of the county; she was asked to speak at numerous clubs and other groups. The speeches worried her because she was shy about the formal approach. One to one talking, or writing—those were her ways of communicating.

On August 30, a month after she returned, she wrote in her journal, "Gradually returning to normalcy—it has been very strenuous. Such crowds here every day and such stacks of letters—always the curious crowding to see a notorious person whether they're murderers, or freaks, or prize winners. Shame to say that, when everyone is so kind and lovely and have taken me to so many nice places."

The trip may have complicated her life too much. She had always admired simplicity. What earned her the award in the first place was the sincerity and simplicity of her writing, written without straining for effect—friendly and objective. That quality in her personality was obvious in New York. Edward Anthony, one of the *Country Home* people who escorted her almost every place she went, said, "Mrs. Mahnkey brought New York the beauty of simplicity." Carl Van Doren said that some of her local news items had the power and simplicity of the poems of old China.

Until that trip she was always the observer, writing her impressions of people and events. Suddenly, she had to endure being thrust into the spotlight, sought after, and written about. Though gratified that her work was receiving attention, she soon realized that most of the attention was focused on her and her Ozark background rather than her writings. It was as if this cultured and attractive woman was some anomaly; she was not the barefoot, pipe-smoking Ozark woman the media had led the rest of the country to expect from the hills. In the midst of all this attention to *her*, she probably inferred criticism of her writing. In the spotlight as she was, she could not withdraw to her hills as she did at home when she sensed some condescending attitudes from the Study Club ladies.

During the fall after her trip, back among her blue hills, she began getting into her accustomed routines. Cooking sweet potato pie, cowpeas—"the humblest of vegetables"— canning tomatoes and piccalilli, eating pawpaws that Bertie brought her, butchering Pres's hogs with Doug and little Pat's help, and playing pitch in the evenings with Pres (and sometimes beating him), all helped to bring her back to the simple basics of family life.

Though the recognition opened a few temporary markets for her writing, it did not change her established pattern of writing weekly news to the local papers, monthly "In the Hills" contributions to the Springfield dailies, and short pieces and poems to other publications from time to time. Rarely did she receive any payment, and if she did it was usually less than ten dollars. Nor did the award alter Pres and Mary Elizabeth's way of life—their business or their personal habits. To her family and friends, she was the same as always.

Concern for the problems of her children and their families and joy at their successes occupied her mind during the coming months. Doug passed his bar examination. When he got the word, his whole family rode over with him to tell her, honking the horn, laughing, and shouting, "We're lawyers." With his law credentials, Doug was elected prosecuting attorney for Taney County.

One day in January after Doug took office, Mary Elizabeth was walking home from Forsyth thinking how proud she was of his accomplishments. He slowed down to pick her up while bringing Pres home. As the men came in sight of her, Doug said to his father, "Look at her. She walks like a girl!" When Pres told her what Doug said, she was pleased. She then took a long look at Pres. That night she wrote in her journal, "Papa is sixty tomorrow—he walks like a boy and talks like a boy and a pretty tough boy at that."

Doug was doing fine, but how much she wished she could do for her other two children, Bertie and Reggie. Bertie and Roy Jones, after a hard time in the difficult early years of the Depression, were recently settled near the former Mahnkey home at Mincy where they owned a little farm. Roy earned some ready cash by carrying the mail from Kirbyville to Mincy. Mary Elizabeth worried about them during the icy winter—Roy on the bad, unimproved roads each day and Bertie at home alone since both Leon and Winnie Bee were in Mincy School. Spring came late in 1936. Roy and Bertie's best cow couldn't get up, wouldn't eat and eventually died. "Too bad—too bad!" Mary Elizabeth wrote, "Always the broken pitcher—the blighted rose for Bertie—and she so dear, so precious."

More than Bertie, she worried about Reggie. In the army since eighteen, her second son left the service when he discovered that he couldn't support his wife and baby son on a soldier's pay. Since there were no jobs in North Dakota where he lived, or anywhere else for that matter, Pres and Mary Elizabeth used a little savings that they had to put him in business. For three hundred dollars they bought a little store and two acres in Mincy across the road from their old home and store, and near Bertie and Roy's farm. They stocked it with five hundred dollars worth of goods and fixed up a place for the family to live in back of the store with a view over the rolling wooded land. Mary Elizabeth and Pres were confident that Reggie and Bertha would do their best to make a go of the business.

For the first time since they were grown, all three Mahnkey children were close by and with a total of five grandchildren. "Gary is a darling—so smart and so good," she wrote after she saw Reggie's baby for the first time. Her life seemed full.

But Mary Elizabeth wasn't contented in their little house east of Forsyth. It wasn't home—too isolated; she missed the companionship of close neighbors. But it did have one big advantage: it was near Doug's new rock house a mile up the road toward town. Pat and little Mary Jo came to see her often.

A Candle Within Her Soul

She didn't feel at home with the ladies of this county seat town as she had with the farm women in the tiny crossroads villages or open country where she'd always lived. Very few people called. One lady "even made snooty remarks about my literary attempts," Mary Elizabeth wrote in her journal.

Though the comment bothered Pres, Mary Elizabeth tried to be indifferent about it. As often when something moved her, she wrote a verse. Her feelings show through the humor in this one she typed off and pasted in her journal.

Small Town Stuff

When we left our old home on the crick
Says I, "No more I'll be a hick.
Beauty parlor, lipstick, paint
Will make me into what I ain't."

But now the stones come hurling in
To bruise my heart, and head and chin—
"Old Mrs. Mahnkey tried to write.
How quaint, did-ya ever see such a fright?

"Old Mrs. Mahnkey puts on airs
Because she climbed the White House stairs.
Old Mrs. Mahnkey's prose and verse
Are silly, weak, and growing worse."

At first this made me pretty blue
But now dear friends, I'm telling you
Although it may sound pretty rough
Mrs. Mahnkey knows this small town stuff.

But winning second prize for poems of spring in a poetry contest in the Springfield *Leader* elated her. Perhaps her luck in contests was changing.

By July life was back to normal. She worried about the basic things, such as the continuing drought. She was thankful all the grandchildren were over the measles, and, as many times in the past, she began to count her blessings. Thumbing through her journal she noted that a year ago she was in Springfield buying the material for her dresses and the white straw hat to wear on her trip. "How much better off we are," she wrote, "every one of us—even Mary Jo and Gary—than we were then." The trip became a memory and she regained her zest for life.

Better times were soon to come. On August 25, 1936, Mary Elizabeth wrote in her journal in a hand that was trembling with excitement. "Something so wonderful has happened that I can hardly write it down. The beloved old Mincy house is ours again—after all the hoping and planning and praying and despairing. C.P. wound it up today. Through our old friend, Charlie Groom, we bought the mortgage of $1,800—70 acres of land, store building, mill, dwelling (O where Bill was so happy), barn, hen house, garage, and little Artie Gardner house over by Strahan's.

"They drew up a contract and relinquished the post office to me—but will not give possession till January 1—only of the store. C.P. will have to go down and fix living quarters in the rear of the store for us.

"O Baby, let us be happy for the little while that's left in the earth." In all the intervening years since the storm, she had never recovered from the death of her little son Bill.

As she said goodbye to the little house, she almost felt guilty that she was leaving it so gleefully because the house was lovely and comfortable. It had the first sink and inside hand pump she'd ever had. It also had pleasant family memories. It was the first house Doug owned and loved—the house where Pat and Mary Jo were born.

She remembered when she and Pres first moved there from Oasis and invited Doug's and Bertie's families to dinner. Doug danced around the kitchen with Mary Jo singing, "O here we are eating dinner in our little house again." Bertie brought a big walnut cake with bananas in the frosting, which Roy called a dedication cake for their new home. Leon put up the old flag on the front porch.

Mary Elizabeth regretted moving away from Doug and Merle and the children and "to leave such quiet loveliness"—yet it was not home. Thoughts of Mincy suffused her with joy. Mincy, the well-beloved place where she and Pres and their four children lived twice before, in 1914-16 and 1917-18. Those were the halcyon years when they were all happy together—when Doug and Bertie outgrew their childhood, and Reggie and little Bill were carefree little boys.

Chapter 20

THEY LAUGH AND I LAUGH
Contentment at Mincy:
August 8, 1937 - Fall 1943

> Each stone, each stick, each flower, each leaf
> Speaks to me of the old time grief,
> Yet when I walk this way in the spring
> They laugh, and I laugh, they sing, and I sing.

Almost a year later Mary Elizabeth was in the big combination kitchen-dining room just to the left of the entrance hall of the beloved house at Mincy. She was expecting Doug's and Bertie's families for dinner. While her dinner was cooking—fried chicken and Kentucky Wonder beans cooked long and slowly with pork fat—she was sitting at her writing desk putting the finishing touches to her monthly "In the Hills" column for the Springfield daily.

Cooking a meal was so natural after forty years of housekeeping that she could concentrate on her article, yet still be conscious that the smell from the blackberry cobbler in the oven was telling her that it was almost done. Also, she was subconsciously aware of Pres's movement across the road at the store where a neighbor interrupted Pres's Sunday morning's relaxation on the porch. Mary Elizabeth read a few lines from her article.

Pres and Mary Elizabeth in the front lawn at Mincy, January 1936.

"Of early mornings down this way, the fog from White River fills all the little hollows." She glanced out the east window of her kitchen in the direction of the river at the velvety Ozark hills.

She turned back to her writing where she was describing this same view. "The east branch of the crossroads passes the old white schoolhouse, where the bell makes such melodious music, and the children's shouts on the playground also make music. Our children went to a school here, and later two of our grandchildren. Down this way is Mincy Creek, that gave its name to the settlement. And clear to the river, long ago, were pleasant little homes, people we knew and loved."

She left her work to take the cobbler out of the oven of the wood cook stove, setting the baking pan on the open oven door to cool.

"I love best, I think, the view toward the south. One of the highest hills in that long blue outline is Huckleberry Mountain. Beyond is Bee Creek, also Fox Creek, and down in there lived Granny McGill, a famous midwife of pioneer days. She was the ancestress of a wonderful people. Until a year or so ago her log cabin, built before the Civil War, was still standing and in good repair. A smart aleck newcomer went over there and tore it down to fix up a hen house and used the rest of it for wood. We all were so wrought up over this blasphemy that the man seemed to know it and left for California."

The good fortune in getting back Mincy caused Mary Elizabeth to remember other happy times during her sixty years, such as the honor that came to her from winning the award for best rural correspondent of 1935.

There were sad times, too, such as Reggie's failure in the store and abrupt departure from Missouri. And her greatest sorrow of over seventeen years ago, little Bill lying on the board across the two chairs where neighbor men had laid him out. His memory was especially strong since she and Pres repurchased the store and moved back to the house where Bill once lived so happily.

Mincy comforted her. Perhaps living again where Bill was such a happy little boy finally helped Mary Elizabeth reach a sort of peace and accept his death. She now had grand-children which reminded her of him. Hearing their voices, she jumped up with surprising quickness in spite of her lame knee, and with smiles on her round face hugged each one.

The children played noisily outside under the big shade trees. Before settling on the front porch to await dinner, the men went to the barn to admire Pres's latest trade, the cow he bought for thirty dollars.

Meanwhile the women put the finishing touches on the meal. Fresh from the thoughtful mood before her family came, Mary Elizabeth began counting her blessings as the two young women chatted and worked. "Dear Merle," she wrote in her journal. "Doug's wife. Always so sweet and patient and faithful. She has fitted into our family just as though she had always been meant for us."

She looked at her daughter. "My girl child, as she was growing up my constant companion, my greatest joy." Finally, after a difficult time during the Depression, things were looking up for the Joneses.

During the meal Mary Elizabeth listened proudly as Doug told some experiences in his work. He was in his second year as prosecuting attorney of Taney County. But more important to his mother than his material success was his devotion and presence. He was always there. "Tender and true," she wrote many times in her journals.

Though known throughout southwest Missouri for her writings, Mary Elizabeth could not find words to describe the joy her grandchildren were to her. They made her feel young again, just as if they were her children, not her grandchildren.

She looked at the two joking and laughing families. A glance at Pres showed her that he shared her pride. A few years later she would say of this last stay at Mincy, "The seven years there were as happy as any years I had known." The magic of Mincy Valley never failed during the three times the Mahnkeys lived there—this last time since August 29, 1936. This day recorded in her journal was Sunday, August 8, 1937.

Though Mary Elizabeth was proud of her children, she was also proud of what she and Pres had accomplished. Starting with nothing when they married in 1899, through all the vicissitudes of economic times and unpredictable and tragic weather conditions, they now owned this house and ran the store and post office in this little crossroads village where they loved their neighbors and were loved and respected in turn. They were still able to handle the business, though it took both to run it.

After everyone left and chores were done, Pres settled down on the porch with his pipe; Mary Elizabeth returned to her desk. She pushed back the little lavender typewriter with the worn roller that she had used for years to type her stories because her handwriting was hard to read. As she picked up the article she was editing earlier in the day, she was amused. People might also have trouble reading her typing because of some broken letters and the worn-out ribbon.

Though pleased with the success of her two older children, she continued to worry about Reggie. Just a few months ago he and Bertha and little son Gary were all here in their little business across the road.

But Reggie had been away from the hills too long and had become accustomed to city living and conveniences. His wife hated the backwoods hills where there was no electricity and she had to drink water from a spring. When Reggie ran up debts, his parents used the last of the resources they so carefully saved through the years to pay his creditors.

In spite of his personal problems, it is doubtful that the store could have succeeded. To stay in business during the Depression years, merchants had to extend credit to many of their customers, or take something in trade, such as cattle or hogs. Reggie was not in a position to do either. Added to that handicap, the improbability of his little store competing with the bigger, established Mincy store during this period of the decline of the county store almost assured failure.

The store closed; Reggie returned to North Dakota. Mary Elizabeth and Pres, always proud and independent, never seeking help, never buying anything they could not pay for, and always keeping their word, were deeply hurt by Reggie's conduct. They were humiliated when he applied for government relief to support his family.

Young Reggie saw nothing wrong with his life style. Borrowing money was a fact of life where he had been. But the Ozark Mahnkeys lived under a different code. Mary Elizabeth herself called the Ozarks the "last post of the rugged individualist." She and Pres didn't believe in government assistance. To them Reggie's behavior was irresponsible and unthinkable.

As the months went by, the parents' love and understanding was great enough to accept the situation. Reggie wrote home regularly and frequently, each letter brightening Mary Elizabeth's day. Other than a visit or two through the years, Reggie never returned. His letters were his life line home. As opportunities opened for him, and his family grew to three boys, Gary, Curtis, and Spencer, Mary Elizabeth's hurt dissipated. Reggie was again the fond, but distant son. He was again, and always, "Dear Reggie."

Before it got too dark to see, Mary Elizabeth put her mind to the article she needed to mail to the Springfield paper.

> Mincy is a strange little old world village, inasmuch as the farms lie back and to the outside, and the folk all build their houses near the road, and so there are several lights twinkling at night quite near. Opie Reade once said in his most delightful way, describing a little country village, where "a blacksmith shop, a store and a mill put their heads together and declared themselves a town."
>
> The little store, painted white within the past few years, stands at the crossroads (an old saying, bad luck to live at the crossroads, but we always disregarded this).
>
> Our house is near the store, and is an old-fashioned house with the two front doors. I think the old house was glad to see us, this last time, and I've worked hard to get shrubbery started again—the last owner pastured the yard. I have iris in abundance, for this flower is my favorite. There is a coral honeysuckle, and pink Ramblers over the front porch, and hollyhocks in the back yard. Blue grass

is coming back, luxuriantly.
Mincy is our home, and we love it.

During the years at Mincy, Mary Elizabeth's journals and notes reveal a dichotomy of reactions—sometimes real contentment and sometimes the old restlessness and yearning. She illustrates that feeling in "Similarity."

> Contentment is a lovely flower
> But it was hard to start.
> It grows like Resignation—
> I can't tell them apart

Mary Elizabeth in the living room at her home in Mincy about 1940.

Perhaps she was resigned to the realization that her dreams were fulfilled as much as they ever would be. Or perhaps she recognized that her restless spirit was finally calmed by age as "The Captive" suggests.

> I started up the mountain
> With step so light and free,
> But before I reached the fountain
> A gray grim shape caught me—
> "You'll do no more wild roaming
> For I've found you, bound you now."
> O, who was this weird monster,
> With the hoar frost on his brow,
> Who shivered in a palsy,
> Who chattered in wild rage?
> Then, sick and faint, I realized
> I was captured by old age.

But she and Pres were too busy operating the store and post office, farming their land, tending to the cows, hogs and chickens, raising a garden, and improving and maintaining their buildings at Mincy to dwell on unpleasant thoughts.

Pres was the main storekeeper and master trader. She kept the books and handled all their customers' credit accounts. She minded the store when Pres was gone and daily handled the post office.

Sometimes customers were surprised when a white-haired woman came to help them, especially when it came to automobile supplies. One time when Mary Elizabeth was alone, the upset owner of an expensive car with a steaming radiator rushed in to buy a fan belt. She had nothing that would fit, though she took one out to see.

Then she suggested, "Couldn't you use a saddle string [narrow leather strips used to tie supplies onto saddles] till you get out to Kirbyville where there are garages?"

"What the hell's a saddle string?"

Undisturbed by his annoyed attitude, she found one the

Mincy Store about 1939. Pres is standing in the door to the post office corner where Mary Elizabeth was postmaster.

exact width of the broken fan belt. With her help he knotted it securely, and started the engine. The improvised fan belt worked perfectly.

"How did you come to think of that?"

"Any woman who has reached my years and has helped rear a family is surely capable of thinking."

The partnership between Pres and Mary Elizabeth was not limited to the business. It extended to their home as well. There Mary Elizabeth was, of course, the main worker, but Pres helped in many ways. Though many women helped their husband in the fields and with the animals, at this time not many men helped in the housework or took any interest in the lawn. Mary Elizabeth tended her flowers; Pres mowed the lawn. She did the weekly wash after he drew the water and carried it in for her. She did the mopping of the floors afterwards, but he sometimes finished mopping for her. She did the cooking and canning, but when she was late getting home from her visits, he had dinner ready. She loved to visit her friends and see interesting places. He did not object, staying home keeping the store.

Pres and Mary Elizabeth shared many things and had many of the same values. They both loved horses, but in 1940 Pres traded off his last horse. They both loved children. They were both Republicans. He did not belong to any church or lodge, but that did not bother her.

To their family and neighbors they seemed always in perfect agreement. She called him the General Manager. She often bragged on his many talents, how quick he was with numbers, how clever he was with his hands, how well he played the harmonica. Every time the grandchildren came, she had something good to say about him, or narrated some tale about his antics while Pres beamed proudly.

Pres, on the other hand, was more taciturn. His "Old Lady" meant everything to him, though he rarely said so. He missed her greatly when she went to New York. He appreciated her help in the business, her skill at household tasks, and her knack with children. He must have been proud of her writings; he certainly never interfered in any way, being quite willing for her to take trips, visit, and spend time at her desk. He probably did not fully appreciate her talent until after her death when he read over and over everything she had saved in her dozens of scrapbooks and journals. During her lifetime he was too busy to pay much attention to what she was writing.

There was, however, one area in which they were not in agreement. Though they both spent most of their childhood years in Taney County, their families were different. Pres, from hard-working people, wanted enough money to be secure. Before Social Security, the specter of the poor house was very real. He saved his money a dime at a time to have cash to pay his taxes. He spent money only on essentials.

Mary Elizabeth's family was different. Life for the Prathers, though erratic, was easier than for the Mahnkeys. They took time to read and to write copious letters. They spent money on cultural activities. When Mary Elizabeth had some money, she wanted to do things, go places, and buy nicer things for her family. Sometimes she spent the money; other times Pres prevailed.

Pasted in one of her scrapbooks dated December 1940 is a sheet of paper with rows of figures in Pres's handwriting. Beside it Mary Elizabeth scribbled, "Figures, figures, figures by C.P.M. Patient, careful always. He figured and I made rhymes."

Undoubtedly she wrote "The Dreamer" to highlight their differences.

> He lived on the fruits of After While
> A spectral, shadowy tree.
> I gathered berries of Now and Here,
> Their taste has been sweet to me.

But they were in perfect agreement on the subject of the grandchildren. They loved to have them visit, both spending time with them and tolerating whatever they did. Children and grandparents had great times.

The old house was the classic grandmother house, airy and light, quiet and tranquil, and full of exotic things people gave Mary Elizabeth. It had a mysterious upstairs for little ones to play and sleep in, a big shady lawn for action games, and a cheery kitchen for snacks of sugar cookies and home-made bread spread with fresh churned butter and some fruity jam.

Both grandparents were jolly with the children, never too

busy to listen to them or play with them. An exception to that was so unusual that it stayed in their memories for years. One day Pat saw Mary Elizabeth in the garden picking a few peas for dinner. He ran up making conversation as usual, but she hardly noticed him. She seemed troubled or maybe ill, though she did not say.

Perhaps she was thinking about Reggie or little Bill. She may have been struggling with the problems of getting old, or more likely, she might have been worried about the ominous war news from Europe. She had experienced one war. Pat bounding toward her all joyful may have made her fear for him, for what his future might be in the different world he was growing up in.

Pat's childish conclusion, however, was that the impossible had happened, and she was angry with him. At noon the peas were in a beautiful dish, and Mary Elizabeth was the usual attentive grandmother. Pat unwittingly had intruded into the inner world she hid from her family.

Winnie Bee had a similar experience in March 1940. She found Mary Elizabeth crying.

"Mama," Winnie Bee asked greatly disturbed for she never saw her grandmother other than smiling and cheerful. "Why are you crying?"

"Little Mama has died," Mary Elizabeth explained and showed Winnie Bee the letter from California telling of Betsy Prather's death at age ninety-five.

But most of the children's activities were fun. They gathered by her desk under the two horseshoes tacked on the wall, "one hanging one way and one another thus satisfying the ancient superstition of a horseshoe hanging up means good luck," Mary Elizabeth explained. "Yet conflictingly, as one version says, the shoe must be hung with the open end up, and one says the other way, as the first way all good luck is held inside and the other says the good luck will all fall out. So I fooled the fates on this, anyway."

She claimed to be superstitious. She didn't allow the grandchildren to rock an empty rocking chair or carry a sharp garden tool through one door and out another. She loved "ha'nt" tales for she believed that childhood would be bleak and colorless without them. She loved it when the children begged her to tell them scary stories from long ago.

The children brought back Mary Elizabeth's youth. After passing sixty, she was very conscious of getting old. Her poetry and her scrapbooks have frequent references to age. The daily account in her journal was a constant reminder of time passing.

"I washed a few pieces. As I glanced back I thought with a sudden pang 'an old woman's washing.' No little frolicsome blouses and rompers and shirts a-dancing in the breeze."

The death of her mother made Mary Elizabeth more conscious of time passing. Though Betsy Prather had lived in California with her daughter Deal for many years, they corresponded regularly. Betsy returned to the hills only twice, but she wouldn't stay. Mary Elizabeth wrote in her journal, "I think that always some thought of Mother's colored my entire life. I tried to cook like she did, and tried to keep house like she did. Always there was the quick running thought of this or that I must write, for she would like to hear it—and now, no more forever."

Neither Mary Elizabeth nor Pres let their growing infirmities hinder them. They were always ready to go whenever the opportunity occurred. "So thankful we old plugs can still jog along."

Perhaps her greatest excitement of the Mincy years was in the summer of 1940 during the Roosevelt-Willkie campaign for President. Mary Elizabeth was commissioned by

Wheeler McMillan, her friend at Crowell Publishing Company, who was now with *Farm Journal* magazine, to go to Colorado Springs to interview Mrs. Wendell Willkie.

Mrs. Willkie thought Mary Elizabeth's face was familiar. She remembered reading the news stories about her while in New York getting her award. "Do you still write?" she asked. Then she asked Mary Elizabeth if she thought the varied agencies the government had set up for relief were really effective.

Mary Elizabeth answered, "As a country woman, I can only give you a country woman's views, not abstract, not ideological, with concrete illustration. I've often had to help my husband treat a sick cow. Maybe she had lost her cud. We forced a piece of fat meat down her gullet. Maybe she was poisoned. Down her poor neck went melted lard. Maybe she needed blood letting, so a dew lap was sliced down. Maybe she had the holler tail, so her tail was split, salt poked in, and the place bound up. Many and many a remedy we tried. Sometimes the cow got well, but more often she died."

The subsequent Republican defeat hurt Mary Elizabeth more than the other times Roosevelt won because she knew the Willkies and liked them so well.

Raised in the old school of self-help and rugged individualism, the Mahnkeys could not adjust readily to the new policies of the Roosevelt administration. Government aid, growing restrictions, and interference in business and farming went against their way of working. They disapproved of relief which they thought made many able-bodied men lazy.

The Mahnkeys' way of life was disappearing, not just because of the new governmental policies, but in many other ways as well.

The most obvious change was caused by the war in Europe and the United States involvement after Pearl Harbor.

For the Mahnkeys and most Ozarkers, the old ways never returned. The effects of the war, better economic times, a benevolent yet more restrictive government, good roads, high schools, radio, and electricity in the rural areas brought the twentieth century to the hills.

Just as they were in 1917 when the United States entered World War I, at the declaration of war on Japan and Germany in December 1941, the Mahnkeys were again keeping a store at Mincy. The community gave a big dinner to each boy who left. Almost overnight the boys were drained out of the country. This time some girls went to join the WAACs (Women's Auxiliary Army Corps) or WAVES (Women's Reserve of the United States Naval Reserve).

Roy and Bertie went to Puyallup, Washington, to join Reggie's family to work in the shipyards, just as Pres and Mary Elizabeth did at the end of World War I. The loss of the Joneses caused Mary Elizabeth and Pres hardships and much loneliness. Doug stayed in Taney County, but with his increased work and added local wartime responsibilities, he could not visit as often as before.

Even in tiny Mincy valley the Mahnkeys discovered that peace-time difficulties of keeping a country store were nothing compared to those of war-time storekeeping. The ration stamps were troublesome to handle and paste into the books correctly.

Mary Elizabeth wrote jokingly in her "In the Hills" column. "We may have to build an annex for the display of all the government stuff sent us for posting. For this small crossroads community, we were sent 600 application blanks for ration book number three."

Bad as rationing was for the storekeeper, Mary Elizabeth decided it was better than the rushing and grabbing. People that never stepped inside a country store rushed in to grab all they could carry of scarce items. One man was determined he was going to buy all the coffee in the store until an angry Pres faced him with, "No, you can't have it! That is for our customers."

Another time when coffee sales were frozen, two city men fishing at the creek came to the store begging for coffee. Though Mary Elizabeth wanted to give them some, she didn't for fear they might be from the Office of Price Administration checking on them. What hurt more than the lack of coffee was people spying like they couldn't be trusted.

Of the rationed foodstuffs, hill people suffered most from the scarcity of coffee and sugar. The rationing of meat, shortening, and canned foods was no hardship since most produced these foods themselves. But there was nothing to take the place of coffee. "Some of the old-timers drank four to eight cups a day, and they drank it so strong it would float an iron wedge," Mary Elizabeth said. "The lack of sugar hurt the country women. How could they put up all the luscious fruits, the wild blackberries and dewberries, the fine peaches and apples, if they had no sugar? Then they were accustomed to baking cakes and that took sugar. In the country, there are no bakeries where one may buy cakes. I quit coffee so Pres could have more coffee and sugar. I had always liked tea anyway."

Mary Elizabeth's sympathy for her neighbors is evident in this free verse, "Rationed." Though she preferred using traditional rhythm and rhyme, she wrote that some themes seemed to require a freer form.

"Now this is the way to use your sugar,"
said the lady with the painted nails.
Wisely she spoke—of plums and
peaches and berries.
and food values and nutrition.

Aunt Lucindy gazed at her
with tired old eyes,
Eyes that had grown dim
watching bubbling pots of richness,
Eyes that had studied
cool cedar shelves
and the best way of marking
jams and jellies,
cunning old eyes that flicked momentarily
from the stained nails to the stained lips.
"Yes-sum" was all she said.
July 20, 1942

Other affairs of the business became too complicated. The little fourth-class post office which netted no more than $140 to $150 a year became ridiculously complex. Difficulties began to mount up. There were no longer telephones in the hills. When storms and time tore down the community-owned lines, no one replaced them. Though the Mahnkeys missed the close contact of neighbors with the telephone, they enjoyed hearing the national news on their battery radio set. Pres had difficulty getting merchandise they needed for the store. They couldn't find hired hands to do any work. For two years the hay crop rotted in the field because they could not hire anyone to harvest it.

In addition to these problems, so many families had moved West that trade fell off. In the fall of 1943, Mary Elizabeth said, "We decided we had had all we could stand. We sold out."

Leaving Mincy and buying back the little house in Forsyth was truly the end of an era for the Mahnkeys. Pres and Mary Elizabeth never operated a country store again.

The Mahnkeys experienced the great changes in the hills that were culminating in the 1940s: the change from working

for self and self-sufficiency to working for wages; from individualism to a social state; from large country populations to
city living; from a simple life with few needs and little money
to a more complicated one dependent on regular income.

Aware of these trends, the Mahnkeys sold the business
while they could save their investment. Charlie Orr, who
bought the store and property from them, operated with diminishing business until 1953 when he closed the store.

When she moved to Mincy this last time in 1936, Mary
Elizabeth had thought that finally she and Press would never
move again. All during their married life, the new places they
moved to, even those that seemed good, had some problems
so that eventually one or both wanted to leave. This was true
at Mincy. Two years before they actually sold the Mincy store,
Mary Elizabeth decided it would be better for Pres to sell,
even though selling the store meant leaving the big house and
the neighborhood.

Yet when they did sell, it was resignation to the inevitable that convinced her to leave. In October 1943 she shared
with her readers the moving of her memories from the beloved Mincy home.

> I've been carefully taking up little pieces of my favorite
> flowers and shrubs. There is the Cynthia Youngblood iris.
> It is gold and bronzy brown. It grew at the left of the gate
> as you entered the cemetery at Oasis, at the foot of this
> young mother's grave. She was the wife of Eli Gibson. I
> took a tiny rootlet from this iris one time. It grew well, and
> I've divided with many others. Then there is the Alta
> Morris iris, a tall, stately plant that holds such a load of
> lavender blossoms and has such a sweet perfume. Alta
> Morris brought it to me at Oasis from her old home near
> Green Forest, Arkansas.
>
> There are the May McCord jonquils and the Effie

Phillips coral honeysuckle and the regal blue iris that came from the old Rogers place in the Skaggs ranch. Rita Mathews was out that way one time hunting hogs and found all this wealth of iris and dug up a start. How come mine.

The bridal wreath, too, has a story. I got a start of it down in the Mincy cemetery. Walking there one day I saw that the bridal wreath by Otis Yarnell's grave was a snowy, feathery cascade of bloom. Bad luck to pick a flower in a graveyard, but this I've always disregarded, for flowers are meant to be caressed and loved and gathered. I broke off a flowering branch and brought it home with me and set it by the west window. It did well. I'm taking a slip with me.

Otis was a dear lad, adored by our children and every one else. He was a dispatch carrier in that other dreadful conflict and did not live long after his return. He had been slightly gassed. Some said if he had taken care of his health, and not at once resumed his fox hunting, he might not have died. But he loved this sport and his dogs and horses. At night, as the planes drone overhead, and no longer do we hear the hounds and the hunter's horn, for they're far away after more savage game, I think of Otis and his splendid young life. Nothing left, only the bridal wreath bush his mother set by his grave.

Chapter 21

LET ME LOVE THEM WHILE I MAY
Retirement at the Little House and Kirbyville:
Fall 1943 - Christmas 1946

> O Life, I wish you were more frowning,
> And not so sweet and gay—
> For then I would not mind the going,
> For I know I cannot stay.
>
> O Life, the lovely things you gave me,
> Let me love them while I may,
> For I know I cannot take them
> When I have to go away.

In the fall of 1943 the Mahnkeys bought back the little house at Forsyth that they had owned before moving to Mincy. Though it was comfortable and available at a reasonable price, Mary Elizabeth never really liked it—too fenced in. She liked to be where she had a view.

Their fifty-acre place was behind a pasture and orchard, with the road ending at their house. But they had a pond and three cows, and by looking between the trees in the right places she could see the White River. The land was rough, rocky and steep. Becoming crippled with arthritis through the years, she was afraid she'd fall and be a burden on her family. Nevertheless, at least once a week she walked through the orchard and, while leaning against a tree to rest her knees, looked over the landscape.

Her general dissatisfaction with the place was partly because of the war. For the three years they lived there, Pres ran a little tavern and hamburger place in Forsyth that was within walking distance; Mary Elizabeth did not help in that business. She worked with her flowers, continued with her writing, and carried on an even greater correspondence than usual. She corresponded with many service men in addition to her family, friends, and writing connections.

She was near Doug's family. Pat came every night and morning to milk the cow he kept there. Mary Jo ran in frequently. Then, on January 20, 1945, Doug's third child was born. The delight in the new grandson helped Mary Elizabeth and Pres take their minds off the war.

She crocheted for the new baby three pairs of bootees exactly like those she had made for his dad when he was a baby. "The baby, a handsome, strong, sturdy little fellow, was born at home, and Cinda Kenner, [Mary Elizabeth's friend from Oasis] came to take care of her. She stayed six weeks and Merle was the envy of all the women in Forsyth, for Cinda was the only efficient help they had seen since before the war. They named the baby Bill, in memory of my little Bill."

Though Doug was nearby, again elected to the state legislature, Bertie, Roy and their children Leon and Winnie Bee were still in the West working in Todd Shipyards. It seemed strange to the family that gentle Bertie was welding steel plates on ships. Mary Elizabeth missed them terribly.

She worried about Leon, just reaching military age. He and Winnie Bee returned to Taney County to visit Pres and Mary Elizabeth the summer of 1944. Leon, approaching his eighteenth birthday, was anxious to get involved in the war.

When the young people left to return to the West, Mary Elizabeth accompanied them as far as Springfield. "My heart ached
to go on where my children were, but Pres didn't want to go.
In the other war, it was the other way around! He was the one
that wanted to go." When Leon left, she kissed his hand as she
did when he was a baby, for she never kissed a baby on the
face, and said, "Well, big boy, if you ever need a friend, you
know where your old Grandma is." Leon soon joined the
Marines.

On her lonely hilltop in Forsyth, Mary Elizabeth made
Leon a quilt. She felt closer to him doing something for him.
She found it difficult to write worrying about him and the war.

> I used to write quite gaily
> Of mossy water mills
> Of cedars and wild asters
> And misty, hazy hills.
>
> But little dancing words I loved
> Have vanished over night.
> I have no somber, solemn words
> For bombing planes in flight.

The war was not her only concern. Mary Elizabeth was
worried about Doug's seat in the state representative because
he had to campaign every two years. In the strong Republican area, winning the August primary won the office, for there
was no Democratic opponent. Some elections were not difficult, but sometimes the Republican opponents were powerful. He did not always win.

On April 7, 1945, she went with him to Jefferson City.
She visited the state legislature to hear the discussions and at
night saw the movie, *National Velvet*. Just when they were to
return home, they went to the boarding house for her bag. The

landlady was sitting at the telephone, apparently stunned by news she just heard.

"Roosevelt is dead!" she sobbed.

After dark on the way home they ran into a storm. Mary Elizabeth described it.

> The wind blew with hurricane force, the rain poured like a waterfall, and the lightning quivered in the air like a curtain of light. Above all was the constant roar of thunder. It was not just a passing storm. It was one of those keep-it-up affairs that seemed to go on forever. I was probably as fearful as I had ever been in my life, for I had the guilty knowledge that I had not been sorry when I heard about Roosevelt's death. The storm, which came so suddenly and with terrific force, seemed to have been sent as a retribution, a direct punishment to me, although I hated to believe Mr. Roosevelt had that much influence with the Heavenly Powers.
>
> Mile after mile we drove, and still the storm was with us—the thunder deafening, the lightning fairly dancing over the hills and valleys with a brilliance that was positively blinding. When we came to all those long metal bridges that we had to cross in the Lake of the Ozarks country, the lightning playing on the iron structures made it seem that we were driving into blazing cages. On one of them, away out in the wilderness miles from any house, our car light caught a flag being whipped to shreds in the wind-driven rain. It was at half mast."

They reached home at midnight to find Pres worried sick about them. He had been in the cellar three times. There were fourteen tornados reported that night.

Mary Elizabeth spent much time listening to the radio and reading war news in the newspapers. From the beginning of Hitler's career she had clipped news items for her many scrapbooks with handwritten comments beside them expressing her concern.

When Germany surrendered in May of 1945, she was happy for the men in Europe, but, she said, "Our boy was in the Pacific. Leon and his mother devised a little code, and she figured he was at Saipan."

> When he was eight
> He threw a rock
> So true and straight
> Across Long Creek
> And hit a tree
> To show his boyish skill
> To me.
>
> Ten years have passed
> And his dear hands
> Toss live grenades
> In jungle lands.

The end of World War II, just as the end of the first world war, brought tearful thanksgiving. On August 14, Pres and Mary Elizabeth were sitting on the porch when they heard the fire siren blowing in Forsyth. "It's a fire!" exclaimed Pres.

"No!" Mary Elizabeth knew. "Japan has surrendered."

Mary Elizabeth moved one more time. Her last home was back in the bald knobs near Kirbyville in the community that was so important to her youth. Two governmental actions made this move possible.

First, when Mary Elizabeth reached sixty-five she was eligible for a Civil Service pension of $30.05 a month from her years as postmaster. "I always say the nickel is for a lead pencil. I still need it for I still do my writing for Springfield and Forsyth papers," she said. The pension gave them financial security.

The second governmental action was the plan for building Bull Shoals Dam on the White River in Arkansas below Forsyth. The waters from the dam would be impounded right up to Powersite Dam which formed Lake Taneycomo. The new lake would ruin the business section of Forsyth, for the impounded water would be capable of rising to four feet in the courthouse. The town would have to move to the neighboring western hill. With all the land speculation and turmoil caused by the plans for the dam, Mary Elizabeth convinced Pres to sell their place, even though their land would not be affected by high water.

Bertie and Roy returned from the West with the end of the war jobs. With Leon gone (he made the Marines his career) the Joneses no longer wanted their house near Kirbyville; they wanted a country store. After buying the John Morrow store in Taneyville, Bertie and Roy sold to Mary Elizabeth and Pres their house near Kirbyville, in Mary Elizabeth's girlhood home territory.

The Kirbyville place of thirty acres was right on the main road, which is now Highway 76. No longer was Mary Elizabeth isolated where she couldn't see anything. She was in the mainstream again. For a couple of years she was content.

In the mid 1940s, with the coming of the rural electric lines, household work became easier. The Mahnkeys first enjoyed electric lights in 1944, and soon after got an electric iron. Perhaps most welcome of the appliances was an electric "ice box" in May 1946. She and Pres enjoyed the ice cream they made in it and the ice cubes for iced tea. Mary Elizabeth's failing health made the electric washing machine a useful addition, especially since Pres or Bertie had to do most of the washing.

On fine days Mary Elizabeth's favorite place was the

rocking chair on the front porch. Amid the flowers in the flower boxes and flanked by blooming spirea bushes, Mary Elizabeth often looked beyond the busy highway and the neatly kept golf course across the road to her distant hills.

Family members dropped in often on their way to other destinations. New friends and old-time friends and neighbors visited the Mahnkeys at their home on the highway as they used to do on the porches of the country stores. Mary Elizabeth caught the mood.

> Uncle Andy comes to our place
> Sometimes to stay a spell.
> We always love to have him come
> He has so much to tell.
>
> But now and then, he gets plum still
> And watches cars go by.
> He counts them all so carefully
> Not one escapes his eye.
>
> One morning when the hearse went by
> He stopped countin' cars and said,
> "Ain't that the rig, they use now-days
> To carry off the dead?"
>
> When we answered yes, he bowed his head
> And laid his old hat down—
> "I fergit 'bout folks a-dyin'
> Here in this busy town."

Mary Elizabeth continued sending her poems and prose to magazines and radio stations. The flurry of interest in her work after her award in 1935 had provided some modest payments, but by the 1940s she rarely received any compensation, even though her poetry was being included in anthologies, and her "In the Hills" column was still popular.

Her friends urged her not to expend her skill on this voluntary column and on her weekly items in the county paper. Ignoring their advice, she continued, even though, as she noted in the margin of one of her scrapbooks, "The *Kansas City Star* has quoted from my work and lots of Ozarkian writers have helped themselves to it." Even her friends, May Kennedy McCord and Marguerite Lyon, used her material in their literary careers. Mary Elizabeth was not bitter, rather awed that her work was worthy of their interest. But sadly she noted, "All the pay I ever got was the daily paper."

Another honor came to her in November 1943. For her poem "Wild Honey," she was given the title Poet Laureate of the Ozarks by KWTO radio station in its yearly contest program. This title is still used in accounts about her, though others won the contest and title in succeeding years.

Her voluntary writings did help her realize some income because of the exposure they gave her. For a few months, until Mirandy's Chicago-based radio program, "Persimmon Hollow," was canceled in December 1945, the popular radio star paid Mary Elizabeth $10 a month to send her ideas, stories, and sayings she could use on the air. Then beginning in 1945, the White River Valley Electric Cooperative commissioned her to write a monthly page for their publication, *Hill and Hollow News*. Her page was entitled "From the Fireside," with a subtitle of "Where the little things of life that mean so much are related." She wrote in her journal, February 24, 1945, "This is a veritable gift—pays for our lights and more, for the bill is only $2.75 a month."

Mary Elizabeth and Pres moved to the Kirbyville house just before Christmas in 1946. Thrilled with the place, secure with the monthly pension check from the Post Office, and glad to have Bertie's family back in Missouri again, she settled in happily. It was good to be in home territory.

On Christmas Day she baked a chicken, mince pies, and a fruit cake. She was confident that the children would come. It would be like the old days. She and Pres were home again in the midst of the excitement of Christmas, cooking a big dinner for hungry mouths. But only Doug came. He ran in for a minute Christmas morning to bring gifts and regrets. All of his family were down with colds, and he was afraid to take them out. Just before noon Bertie, Roy, and Winnie Bee sent word they would be busy in their store all day. Because they couldn't come, because there was no mail delivery and he couldn't read his daily paper, Pres moped in the house.

At first Mary Elizabeth was also sad and lonely. Thoughts of her family crowded in. She thought of her wandering brother Joe who had just died of a heart attack alone in San Antonio, Texas. "How much he did without—home, wife, child—even maybe he knew cold and hunger." Only Dick, Deal, and herself were left of all the Prathers, and Deal was ill in the same tuberculosis sanitorium where sister Mag died.

Since Christmas was a holiday to be celebrated as each person wanted, she indulged in one of her favorite pastimes. She took a walk. Leaving the dinner untouched and climbing through the fence with her stiff knee, she walked to the top of the hill behind their house. She looked over the scene below her. She told Marguerite Lyon who interviewed her the next summer:

> There was Bald Knob that had given its name to the band of men starting out so loyally and with such high ideals, and ending with murder and shame to fine family names. Here and there, I could see faint traces of the old road that my brothers used to travel on horseback—Bob, Ben,

Frank, Dick, and Joe—the same road that Deal and Mag raced their ponies to parties, and that Pres traveled on a trying freighter's job, driving his black mules, Julie Beck and Peter Jack, to Springfield and back. There was the road along which Father had ridden on old Nell, each stately, dignified, unhurried. Sometimes he rode along reading his paper, or making one of his fiery speeches. In my fancy, I could almost see on big dappled gray Dan, the slender, lithe lad with the shining curly black hair and sparkling black eyes, Paul Kinney. With him was a girl, myself, so full of dreams and ambitions, riding along on a little brown mare.

As the winter wind rose in the trees, I fancied it was the music the girl used to play on her harmonica, smiling to herself to see Kit nodding her little head up and down in perfect time with the music. Kit, Carl, Paul, Bob, Father. How many had passed along that fragment of road with me. I turned to look at the broad curving white highway that led to the sparkling blue water of Lake Taneycomo. Even on that stormy day cars were speeding along, hurrying as senselessly as tourist cars always seem to be doing. Remembering us sitting on the wagon boards snugly wrapped in Mother's quilts and comforters as the horses plodded along that tree-lined road suddenly made me feel very sorry for those smug people wrapped in their smart furs. How could they feel the magic of the great hills that neither storm nor flood nor dam nor highway could destroy!

In those hills I had known heartbreak and ecstasy, joy and dismay, agonizing worry and richest contentment. The great wooded hills had shared in every mood. When I was happy, they seemed to have the same sunshiny glow I felt in my heart. When I was fearful, they seemed to close around me with sheltering protection. When I was sad— even during those dreadful months after the storm had taken my little Bill—they seemed to be pointing upward as if trying to lift my spirits from that terrible black sea of gloom to the beauty of their trees and flowers and shining springs. Always they brought peace to my heart. Small wonder, I reflected there on that hilltop on that Christmas morning, that the hills forever draw to their bosoms the children born within their shadow!

Mary Elizabeth Mahnkey about 1945.
Photographed by Townsend Godsey.

Chapter 22

WHEN THEY PUT AWAY MY SILKEN SCARF
Last Home near Kirbyville: 1947 - August 13, 1948

> When they put away my silken scarf
>   My beads and thin gold rings
> Will they think of my old washtub
>   My broom and other things?
>
> The little hoe I kept for flowers
>   The basket for dead leaves:
> No one to use them anymore
>   And so my spirit grieves

Though written a few years earlier, the above poem entitled "Service" illustrates Mary Elizabeth's philosophy during this last year. Even when anticipating her own death, she still uses common things as metaphors. Although the simplicity of this poem may hide its depth, it sums up her values and life work as she asks that the things she values be remembered and continue to serve.

The spirit of Mary Elizabeth Mahnkey should not grieve. Her soft flame continues to touch us and remind us of our need for beauty and commonplace values. In this verse, she says we need to treasure not only the valuable silk and jewelry (beauty and finer things), but also essential for a satisfying life we must preserve simple household tools. Washtub and broom for cleanliness (purity, virtue), a hoe to cultivate the good and remove the undesirable, and a basket for dead leaves (end of season, memories, life). The basket is a simple metaphor that encompasses the results of natural and human endeavor.

Mary Elizabeth used simple metaphors her contemporaries understood. If she were writing today, she'd probably use washing machines, dust busters, and power mulchers instead of washtub, broom, and basket. The message would be the same. Powerless as she was in many ways in a male-dominated society—tied to her man and his decision—she used common things, over which she had control, to express the larger issues that never become out-dated.

In her time Mary Elizabeth helped women to understand their importance and to be proud of their own worth. Her subtle message helped men to become more sensitive to women's problems, thoughts, and importance. Up to the last few days of her life she continued to portray the beauty of the Ozarks and the worth of its people. Mary Elizabeth Mahnkey was an Ozark writer who made a difference in her own time and continues to speaks to us today.

Young women still enjoy her poetry. In 1994 a graduate student wrote, "Mrs. Mahnkey speaks of commonplace objects and events that we encounter every day. Somehow, she makes them no longer commonplace. She makes us see these 'everyday' things with the eyes of one who might be seeing and experiencing them for the first time. Thank goodness for people like Mrs. Mahnkey who possess the ability to open our eyes and our hearts to the unending wonder that is the birthright given when we were placed upon this earth."

At her last home among the balds near Kirbyville, with diminishing ability because of her rapidly failing health, Mary Elizabeth continued as usual her house, garden, and lawn work, sewing, visiting, and writing. Though her pensive mood was not as evident in her columns, her poetry was more and more about death. Even there her themes of beauty and details of commonplace living are foremost.

Since her forties, Mary Elizabeth had been reflective. Her readers enjoyed her descriptions of long ago daily occurrences, old superstitions, and folk tales from her family and other old-timers. Much of her writings in the two years in Kirbyville were reminiscences. Her poetry became more lyrical and reflective.

> Perhaps sometime, somewhere, someplace
> Beside a distant shining sea,
> We may be judged, not as we are,
> But as we've tried to be.

In February of 1948, she began her last journal which covered five months. Her persistent back pain began to escalate.

Feb. 20, 1948, Thursday
Doug gave me this nice book about two years ago. So I'm starting out on another record—wonder where all I'll be writing in this one?

Monday, the 23rd
It is cool today and Pres went out to cut wood. Really he shouldn't be out in this wind, but would like to see the color of the person's eyes that could stop him.
I sent for a box of Doan's Kidney Pills. Back hurts now and I always was proud of my back. But they didn't help and I took them all. I was complaining about it to Pres

about it and he said, "No pills will cure *old age*."

Feb. 26
(My little jonquil bed at the yard gate at Mincy is almost
in bloom, I know. Oh, why do we suffer so in this old
world?)

As spring unfolded she wrote about her pleasure with
flowers, especially with the plants she had brought from
Mincy. Since she was unable to get outside to gather the blossoms herself, Pres, without being asked, gathered bouquets
for her, even going to the little pasture for some redbud. When
Roy stopped by to leave a package of jonquil bulbs sent by
the wife of the man who bought Mincy store from them in
1943, Pres asked her where to plant them. She remembered
how different he was back in 1914 when he, little Bill, and
Mary Elizabeth got the first start of those jonquils. Grumbling
and swearing, he wouldn't put them where she wanted them.
    In spite of the incessant pain the doctor said was her gall
bladder, she was happy about several things. They received
$15 a month rent from a house they owned in Powersite.
(Even then they planned to move again when she was able,
for the busy road that she had enjoyed at first, now made her
nervous.) Her Civil Service Retirement annuity was raised to
$38 a month. Pres papered the kitchen and put down some
new linoleum, brightening up the house. Pat graduated from
high school with high honors, though she wasn't well enough
to attend. Letters and gifts from Reggie in Oregon cheered her.
He was doing well now, not drinking, working steadily, and
attending church. Gary was bugler for his Boy Scout troop,
using the bugle she and Pres had sent him.
    Bertie and Roy bought a good 240-acre farm with
springs and ponds and a fine remodeled house. Mary Eliza-

beth was glad to have a farm in the family again. She remembered what a friend had told her long ago. "As long as you've got you a little farm, you've got you a comin' up place." Knowing they had it was a comfort to her, for she realized, "Papa and I might have to take a room or so [with Bertie], for the time is arriving when he will have to have help."

She commented frequently on national events. March 9: "Listened to Truman's speech yesterday, full of F.D.R. clichés—defying Russia as F.D.R. defied Ja-

While photographing Mary Elizabeth, Townsend Godsey asked her, "Is there some pose you often take when you write?" She answered, "Sometimes I put my finger to my mouth like this." Photo by Townsend Godsey from *These Were the Last.*

pan—urging a draft, Marshall plan speeded up, and so on." June 25: The GOP Convention with Dewey and Warren and the draft bill. "Truman has signed it and it is said the boys will be in uniforms by September. Poor children. May God have mercy." She thought of Pat who would soon be eighteen

She greatly enjoyed attending the meeting W.E. Freeland, the editor of the *Taney County Republican*, held in Forsyth for country correspondents. Part of the reason for the meeting was to honor her. "It was wonderful and they were all so kind to me," she wrote March 22.

She continued to write as usual. "They Got the Blue Hills," probably the last poem she wrote, was published in June, just before Bertie and Roy bought the Snapp place. Thinking of them moving and recalling the many moves she had made in her life probably inspired this poem which she copied in her journal June 12. Once again it was the simple things and beauty of nature that were important.

> We got these with the Snapp place
> This rug—this range, these shades
> And all the tools out in the sheds
> Tractor, hoes and spades.
>
> (They got the vista of blue hills
> the catbird and the quail
> Silver lining of hawk wings
> The cloud with new-moon sail.)

Winnie Bee had married the summer before in 1947, and Leon brought his new East Coast wife by on his way from Virginia to his new Marine assignment in San Diego. Though Leon's marriage should have been happy news, when Roy brought her Leon's telegram saying he was married, she reacted sadly. "Silly, I know," she wrote March 11, "but (I was lying on the couch) I turned my face to the wall and wept." Life was passing too quickly for her.

In May when it was obvious even to Mary Elizabeth that her back pain was more serious than gall bladder trouble, her family and doctor convinced her to go to the hospital. On May

10 Doug took her to St. John's Hospital in Springfield for extensive tests. After she returned home, she wrote on May 18: "Not very promising—the discoveries made by x-ray pictures and agonizing tests. 'A rock in the gallbladder as big as a walnut, cancerous condition of the bladder.' Supposed to go back for x-ray treatments of the latter condition, but don't think I shall. I couldn't stand much more and can drag along some with opiates."

Even after learning that her illness would be fatal, she continued to be interested in and write about the commonplace things around her. Her next sentence in that entry was, "The little chickens were fine and the garden growing beautifully."

During her final illness she included in her journal only scattered comments on her condition, recording more about her family and friends than herself. Almost every entry included such phrases as: "Dear friends came to see me. Lots of flowers.... Berta did our washing yesterday, brought part of the things yesterday ironed. C.P. ironed the rest.... Reggie and Bertha sent a nice pair of silk hose and a pretty card for Mother's Day. It almost broke my heart some way. This is all so hard on Papa and them.... A familiar voice—Mary Young with loads of flowers. They make me happy and sort of at peace, to think of her gathering them—of where they grew [from little Bill's grave].... Papa is sitting out in the yard. Berta looked so frightened and pitiful. I'm so sorry for all of them."

On June 12 she wrote, "A pleasant visitor night before last was Steve Miller, the artist who makes the wonderful pictures for the *Hill and Hollow* magazine. He is more than an artist. He is a deep thinker, and kind and thoughtful. He said all of my poems had a certain quality that just naturally made them easy to illustrate."

Her illness did not prevent her from experiencing, and

recording, unkind remarks from visitors. Her sensitivity to those who criticized either her or her family, even when the people had her best interests in mind, continued to rankle her. On July 8 she recorded the brief but pleasant visit of Rev. and Mrs. Guy Howard, the "Walkin' Preacher."

But her experience the next day was not pleasant. She wrote: "Sunday afternoon another preacher (I have called him the Singing Preacher) and his wife came—stayed all afternoon, very pain-in-the-neck-ful. He was talking to Pres round and round about the condition of my soul. (We shall soon have been here 3 years. That's their *first visit*.)

"Then Monday morning Dean Hall Jackson came. He did not talk about the condition of my soul, but as he was leaving he said, 'May we have a word of prayer?' and I held to his hand as he prayed, solemnly—rather portentously.

"I never knew much about my soul, but I've tried to do the best I could—like a million other poor old broken down grandmas just like me."

Saturday July 24th she wrote: "Sunday afternoon it cleared off and May McCord stopped with Emma Galbraith, Maude Horine and Henry McCann. May kinda poured it out on me for not going away for surgery, and Maude Horine insulted Pres by coming right out and saying, 'Mrs. Mahnkey is not getting proper care or attention.' I'll not 'look over' that. I've got along with people often by looking over things but this was too much!"

This last entry in her journal ended with a comment about Doug. "Doug stopped Wednesday and read us such a fine piece he had written. It was in yesterday's *Daily News*, there where they put my piece. It really reads like mine--only better composed and organized."

Three weeks later, Friday, August 13, 1948, shortly after eleven o'clock in the morning, Reggie arrived from Salem,

Oregon. Pres, Doug, Bertie, and Roy were all there in her bedroom. Doug bent over Mary Elizabeth's bed and said, "Reggie is here." Her family caught a glimpse of a fleeting, feeble smile. Mary Elizabeth Prather Mahnkey died at 11:20 a.m.

PRESENCE

The door blew open,
  And the wild rainy wind
Blew out my candle,
  Did some one come in?
For I, who never knew
  Terror or fear
Listen and listen
  For something is near.

MOUNTAINEER

No floral doo-dads for my grave, please
No roses, no lilies, none of these
But go to the hills, to my cedar trees

And twist off a bough, spicy, sweet
From some gnarled old tree that had fought defeat
And battled the winds and rain and sleet.

NOTES

Most of the research for this biography has come from four sources: Mary Elizabeth's own writings; an unpublished manuscript of interviews with Mary Elizabeth by Marguerite Lyon in 1946-47; memories and writings of Mary Elizabeth Mahnkey's surviving family and friends; and my own knowledge of and experience in the Ozarks.

There are no fictionalized accounts. Since the source material was often told to me in oral history fashion, or written that way by Marguerite Lyon, Mary Elizabeth Mahnkey, or others, I have been able to tell her story in narrative form using dialogue, based on direct quotes I have read or captured on tape recordings. If the words are not the exact words the people said, at least they are the words quoted by someone who was there.

I have not used footnotes for three reasons. I think footnotes get in the way of popular reading. To document every source would necessitate footnoting almost every paragraph; instead, when possible I have indicated in the text the source. And, I don't believe there is need for documenting since most material came from Mary Elizabeth herself. To indicate just where she wrote it does not seem important. When she wrote it is important; I indicated the date in the text when available.

My four primary sources need some explanation.

1. Mary Elizabeth's writings: Douglas Mahnkey and Winnie Bee Jones Wolf lent me thirteen journals and thirty-three scrapbooks of Mary Elizabeth's filled with clippings and memorabilia. As is often the case, though she carefully clipped out her articles to paste in the scrapbooks, she did not always indicate the source or date. Most of her clippings were from four newspapers: *Taney County Republican* at Forsyth, *White River Leader* at Branson, and the Springfield dailies, *News and Leader* and *Daily News*.

2. The Marguerite Lyon manuscript: In the summer of 1946 Mary

Elizabeth visited Marguerite Lyon for four weeks in the Lyon home in Eureka Springs, Arkansas. They were together an additional two weeks the next summer in Taney County. Mrs. Lyon, feature writer for the *Chicago Tribune*, was known as Marge of Sunrise Mountain Farm from her "Fresh from the Hills" column and as author of two popular books about the Ozarks, *Take to the Hills*, 1941, and *And Green Grows the Grass All Around*, 1942, Bobbs Merrill. Marge recognized Mary Elizabeth's talent and realized that her life would make a good story. Though Mary Elizabeth was not very willing, Marge persuaded Mary Elizabeth to tell her the story of her life.

Mrs. Lyon wrote the manuscript from what Mary Elizabeth told her and from some journals and scrapbooks Mary Elizabeth lent her. The 235-page manuscript is written almost entirely in the form of direct conversations from Mary Elizabeth—an as-told-to narrative, though Mrs. Lyon adapted much of the "conversation" directly from Mary Elizabeth's own published writings. Though submitted to Mrs. Lyon's publishers, the manuscript was never published. A few years later, before her death, Mrs. Lyon gave the only copy of it to Douglas Mahnkey as his exclusive property. It sat in a drawer in his house for over twenty years.

In most places where I write, "Mary Elizabeth said," I am using material from this manuscript, though not necessarily verbatim. I did some editing and expanding; there are numerous inaccuracies and omissions of information the reader needs to know. Where I found Mary Elizabeth's original work, I used it.

Mary Elizabeth did not read the completed manuscript. By the fall of 1947 when it was completed, her health was deteriorating rapidly. She was not disappointed when the publisher rejected it. She died the summer following the last interviews.

3. Family and friends: Douglas Mahnkey, Mary Elizabeth's eldest son and only surviving child, gave me permission to use material from two books he has written about Taney County, *Bright Glowed My Hills* (1965) and *Hill and Holler Stories* (1975). In addition he visited with me in person or on the telephone many times, wrote many letters, and sent me several hours of taped memories and information about his parents and Taney County. His son Pat wrote several letters about his memories of his grandparents. Together Pat and I talked with his sister, Mary Jo Mahnkey Kirkey, his cousin, Winnie Bee Jones Wolf, and many of Mary Elizabeth's friends and neighbors (or their children). We visited most of the places important in her life.

Notes

4. My own knowledge of the area: I was born on a farm in Vernon County, and in 1946 I came to the central Ozarks as home agent of Laclede County. There I married and farmed, having diverse experiences that helped me understand many of the things Mary Elizabeth Mahnkey went through fifty years before me. Then from 1973 to 1983 I was teacher/advisor to *Bittersweet*, a quarterly by high school students about Ozark culture and heritage. I accompanied the students on hundreds of interviews all over the Ozarks of older men and women, gathering much knowledge and understanding of the Ozarks and its people. Where my source material about some aspect of her life was missing, I filled it with my own knowledge and experience.

FAMILY CHARTS

PRATHER FAMILY

Ada Marie (Betsy) McMillian m. 1863 Alonzo Smith Prather(Colonel)
1844-1940   1840-1910

1. Robert Hiram (Bob)   m. 1887 Gertrude DeLong
   1865-1895

2. Benjamin Hargrove (Ben) m. 1898 Janie Ray
   1866-1905

3. Frank Walker   m.   Molly Brumley
   1868-1922

4. Richard Lee (Dick)   m.   Mabel Collier
   1871-1949?

5. Baby girl
   1870

6. Gracie
   1873-1874

7. Mary Elizabeth (Mamie) m. 1899 Charles Preston Mahnkey
   1877-1948   1875-1965

8. Joseph McMillian (Joe)
   1879-1946

9. Adelia Marie (Deal)   m.   Jack Pruden
   1882-1949

10. Margaret Minerve (Mag) m. 1907 Charles Russel
    1986-1930

MAHNKEY FAMILY

Mattie J. Rudder   m.   Charles Mahnkey
? -1927   ? - 1905

1. Tommy
   1872? - unknown

2. Emma   m. 1893   Saul (Sol) Wheeler

3. Sopha Anna (Annie)   m. 1893   James L. Wheeler

4. Charles Preston   m. 1899   Mary Elizabeth Mahnkey
   1875-1965   1877-1948

5. Andrew Benjamim   m. 1922   Cordie Cobb

6. George S.   m. 1913   Bessie Russell

7. Cecilia   m.   Sam Swartz
   1887-?

8. John Henry
   1890-1933

9. Mattye   m.   Roy House

10. William (Bill)   m. 1921   Elsie Casey

Genealogy

MARY ELIZABETH AND PRES MAHNKEY FAMILY

Mary Elizabeth Prather (Mamie)   m. 1899   Charles Preston Mahnkey
    1877-1948   1875-1965

  1. Baby girl
    1900

  2. Charles Douglas (Doug)   m. 1928   Merle Walker
    1902-   1907-1985

      1. Charles Patrick (Pat)
        1930-
      2. Mary Jo
        1933-
      3. William Donald (Bill)
        1945-

  3. Roberta Marguerite (Bertie) m. 1925 Roy Jones
    1905-1983   ? - 1985

      1. Reginal Leon
        1926-1984
      2. Winifred Elizabeth (Winnie Bee)
        1929-

  4. James Reginal (Reggie)   m. 1928   Bertha Klein
    1907-1979

      1. Gary
        1934-
      2. Curtis Preston
        1937-
      3. Spencer Dee
        1940-

  5. William Richard (Bill)
    1912-1920

BIBLIOGRAPHY

Batson, Marilyn. Book review of *Marigold Gold*. Culture of the Ozarks
  Class. Drury College. Springfield, Missouri. August 8, 1994.
Box, Pete and Clarabel. Interview. Kirbyville, Missouri. July 10, 1984.
Clark, M. Graham. Interview. Point Lookout, Missouri. July 18, 1984.
Church, Robert. Letter. January 29, 1985. containing Prather men's Civil
  War record.
Christian Science Monitor. "A Woman in the News." July 31, 1935.
Cummings, Dorothy. "Melva." *White River Valley Historical Quarterly.*
  Fall. 1963.
Daily News. Springfield, Missouri. clippings. 1930 to 1948.
Freeland, Maude. Interview. Forsyth, Missouri. July 18, 1984.
Freeland, W.E.. "Mrs. Mahnkey's Honor." *Taney County Republican.*
  September 23, 1964.
_____Editorial. *Taney County Republican*. 1935.
Globe Democrat. St. Louis, Missouri. clippings. 1935.
Haworth, John J.. "Taney County Baldnobbers." Kirbyville, Missouri.
  Library of Elmo Ingenthron. typescript. 1941.
Ingenthron, Elmo. *The Land of Taney*. Ozarks Mountaineer. Branson,
  Missouri. 1974.
Kansas City Star. Kansas City, Missouri. clippings. 1935.
Kenner, Alva. Interview. Clear Water Acres. Missouri. August 6, 1984.
Kirkey, Mary Jo Mahnkey. Interview. Rogersville, Missouri. August 15,
  1984.
Layton, Ben. Interview tape made by Douglas Mahnkey. Taney County,
  Missouri. 1977.
Literary Digest. "They Stand out from the Crowd." August 3, 1935.
Lord, Russell. *Voices from the Field*. Houghton Mufflin, Co. 1937.
Lyon, Marguerite. *Lady of the Hills*. Manuscript. 1948.
Mahnken, Lorene. Interview. Swan, Missouri. August 18, 1984.
Mahnkey, Charles Preston. Letters. 1898, 1903.
Mahnkey, Douglas. *Bright Glowed My Hills*. School of the Ozarks Press.
  Point Lookout, Missouri. 1968.
_____*Hill and Holler Stories*. School of the Ozarks Press. Point Look-
  out, Missouri. 1975.
_____ Interview. Forsyth, Missouri. September 15, 1982.

_____Transcribed tapes. July 6, June 25, July 20, December 13 and 14, 1984. Interviews July. August, September 1984 and Spring 1985.

Mahnkey, Mary Elizabeth. 13 volumes of *Journals*:

    March 10, 1892 - April 23, 1892

    March 4, 1901 - February 19, 1902

    December 12, 1902

    1906 - 1908

    June 25, 1910 - December 1911

    February 1912 - July 1914

    July 1, 1915 - March 2, 1920

    June 6, 1931 - December 26, 1933

    January 4, 1934 - December 29, 1941

    1935

    July 1940

    February 16, 1945 - February 17, 1948

    February 20 - July 28, 1948

_____ "The Forum." *The Country Home*. August 1935.

_____ "From the Fireside." *Hill and Holler News*. White River Valley Electric Coooperative. Hollister, Missouri. 1945-1948.

_____ "In the Hills." and "Backwoods Contributor." in "The Wastebasket" column. *News and Leader* and *Daily News*. Springfield, Missouri. 1930-1948.

_____ "Kirbyville." "Forsyth." "Oasis." "Mincy." and others. *Taney County Republican*. Forsyth, Missouri. 1890 to 1948.

_____ "Ozark Correspondent." *The Country Home*. Crowell Publishing Co. New York. 1935-1936.

_____ *Ozark Lyrics*. Third Edition. School of the Ozarks Press. Point Lookout, Missouri. October 1, 1935.

_____ *Ozark Lyrics: the Song Poems of the Ozarks*. School of the Ozarks Press. Point Lookout, Missouri. 1972.

_____ "Under the Sky." *Missouri Magazine*. October 1930.

_____ 32 volumes of scrapbooks.

_____ Various articles in *Missouri Magazine*. Jefferson City, Missouri.

Mahnkey, Patrick. Letters. July 6. July 20, 1984; Interviews July, August, and September 1984, Spring 1985, July and August 1985, April 1986.

McClary, Cecil. Interview. Kirbyville, Missouri. July 10, 1984.

McCord, May Kennedy. "Hillbilly Heartbeats. *News and Leader*. Springfield, Missouri. July 28, 1935.

Bibliography

McCullough, Florence Woodlock. *Living Authors of the Ozarks and Their Literature*. 1941.

McFarland, May and Leonard. Interview. July 18, 1984. Hollister, Missouri.

McHaffie, Ella. "Journal of New York Trip." Manuscript. July 19-29, 1935.

Moore, Charles and Ella. Interview. August 6, 1984. Twin Island Estates. Missouri.

Moore, Charles A. *Moore Family History*. 1979.

"Mrs. Mahnkey's New York Scrapbook." *The Country Home*. Crowell Publishing Co. New York. 1935.

NBC-WEAF. New York City. Radio Address 6:35 EDST. July 22, 1935.

News and Leader. Springfield, Missouri. clippings 1930 to 1948.

Prather, Ada Marie. Journal and Account Book. July 6, 1910 to 1916.

Prather, Richard L. Private papers.

_____ "The Big Road in Missouri and Arkansas Ozarks - 1880-1900." *Taney County Republican*. August 14, 1957.

Randolph, Vance. *Ozark Folksongs*. Revised Edition. University of Missouri Press. Columbia, Missouri. 1980.

Strahan, John, Jr.. Interview. August 6, 1984. Forsyth, Missouri.

Taney County News and *Taney County Republican*. Forsyth, Missouri. clippings from 1889 to 1948.

Taney County School District No. 1. T. 21. R. 21. Record book of Turkey Creek School. 1892-1894.

Taneyhills Study Club. Branson and Hollister. Missouri. Scrapbook. 1930s.

Taneyhills Study/Library Club Treasury Book I. September 1933-February 1945.

Upton, Lucile Morris. *Bald Knobbers*. Caxton Printers, LTD.. Caldwell, Idaho. 1939. Second Edition. School of Ozarks Press. Point Lookout. Missouri. 1970.

Van Buskirk, Kathleen. "When School Bells rang in Ridgedale." *The Ozarks Mountaineer*. Branson. Missouri. July-August. 1981.

White River Leader. Branson, Missouri. clippings from 1913 to 1948.

Wolf, Winnie Bee Jones. Letters and Interviews. Wichita Falls, Texas. July 27-28, 1985; Harrison. Arkansas. May 1989.

INDEX OF MARY ELIZABETH'S POETRY QUOTED

First Lines

INDEX

A

Aging: 148, 296
Anderson, Addie: 46
Animals: (see names of animals)
Anthony, Edward: 255
Anti-Bald Knobbers: 43ff
Appleton City, MO: 28, 30, 34, 38
Arkansas River: 286
Atchinson, Augusta: 222
Automobiles: 153

B

Baersfield, Mrs. Fred: (see Mirandy of Persimmon Hollow)
Bald Knobs (Taney County, MO): 33, 289
Bald Knobbers: 39ff
Bald Knobber Era: 39-48, 49
Barrett, James W.: 12
Baseball: 159
Beck, Thomas: 3
Bedding (straw ticks): 87
Bedford, Authur: 60
Bee Creek (Taney County, MO): 200, 262
Benton, Thomas Hart: xvii, 237
Berry, J.S.: 44
Blacksmith shop: 155
Blue Eye, MO: 218
Bolin, Alf: 40
Box, Anna: 182ff, 199
Box, Florence: 180ff, 195, 199
Box, Hubert: 176, 180, 190

Bradleyville, MO: 64, 74
Bradleyville Normal School: 64ff
Branson, MO: 4, 15, 49
Branson, Betsy: 47
Branson, G.E. (Gabe): 46ff
Branson School, Old (Roark Creek, MO): 77ff
Breakenridge, Cil: 166ff, 173
Broun, Haywood: 13ff
Brushy Creek School: (see Union Flat School)
Bryan, Hiram: 60ff
Bull Shoals Dam, AR: 286
Burnett, John: 245
Bushwackers: 40f
Business College, (Springfield, MO): 75ff
Buttercup (cow): 250

C

Camp House (for wagons): 91ff, 123
Caney Creek, (Taney County, MO): 174, 180-190
Carthage, MO: 15
Cedar Valley School, (Taney County, MO): 226
Chadwick, MO: 99
Chickamauga (Battle): 22
Chickens: 90, 114
Child Care: 106, 114, 124, 171, 208
Childbirth: 94, 105, 119ff, 208ff, 220ff
Childhood games: 35ff
Christian County, MO: 44

319

Index

Fox Creek (Taney County, MO): 262
Free Jack Spring: 53, 91
Freeland, W.E.: 7, 240, 298
Funerals: (see Death and burial customs)
Funk, Edward: 46ff

G

Gailbraith, Emma: 300
Gardening: 90
Gardner Mountain, (Taney County, MO): 149, 197, 199
Gibson, Eli: 278
Globe Democrat, (St. Louis, MO): 15
Godsey, Townsend: ill. 292
Grist Milling: 139, 156, 205, 214
Groom, Charlie: 259
Groves, Martha: 65ff
Gypsies: 66ff, 212

H

Harrison, AR: 18ff, 23, 42
Hay baling: 133
Heating (house): 89, 168
Hill and Holler News: 57, 288, 299
Hilsabeck, Nellie: 60
Hollister, MO: 110, 149, 186
Homestead Law: 98
Homesteading: 59ff, 98ff
Honesty: 154ff, 211
Honeymoon: 85
Horine, Maude: 300
Horseback riding: 57, 80, 94, 118, 129ff
Housekeeping: 86ff

Housewarming: 72ff
Houston, MO: 166
Howard, Alva: 188
Howard, Cora: 188

Howard, Mr. and Mrs. Guy (Walking Preacher of the Ozarks): 300
Hublar: 250
Huckleberry Mountain, (Taney County, MO): 262
Huckstep, Huldah: 222
Huff, Marion: 156
Hyde family: 166

I

Illnesses: (see Sickness)
"In the Hills" (column): 59, 205, 218, 256, 261, 275, 288
Indians: 24ff
Infare dinner: 85
Iron Mountain Railroad: 110ff

J

Jackson, Dean Hall: 300
Jackson, Frank: 222
Jackson, Johnny: 218ff
Jefferson City, MO: 82, 283
John Morrow Store: 286
Johnson, Joel: 139
Johnson, Masie: 127ff
Jones, Roberta (Bertie) Mahnkey: 15, 119ff, 141, 144ff, 166ff, 180-188, 195ff, 197, 226ff, 240, 246, 251, 255, 256ff, 275, 282, 286, 289, 296ff, 301. ill. 122, 124, 145

Index

Salesmen, traveling: 125, 210
Scarlet Letter: 220
School of the Ozarks: xvii, 166, 177, 240
Schools and schooling: 30ff, 68ff, 75ff, 125, 133, 145, 158ff, 167, 172, 177, 195, 226, 262
Sherman, General William Tecumseh: 22
Shiloh, Battle of: 22
Shivaree: 84ff
Show-Me Missouri Women, Vol.1: xvi
Sickness: 36ff, 90, 118, 123, 129, 154, 167, 168, 208, 234, 245, 257, 295ff
Sixth Regiment of Indiana: 22
Smith, Al: 12
Smith, Andy: 225
Snakes: 30, 70
Snapp, Harrison: 91
Snapp Place, (Taney County, MO): 298
Snobbery: 76ff
Springfield, MO: 5
Springfield-Harrison Road: 54, 91, 123
Southwest Missouri State Teachers College: 199
Stores and Storekeeping: 122, 139ff, 143ff, 150ff, 155, 205ff, 257, 263-279. ill. 207
Storms: 175-190, 284ff
Story telling: 136, 220ff
Stottle (merchant in Kirbyville): 150
Stout Farm: 109ff, 118
Strahan, Issac: 159ff, 259

Sunshine Press, (Springfield, MO): 238
Superstititions: 66ff, 73ff, 119, 134, 136, 168, 274
Swan, MO: 118
Swan Creek and farm, (Taney County, MO): 49, 74, 101ff, 109

T

Table Rock Dam and Lake: 5, 245, 248ff
Tacoma, WA: 170ff
Taney County, MO: xiv, 27, 40
Taney County clerk: 226
Taney County Courthouse: 40
Taney County Republican: 4, 7, 115, 162, 240, 298
Taney Hills Study Club: 238ff, 242ff, 238. ill. 243
Taneyville (Taney City), MO: 49, 74, 99, 100, 118, 161, 192, 286
Teachers' Examination: 68, 77
Teachers' Institute Law: 77
Telephones: 180, 277
Texas County, MO: 166ff
Time (magazine): 3
Todd Shipyards, (Tacoma, WA): 170, 282
Tourists: 158, 206, 223ff, 245
Toys: 124ff,134ff
Traveliing Salesmen: (see Salesmen)
Trixie (dog): 176, 180, 192, 197
Truman, Harry S.: 297
Turkey Creek, (Taney County, MO): 68ff, 174, 180-190, 192

ABOUT THE AUTHOR

Ellen Gray Massey has written most of her life and has been a teacher for thirty-nine years, mainly at Lebanon High School in Lebanon, Missouri, and since 1986 on the adjunct faculty of Drury College's Graduate Education program teaching writing and Ozark studies. In addition, she teaches Culture of the Ozarks classes at Elderhostel groups at the YMCA of the Ozarks at Potosi, Missouri, since 1990. She is active in promoting appreciation of the Ozarks as a speaker for many regional groups and for the Missouri Humanities Council (1991-1993).

Many of her talks are on writing based on her experience as a writer and as an editor of several publications. She was teacher/advisor from 1973-1983 of *Bittersweet, the Ozark Quarterly,* published by students at Lebanon High School, and editor of two books, *Bittersweet County* (1978 and 1986) and *Bittersweet Earth* (1985 and 1993). She was editor of *Briarwood* (1988-1989), Lebanon Publishing Company's regional magazine. She is author of numerous short stories and articles and five recent novels, *Moon Silver* (1991), *Too Many Secrets* (1992), *The Bequest* (1993), *Equestricat* (1994), and *A Grave Situation* (1994), all published by Avalon Books of New York.

In 1995 she was one of the first three inductees into the Writers Hall of Fame. She has won awards from the Missouri Writers Guild three times for Best Book and two times for Best Adult Fiction Story. She received recognition as finalist from Western Writers of America Spur Awards for short fiction.